APPLIED WISDOM

Also from Alexander M. Ineichen

Nowcasting and Financial Wizardry
IR&M, 2015

Roadmap to Hedge Funds
AIMA, 2008/2012

Asymmetric Returns
Wiley Finance, 2006

Absolute Returns
Wiley Finance, 2002

In Search of Alpha
UBS Investment Bank, 2000

Praise for *Applied Wisdom*

"Alexander Ineichen has put together a wonderful collection of market wisdom by extraordinary people and put them in the right market context. It is a must-read for any serious investor, as it is simply outstanding!"

—FELIX W. ZULAUF,
founder of Zulauf Asset Management
and long-term Barron's roundtable member

"When an email from Alexander Ineichen lands in my inbox, I nearly always stop what I am doing and begin to read. I find his insights, research and indeed wisdom to be of lasting value. And the book of those insights? Priceless. And one which will be on a shelf near me, for constant perusal and meditation. Nobody has mastered the art of quotation and wisdom like Alexander. He is in a class of his own, and for the price of a few dollars and some time, you can attend that class. Now pay attention."

—JOHN MAULDIN, four-time *New York Times*
bestselling author and writer of the popular
Mauldin Economics online newsletter

"If you enjoy investing and like to listen to the best thoughts of clever observers of what works and why in investment management, the wisdom collected into this book will give you great pleasure."

—CHARLES D. ELLIS, CFA
and author of *The Loser's Game*

"One of the best investment books I ever read. Alexander's nowcasting methodology helped substantially to optimize my investment activities."

—CUNO PÜMPIN, PhD, Professor emeritus,
University of St. Gallen, Switzerland,
the top business school in Switzerland

"It was the sixteenth century English poet by the name of Thomas Tusser who quipped 'a fool and his money are soon parted.' That echo resounds throughout this very cleverly written book by Alexander M. Ineichen as he uses common sense and wit as his weapons of choice, all the while, holding a mirror up to our capital markets."

—WILLIAM J. KELLY,
CEO of the CAIA Association

"Similar to the 'modern' classic *The Money Game*, written nearly fifty years ago, Alexander uses quotes and sayings and his own analysis to bring great insight to the financial, economic and political situation we find ourselves in today. Alexander knits the quotes together with his own depth of knowledge to provide an important book in a very clever and humorous way."

—ANDY LEES, Founder of The Macro Strategy
Partnership, a UK based research firm
with 120 institutional clients globally

"Alexander brings his attention to detail and thoughtful perspective to remind us all about timeless truths regarding the markets and investing. This is the one book every investor should keep on our desks for regular review!"

—JANE BUCHAN, cofounder of PAAMCO
and CEO of Martlet Asset Management

APPLIED WISDOM

700 Witticisms To Save Your Ass(ets)

Alexander M. Ineichen

Radius Book Group

New York

Radius Book Group
A Division of Diversion Publishing Corp.
New York, NY 10016
www.RadiusBookGroup.com

For more information, email info@radiusbookgroup.com.

First edition: November 2021
Hardcover ISBN: 978-1-63576-814-5
eBook ISBN: 978-1-63576-812-1

Library of Congress Control Number: 2021901841

Manufactured in the United States of America

10 9 8 7 6 5 4 3 2 1

Cover design by Tom Lau

Interior design by Neuwirth & Associates

Radius Book Group and the Radius Book Group colophon are registered trademarks of Radius Book Group, a Division of Diversion Publishing Corp.

To Claudia, Natasha, Thomas, Oliver, and Nicholas (who else?)

CONTENTS

PREFACE

The most important things in life are survival and reproduction. While the topic of the latter is fascinating, this book is mainly about the former.

I started my career in finance as a trainee in 1988. An early station was in the brokerage of equities and derivatives at an investment bank. I remember well asking the then-head of research on the trading floor why they had produced a two-hundred-page research report, a buy recommendation for a stock, and inquired whether anyone was going to read the lengthy tome. His response: "No, of course not, but if something goes wrong, they can blame the bank."

I turned into one of the lads producing those reports no one read. However, ending up in research more by accident than by design, I did have an incentive to spice things up a bit, literally. Early on I adapted a simple writing style that included small pieces of wisdom and wit in the side text of my reports. The feedback was positive from the start. This was good as well as bad. Good, because the feedback giver at least glanced over what I had produced. It got noticed. Bad, because the hard work was not in the witty quotation in the side text but in the content. I often heard that it was enough for the reader to grasp the content by just reading the side text. Someone else's *wisdom* in the side text was *applicable*.

In this book, I turn things around. I have not written this book because I have something clever to say. I have written this book because I have quoted so many clever people over the past three decades who themselves had something clever to say. I now have a collection of wit and wisdom that is applicable to capital preservation and risk management. In this book, essentially a compilation of wit and wisdom, I do not start with the content and add someone's quip to spice things up. I start with a nugget of wisdom, check if it is applicable to capital preservation, and then add some content.

I herein also quote foolish people, not just for entertainment purposes but because the closest we can get to wisdom is avoiding the other side of that proverbial coin, foolishness. We learn silence from the talkative, tolerance from the intolerant, and kindness from the unkind, so we can learn wisdom from buffoons. It is for this reason that concepts such as the basic law of human stupidity, the bozo-explosion, the BS asymmetry principle, and the greater fool theory are discussed.

Along the way, you will learn that Barack Obama and Horace said the same thing, what Marilyn Monroe and Mike Tyson have in common with Leonardo da Vinci, and that both Muhammad Ali and George Soros applied Confucius's wisdom.

For this book, I took extra care to find the origins of the quotations I have used during my career. The Internet was helpful in this regard. However, one cannot be too careful. As Voltaire once said: "The problem with quotes found on the Internet is that they are often not true."

THE GREATER FOOL THEORY

Don't do stupid shit.
—Barack Obama

Applied wisdom means keeping the number of times you shoot yourself in your foot to a minimum and surviving every single attempt at self-mutilation. It also involves knowledge of life, knowledge of yourself, acknowledgment of uncertainty, open-mindedness, tolerance, coolness, naivete-aversion, discernment, instinct, the ability to see the big picture, diligence, prudence, intellectual thoroughness, courage, tenacity, experience, down-to-earth-ness, reflection, happiness, prosperity, and a sense of humor. Applied wisdom can be earned or learned, but not taught.

Applied wisdom is also the avoidance of folly, unwisdom, faux sophistication, dogma, stupidity, ignorance, arrogance, hubris, and includes doubt, skepticism, and a healthy baloney-detection approach.

Applied Wisdom and the Greater Fool Theory

Foolishness and Mathematized Wisdom

The Boxing Day tsunami of 2004 off the west coast of northern Sumatra killed approximately two hundred and thirty thousand people in fourteen countries. All the science of Western civilization did not help to foresee the earthquake or prevent devastation and death. One interesting aspect of this tsunami was that hardly any members of the aboriginal tribes were killed. They were able to conclude from the behavior of their animals that something bad was about to strike, and they moved inland prior to the disaster. They applied wisdom.

> *Wisdom is the quality that keeps you from getting into situations where you need it.*
> —DOUG LARSON *(1926–2017), American columnist*

An apple a day keeps the doctor away. This is not just a saying or grandmotherly advice; it is an old piece of wisdom that has traveled well through time and is still applicable today. There are much fancier ways to say that fruit is good for you. Modern science helps us understand why there is truth that an apple, here a proxy for healthy food, is beneficial to our physical health.

In this book I do not focus on the science bit. I focus on the wisdom that has traveled through time and has its origins in the distant past. In finance, for instance, modern portfolio theory (MPT) proves the benefits of reducing risk through diversification. However, these benefits have been known for thousands of years. In economics we did not need to wait for economists to tell us that excess public debt is not good for societal well-being. David Hume knew it three hundred years ago and Solomon three thousand years ago.

This means the applicable wisdom of diversification is ancient, as is the folly of excess leverage and debt. A quotation or a proverb is just the medium that something used to travel through time and survive until today. A quotation, proverb, or saying ought to contain condensed knowledge, experience, and, ideally, wisdom. Miguel de Cervantes, author of *Don Quixote*, knew this.

> *Proverbs are short sayings drawn from long experience.*[1]
> —MIGUEL DE CERVANTES *(1547–1616), Spanish novelist,*
>   *dramatist, and poet*

In the social sciences, as, for example, in economics and finance, academic research is often "mathematized wisdom," the benefits of diversification being just one example. This book is indeed about capital preservation and risk management, even if some of the excursions might appear to suggest otherwise. Given that the mathematization of old tricks of the trade distorts the wisdom, confuses the practitioner, and adds unnecessary complexity, I often opted for simplicity rather than sophistication. One implicit and important assumption, therefore, is that, as investors, it is better to be street-smart than book-smart:

> *A knowledgeable fool is a greater fool than an ignorant fool.*[2]
> —MOLIÈRE *(1622–73), French actor*

This old quote is shockingly consistent with the phenomenon of expert failure and *dysrationalia*, i.e., the concept of *really* smart people making *really* stupid mistakes. It is also consistent with the Nobel disease, i.e., the concept of highly educated people like Nobel prize-winners endorsing or performing "research" in pseudoscientific areas in their later years. Award-winning science journalist David Robson even goes as far as suggesting that really smart people can be more susceptible to nonsense or pranks:

> *Not only do general intelligence and academic education fail to*
> *protect us from various cognitive errors; smart people may be*
> *even more vulnerable to certain kinds of foolish thinking.*[3]
> —DAVID ROBSON *(b. 1985), British science writer*

Robson reminds us that Albert Einstein was shunned in his later years by other scientists for his foggy thinking and ignorance of facts, and Steve Jobs could still be alive today had he listened to his doctors instead of trying to cure cancer himself with spiritual healing and fruit juice diets.

Practical Wisdom and Faux Sophistication

Wisdom is a path; an ideal. It involves learning, effort, curiosity, intellectual humility and autonomy, open-mindedness, perspective, and failure. Wisdom, like happiness, is not a destination but a journey. Socrates, for example, did not claim to *have* wisdom, but only to *seek* it lovingly. He was wisdom's amateur, not its professional.[4]

The ancient Greeks had a word for a special type of wisdom, one that was more practical than wisdom or intelligence. They called wisdom with practical applicability *phronesis*. This was sometimes translated as "practical virtue" and involved both good judgment and excellence of character.

Aristotle, whose philosophy greatly influenced both the Christian and Islamic religions, distinguished between two intellectual virtues: *sophia* and *phronesis*. *Sophia* is designing and constructing a Formula One car. *Phronesis* is applying the rubber to the tarmac. *Sophia* is often translated as science; it is serious, logical, teachable, and reasonable. It's Mr. Spock. *Phronesis* is much broader, is not teachable, and involves converting theory into practice, diligence, prudence, intellectual thoroughness, courage, tenacity, and experience. It's a cross between Captain Kirk, Yoda, and Forrest Gump's mum. *Sophia* involves searching for universal truths. *Phronesis* involves good decision-making in real-world situations where there is no playbook to follow. It involves reflection, human flourishing, happiness, and prosperity.

Aristotle's *phronesis* is often translated as "practical or ethical wisdom," which is close to terms such as "worldly wisdom" or "applied wisdom." At the most simplistic level, applied wisdom means keeping the number of times you shoot yourself in your foot to a minimum and surviving every single attempt of self-mutilation. It also involves knowledge of life, knowledge of yourself, acknowledgment of uncertainty, open-mindedness, tolerance, coolness, naivete-aversion, discernment, instinct, the ability to see the big picture, and a sense of humor. Applied wisdom can be earned or learned but not taught.

Peggy Noonan, a speechwriter to both Ronald Reagan and George H. W. Bush, and to some on the political right, the greatest essayist of our generation, makes the distinction between *sophia* and *phronesis* when criticizing Barack Obama's judgment in an article titled "The Unwisdom of Barack Obama."

> *Mr. Obama can see the trees, name their genus and species, judge their age and describe their color. He absorbs data. But he consistently misses the shape, size and density of the forest. His recitations of data are really a faux sophistication that suggests command of the subject but misses the heart of the matter.*[5]
> —PEGGY NOONAN *(b. 1950), American author and columnist*

Unwisdom, faux sophistication, and folly, in this book, are the opposite of applied wisdom. As investors we should try to avoid folly. However, in active asset management, where relative performance matters, folly is a prerequisite:

> *Let us be thankful for the fools. But for them, the rest of us could not succeed.*[6]
> —MARK TWAIN *(1835–1910), American author and humorist*

Warren Buffett, who was rejected by Harvard Business School after graduating from the University of Nebraska, once jested that he would like to fund university chairs in the EMH (efficient market hypothesis) so that the professors would train even more misguided financiers whose money he could win. He called the orthodox theory "foolish" and plain wrong. Yet none of its proponents "has ever said he was wrong, no matter how many thousands of students he sent forth misinstructed. Apparently, a reluctance to recant, and thereby to demystify the priesthood, is not limited to theologians."[7]

Meir Statman, a professor of finance who rolls his eyes when friends claim they can distinguish good wines from mediocre wines but is confident that he can easily distinguish good olives from mediocre ones, draws the important link between markets being irrational and the irrationality being helpful for the "rational" among us.

> *The market may be crazy, but that doesn't make you a psychiatrist.*[8]
> —MEIR STATMAN *(b. 1947), German-born Israeli American professor of finance*

While markets may behave crazily, and while we are not rational, we still try to make sense of things. I believe the following to be both true and the bottom line of any debate on human rationality and efficient markets. It is one of my top ten quotations in this book.

> *Man is not a rational animal; he is a rationalizing animal.*[9]
> —ROBERT A. HEINLEIN *(1907–88), American science fiction author*

Thinkers throughout the ages agree that one cannot apply wisdom without being self-aware, i.e., acknowledging one's own ignorance to some degree.

Predictable Folly and First Principles

One idea in finance goes by the name "greater fool theory," which states that the value of a security or asset class does not matter that much as long as you can sell to a greater fool than yourself at an even more ridiculous price than you paid. According to this "theory," it was perfectly rational to buy Internet stocks in the 1990s, as it was rational to buy Japanese stocks in the 1980s, as it was rational to buy Bitcoins at $20 or $10,000 per coin more recently. Whether financial markets resemble a random walk down Wall Street or not does not matter that much in this regard.

> *There is no reason, only mass psychology. . . . It's perfectly all right to pay three times what something is worth as long as later on you can find some innocent to pay five times what it's worth.*[10]
> —BURTON G. MALKIEL *(b. 1932), American economist*

As with everything else in life, risk is involved. The greater fool theory works if you are not the greatest of fools. This is how the "Oracle of Boston" put it:

> You may find a buyer at a higher price—a greater fool—or you may not, in which case you yourself are the greater fool.[11]
> —SETH KLARMAN (b. 1957), American hedge fund manager

Avoiding folly is a first principle:

> The first principle is that you must not fool yourself—and you are the easiest person to fool.[12]
> —RICHARD FEYNMAN (1918–88), American physicist

Buying General Electric, Thomas Edison's company, at $0.5 trillion market capitalization, or buying the Nikkei 225, a Japanese equities index, at forty thousand index points did not work. There is a limit to everything.

> Unfortunately, the greater fool theory only works until it doesn't. Valuation eventually comes into play, and those who are holding the bag when it does have to face the music.[13]
> —HOWARD MARKS (b. 1946), American investor

Even if wisdom is an unreachable ideal, its pursuit is worth it:

> Of all human pursuits the pursuit of wisdom is the most perfect, the most sublime, the most profitable, the most delightful.[14]
> —THOMAS AQUINAS (1225–1274), Italian priest and
>   philosopher

The pursuit of wisdom has many drawbacks, though, the loss of muscle mass being just one:

> If it is wisdom you're after, you're going to spend a lot of time on your ass reading.[15]
> —CHARLIE MUNGER (b. 1924), American investor and vice
>   chairman of Berkshire Hathaway

Investors who can spot folly have an edge over those who cannot, and especially over those who cannot and do not know that they cannot. Folly might even take a bit of randomness out of markets.

> *The fact that people will be full of greed, fear or folly is predictable. The sequence is not predictable.*[16]
> —WARREN BUFFETT *(b. 1930), American investor and*
>   *chairman of Berkshire Hathaway*

Wisdom and Stupidity

Foolishness is something one can count on: it is not going away. While applied wisdom is scarce, there might be an oversupply of folly:

> *There are more fools than wise men;*
> *and even in the wise men more folly than wisdom.*[17]
> —SÉBASTIEN NICOLÁS DE CHAMFORT *(1741–94), French*
>   *writer*

The main content of this book is about avoiding folly, foolishness being the opposite of applied wisdom, as mentioned. Avoiding foolishness is sometimes referred to as the Obama Doctrine:

> *Don't do stupid shit.*[18]
> —BARACK OBAMA *(b. 1961), American politician and*
>   *forty-fourth president of the United States*

Avoiding foolishness is easier than applying wisdom. But then, avoiding foolishness *is* applying wisdom. The Obama Doctrine can be traced, its "wisdom" old:

> *Virtue's first rule is to avoid vice,*
> *wisdom's is to not be stupid.*[19]
> —HORACE *(65–25 BC), Roman poet*

Some things just never change. This book contains many quotations, as outlined in the preface. I obviously hope Benjamin Disraeli's dad was right:

The wisdom of the wise, and the experience of ages, may be preserved by quotations.[20]
—ISAAC D'ISRAELI *(1866–1948), British writer and scholar*

Charlie Munger, Warren Buffett's lifelong partner, who also worked with Warren Buffett's grandfather, most likely agrees with Isaac D'Israeli, as he uses it in his *Almanack*. He recommends the acquisition of what he likes to call "worldly wisdom":

Acquire worldly wisdom and adjust your behavior accordingly. If your new behavior gives you a little temporary unpopularity with your peer group... then to hell with them.[21]
—CHARLIE MUNGER

Foolishness can persist for a long time. Trends, therefore, can go on for a long time, but trees do not grow to the sky. Everything ends eventually, but trying to predict the end has widow-making potential.

Stein's Law and the Widow Maker

Feedback Loops and the Madness of Crowds

Stein's law, sometimes referred to as Herbert Stein's law, is a hugely valuable concept but a horrible timing device for investors. Named after Herbert Stein, Stein's law is defined as follows:

If something cannot go on forever, it will stop.[22]
—HERBERT STEIN *(1916–99), American economist*

Herb Stein was a common sense–laden economist. Stein's law is often adapted to finance and investments as something along the lines of "a trend that cannot continue, won't." It was first pronounced in the 1980s, arising first in a discussion of the balance-of-payments deficit, and was a response to those who think that if something cannot go on forever, steps must be taken to stop it.

In economic terms, Stein's law is often referred to as a feedback loop. A feedback loop can be both positive as well as negative. A feedback loop is self-reinforcing and can go on for much longer than experts predict. For instance, when Japan's 1980s bubble burst in the early 1990s, Japanese interest rates started to fall from around 8 percent in the case of the ten-year government bond yield. At one point in the mid-1990s, there was the idea that Stein's law applied, i.e., that interest rates could not fall any further.

With interest rates low, the investment idea was to sell short JGBs (Japanese government bonds), thereby benefiting from "inevitable" falling bond prices. (Bond prices typically fall as yields rise.) However, the rise in yields never came in a meaningful way. Selling short Japanese government bonds has been called "the widow maker," as the trade produced losses for years. The yields just kept falling, and the bonds rising. Being long the bonds, more or less the opposite of being short the bonds, has been the better option to this day.

A bit of sailing wisdom would have avoided much of the pain from the widow maker, and investments just like it. This wisdom is applicable to nearly anything going against you.

> You cannot fight the water, you've gotta learn how to live with it.
> —Sailing wisdom

Lemmings and Public Opinion

Applying Stein's law for timing purposes can be dangerous. This is especially true if it becomes the consensus view; that is, a view shared by most investors. The widow maker mentioned before is just one example. The view that yields cannot fall forever, implying mean reversion, i.e., a reversal of the ensuing trend is just around the corner, is widely held. While Stein's law might apply and seem logical and mass-agreeable, an element of caution and an element of skepticism seem wiser than joining the lemmings running off the cliff. (Lemmings are rodents and, according to public opinion, have an urge to commit mass suicide by jumping off a cliff.)

In 2016, investments in Japanese government bonds had had a great quarter-of-a-century run. Albert Edwards, ranked first in global strategy in the annual Extel Survey for fifteen years in a row through 2018, who cannot be counted among equities greatest bulls, whose annual gathering is dubbed the "Woodstock of the Bears," wrote the following in a related context:

> *One thing that has served me well in my personal finances and*
> *professional career is that when The Establishment is firm in its*
> *view that View X is the correct stance to take, I treat that with a*
> *healthy dose of scepticism as a starting point.*[23]
> —ALBERT EDWARDS *(b. 1961), British global investment*
>   *strategist*

This is closely related to Bob Farrell's rule no. 9, from his ten timeless rules for investors:

> *When all the experts and forecasts agree, something else is going*
> *to happen.*[24]
> —BOB FARRELL *(b. 1932), American financial analyst*

Skepticism toward lemming-like behavior or crowd-thinking, as are many other ideas, approaches, and concepts discussed in this book, is not new. Mark Twain, a riverboat pilot turned author, who put money into a number of bad investments and eventually went bankrupt, speaks on the subject:

> *The Majority is always in the wrong. Whenever you find you*
> *are on the side of the majority, it is time to reform—(or pause*
> *and reflect).*[25]
> —MARK TWAIN *(1835–1910), American writer, humorist,*
>   *and publisher*

We can trace this idea even further than to Mark Twain. I am quite confident that the further back we can trace an idea or a nugget of wisdom, the more powerful it is. (Whether it is also applicable to finance is a different thing entirely. Counting sheep when sleep-deprived is good old grandmotherly advice but is not applicable to finance.) Skepticism toward consensus thinking was not lost on nineteenth-century philosopher Søren Kierkegaard, who wrote under pseudonyms to disagree with himself:

> *The more people who believe something, the more apt it is to be*
> *wrong. The person who's right often has to stand alone.*[26]
> —SØREN KIERKEGAARD *(1813–55), Danish philosopher and*
>   *father of existentialism*

Some proverbs can be traced back thousands of years, being delivered by all sorts of media, poetry, songs, books, tablets, scripture, etc. A Chinese proverb states pretty much the same thing as Mr. Kierkegaard's remark:

> *A wise man makes his own decisions;*
> *an ignorant man follows public opinion.*
> —*Chinese proverb*

Contagion and the Hipster Effect

Going with the consensus is, I believe, very human. It is also contagious. Gustave Le Bon, a doctorate in medicine, who wrote several books on anthropology and archaeology before moving to natural science and social psychology, put it well in 1895. Contagion is a phenomenon that applies to any social behavior, of which financial markets are only one example.

> *Man, like animals, has a natural tendency to imitation. . . . The*
> *opinions and beliefs of crowds are specially propagated by con-*
> *tagion, but never by reasoning.*[27]
> —GUSTAVE LE BON *(1841–1931), French polymath*

Fashion is an example of lemming-like behavior and contagion. Some call the contagion the "hipster effect," whereby people who oppose mainstream culture all end up looking the same. René Girard (1923–2015), the French polymath, when formulating his mimetic (desire) theory, argued that imitation is inevitable, mimetic theory being beyond the scope of this book. (In a nutshell, it stipulates that you fancy holidays in Barbados because others do.) The herd mentality phenomenon was put well by one of the Founding Fathers of the United States:

A Mob's a Monster;
Heads enough, but no Brains.[28]
—BENJAMIN FRANKLIN *(1706–90), American polymath*

Hoodies and the latest financial fad are all related. Nietzsche, arguably an authority on madness, who wrote about the triumph of the overman but was himself sickly for most of his life, said the following on groupthink:

Madness is rare in the individual—but with groups, parties,
peoples, and ages it is the rule.[29]
—FRIEDRICH WILHELM NIETZSCHE *(1844–1900), German*
   philosopher

The classic and probably most often used quotation on the subject is from nineteenth-century Scottish author Charles Mackay, who wrote the all-time classic and must-read *Extraordinary Popular Delusions and The Madness of Crowds*, first published in 1841 under the then-title *Memoirs of the Extraordinary Popular Delusions*:

Men, it has been well said, think in herds, it will be seen that
they go mad in herds while they recover their senses slowly and
one by one.[30]
—CHARLES MACKAY *(1812–88), Scottish author*

Worldly Wisdom and Collective Idiocy
Bernard Baruch (1870–1965), one of the most famous Wall Street traders at the beginning of WWI, quoting Schiller, the German writer, not Shiller, the American Nobel laureate, a phonetical namesake, thought that collective idiocy is applicable to Wall Street:

Anyone taken as an individual is tolerably sensible and
reasonable—as a member of a crowd, he at once becomes a
blockhead.[31]
—FRIEDRICH SCHILLER *(1759–1805),*
   German writer

The practical relevance related to applied wisdom and risk management is that we can learn from everyone, not just from buffoons:

> *Who is a wise man?*
> *He who learns from all men.*[32]
> —*The Talmud*

Whether it's fashion, gimmicks, Pokémon, cryptocurrencies, underarm tattoos of football players, or investment products, does not matter that much. Groupthink and herding apply. One aspect of professional investment management is that the manager has an incentive to hug the consensus, to be conventional, to think inside the box. The portfolio managers of a fund are often serious employees of a firm, rather than eccentric, entrepreneurial college dropouts. This means they are exposed to career risk, rather than entrepreneurial risk. Keynes, the famous economist who studied not economics but classics and mathematics, made this point well on what he called "the game of professional investment":

> *Worldly wisdom teaches us that it is better for reputation to fail*
> *conventionally than to succeed unconventionally.*[33]
> —JOHN MAYNARD KEYNES *(1883–1946), British economist*

The incentive to be conventional might even be higher today than in Keynes's times:

> *My friend Gary Shilling, the first Chief Economist at Merrill*
> *Lynch, was summarily fired on three different occasions at my*
> *old shop for making three separate recession calls and he was*
> *spot-on each time.*[34]
> —DAVID ROSENBERG *(b. 1960), Canadian economist*

Conventional Wisdom and Contrarianism

The incentive to seek conventionalism is high. In institutional money management, equities were long perceived as too speculative, and institutional investors were mostly invested in bonds and cash-like instruments. This changed in the 1980s and 1990s. I remember well that some

European institutional investors bought their first stock in the late 1990s, i.e., just before they halved for the first time in the 2000s. History repeated itself some years later; it had to:

> History repeats itself.
> Has to; no one listens.[35]
> —STEVE TURNER (b. 1968), English music journalist,
>   biographer, and poet

In the 2000s it was hedge funds that were the "alternative asset class." In the early 2000s, many equity markets fell by 50 percent. Losing 50 percent of a 50 percent allocation to equities resulted in a 25 percent portfolio loss. No careers were lost though. Losing 25 percent was, as Keynes put it earlier, "failing conventionally" as equities were a traditional asset class at that moment in time. However, if an employed portfolio manager lost 20 percent of a 5 percent allocation to hedge funds, resulting in a 1 percent loss at the portfolio level, that employee's career was unlikely to remain fast-tracked for long. The failure was small in percentage terms but career-damaging because the investment, and therefore the loss, was unconventional.

Skepticism toward consensus thinking is part of many investors' DNA. It is probably a *sine qua non* for the greatest investors. Mario Gabelli, an American value investor and frequent Barron's roundtable participant, put it as follows:

> Conventional wisdom results in conventional returns.[36]
> —MARIO GABELLI (b. 1942), American investor

This was sort of not lost on Coco Chanel, not of Barron's roundtable, but of No. 5 fame:

> In order to be irreplaceable, one must always be different.[37]
> —GABRIELLE "COCO" CHANEL (1883–1971), French fashion
>   designer and businesswoman

The funny thing is that nearly all investors know this. Average thoughts result in average ideas, resulting in average performance. Since everyone knows this, it is not enough to be a contrarian. At times it feels as if contrarianism is the consensus (which it cannot be by definition). One ought to be, to use Barton Biggs's wit, a contra-contrarian.

> *Being a contrarian is very chic. The only trouble is that now everyone is a contrarian. . . . Therefore, instead of being contrarians, perhaps we should be contra-contrarians.*[38]
> —BARTON BIGGS *(1932–2012), American strategist, investor, and Wall Street legend*

A contrarian still needs an edge, as one contrarian put it:

> *The trick of being contrarian is to be early, not just different.*[39]
> —DEAN LEBARON *(b. 1933), adventure capitalist*

It goes without saying that there are exceptions to all rules. Stein's law is not excluded from this. There are situations where it might make sense to follow. Voltaire mentioned one:

> *If you see a Swiss banker jumping out of a window, follow him. There is sure to be a profit in it.*[40]
> —VOLTAIRE *(1694–1778), French philosopher*

Unconventional Wisdom and Reason

Intellectual Humility and Autonomy

It is said that John Maynard Keynes, who was a pioneer of women's reproductive rights and took a philosopher, Ludwig Wittgenstein, on his six-day honeymoon with his ballet dancer wife, once explained contrarianism to fellow investment committee members who were questioning one of Keynes's investment ideas, as follows:

> *I want to again explain my investment philosophy. It's called contrarianism. And what that means is that the stuff I like is stuff that the average person, when they look at it, won't like,*

and, indeed, will think it imprudent. So, the fact the committee
doesn't like it is the best evidence for it being a good investment.[41]
—JOHN MAYNARD KEYNES *(1883–1946), British economist*

Barton Biggs, who famously and often argued that "in the long run you want to be an owner, not a lender," translated this into the parlance of institutional investment management in 1999:

> *On an investment committee, it is almost better to be wrong*
> *with the group than to express a contrary view, even if it is right,*
> *because if by chance you are both wrong and a dissident, you*
> *are finished as a functioning member of the committee or firm.*[42]
> —BARTON BIGGS *(1932–2012), American strategist and*
>   *investor*

Contrarianism is a tricky concept. One aspect was already highlighted by Barton Biggs just before: the contrarianism-being-very-chic problem. One further complication is that the contrarian not only needs to think for himself but needs to be humble too. The following quotation is by Ray Dalio, a native of Queens and on this planet's richest top hundred list, and the title of the article in which it appeared was "Unconventional Wisdom."

> *To make money in the markets, you have to think independently*
> *and be humble. You have to be an independent thinker because*
> *you can't make money agreeing with the consensus view, which*
> *is already embedded in the price. Yet whenever you're betting*
> *against the consensus, there's a significant probability you're*
> *going to be wrong, so you have to be humble.*[43]
> —RAY DALIO *(b. 1949), American hedge fund manager and*
>   *author of* Principles

The problem with unconventional wisdom is that once a successful investor promotes it, it is copied—the lemmings and hipster effect. This then circles back to Mr. Biggs's point of being a contra-contrarian.

Pride and Failure

The consensus is not always false; the majority not always wrong. For quite a long while the Bitcoin crowd looked wise. Then Stein's law "happened," and Bitcoin crashed. By the end of 2020, the Bitcoin crowd looked wise again. There is indeed wisdom in crowds intermittently.

Another complication of contrarianism is that many contrarians fail. The celebration of a successful contrarian is an extreme form of *survivorship bias*. You see the winners, but not the losers. The losers have no historians:

> *Until lions have their historians, tales of the hunt shall always*
> *glorify the hunters.*
> —*African proverb*

Benny Hill of *Benny Hill Show* fame, who was allegedly already earning money at the age of six by entertaining punters at the beach with popular songs, understood survivorship bias:

> *Just because nobody complains doesn't mean all parachutes are*
> *perfect.*
> —ALFRED HAWTHORNE HILL *(1924–92), English comedian*
> *known as Benny Hill*

If an investment manager is celebrated at the end of a stellar decades-long track record, it nearly always transpires that he was a contrarian. He did something different, either at an important juncture of his career or regularly. But, as so often in science, life, and everything, it is the omissions that complete the full story. For each celebrated contrarian, there must be thousands who also did something extraordinarily different but failed. For many, the extraordinary contrarian behavior resulted in failure, and no champagne bottles were opened; no books were written; and no celebration took place. After the fact, failing unconventionally is often called stupidity or hubris.

The gentlemen from Long-Term Capital Management ("LTCM"), an American hedge fund, were contrarians too. They leveraged their exposure like no one else. They were different. Their behavior was not aligned with that of the mainstream investment manager, not even with the mainstream hedge fund.

LTCM, although legally a hedge fund, was more like a risk-intermediating investment bank, just without the then-implicit safety net of the taxpayer. (Up until the Great Recession of 2008/2009 the safety net, the too-big-to-fail phenomena, was *implicit*. Today the guarantees are *explicit*, as large losses have been socialized.)

Contrarians and Fools of Randomness

What this means is that for extraordinary success, one needs to be a contrarian, but not every contrarian is an extraordinary success. Nassim Taleb, author of the wonderfully titled best-selling book *Fooled by Randomness*, on a related topic of causality not working both ways symmetrically:

> *Plenty of unsuccessful entrepreneurs were persistent hard working people. . . . Clearly risk taking is necessary for large success— but it is also necessary for failure.*[44]
> —NASSIM NICHOLAS TALEB *(b. 1960), Lebanese American risk analyst and author*

The idea of contrarianism is not new. Again, as with many other aspects of human behavior, it can be traced:

> *Follow the course opposite to custom and you will almost always do well.*[45]
> —JEAN-JACQUES ROUSSEAU *(1712–78), Swiss-born French philosopher*

It goes without saying that a Rousseau quotation is the romanticized perspective on any topic, including contrarianism. Just being different, as mentioned earlier, is not enough. To be successful, one ought to be right. Quite often, but not always, that involves thinking both inside as well as outside the box. The latter, contrarianism, might or might not result in positive results. There's risk involved.

Going against the majority is risky, and success is a possibility, not a guarantee. While there sometimes is wisdom in crowds, as James

Surowiecki (b. 1967), an American journalist and author, suggested in his 2004 book, *The Wisdom of Crowds*, at other times there is not. The author of *The Art of Contrary Thinking*, Humphrey B. Neill, the "father of contrary opinion," as *Life* magazine dubbed him in a 1949 piece, argued:

> *The public is often right <u>during</u> the trends but wrong at both ends!*[46]
> —HUMPHREY B. NEILL *(1891–1977), American author and newsletter writer*

This means throughout the 1990s, when the Nasdaq Composite Index went from four hundred and fifty to forty-five hundred, it was not profitable to be a contrarian. In the year 2000, the market peak, it was. Newer research suggests that there is wisdom in smaller crowds, rather than in larger ones:

> *When problems are difficult, the wisdom of crowds tends to fail, and small groups make better decisions.*[47]
> —MARK BUCHANAN *(b. 1961), American physicist and author*

In his blog, which the above quotation is from, Mark Buchanan references a 2015 Santa Fe Institute working paper with the title "Can Small Crowds be Wise?", to which the four-word answer is: "Yes, under certain conditions." In 1907 Francis Galton, a cousin of Charles Darwin, for example, asked passersby at a county fair to estimate the weight of an ox for an article in *Nature*, a scientific journal. The median estimate was only 0.8 percent from the correct value.

Investment life would be too easy if one ought to just figure out what the consensus opinion is and then go the other way. One needs to reason, irrespective of what the big crowd, the smaller crowd, or your in-laws think. Skepticism is a good starting point for reasoning.

> *Reason is the main resource of man in his struggle for survival.*[48]
> —LUDWIG VON MISES *(1881–1973), Austrian School economist*

One of the best quotes on contrarianism, and proof that the idea is not novel, is attributed to N. M. Rothschild. I think it is one of the top quotes/concepts in this book.

> *Buy when the cannons are thundering and sell when the violins*
> *are playing.*[49]
> —N. M. (NATHAN MAYER) ROTHSCHILD *(1777–1836),*
>   *London-based German banker*

Greed and Fear

There are many variations of the cannons and violins quote. Apparently, one variation of the Rothschild quotation is also a French proverb. It manifests itself in the Wall Street aphorism of "buy cheap and sell dear." Benjamin Graham, author of *The Intelligent Investor*, which Warren Buffett once called the best book about investing ever written, translated the cannons and violins idea into finance parlance as follows:

> *The intelligent investor is a realist who sells to optimists and buys*
> *from pessimists.*[50]
> —BENJAMIN GRAHAM *(1894–1976), American investment*
>   *manager*

Graham taught a reason-based approach at Columbia Business School from 1928 to 1961. Among Graham's students was a young man from Omaha. The young man from Omaha phrased it as follows:

> *Be fearful when others are greedy.*
> *Be greedy when others are fearful.*[51]
> —WARREN BUFFETT *(b. 1930), American investor and*
>   *Graham disciple*

(Fun fact: the young man from Omaha got an A+ from Ben Graham at Columbia in 1951, and never stopped making the grade.)

The cannons-and-violins argument, i.e., the buy-cheap-and-sell-dear idea, has a second application, namely that when something is good, it is potentially a bad investment. If everyone agrees that things are going well, chances are that a lot of the "good news" is already in the price. Take US real estate around 2006/2007 as an example. Everything was well: every buyer got a deal; even NINJAs (no income, no job or asset, a term related to the US subprime mortgage crisis) got loans; real estate brokers were happy; bankers too. Early retirees were flipping real estate and making money. The president was encouraging "folks to own their own home,"[52] and the then-Fed chairman was cheerful too:

> [W]e do not expect significant spillovers from the subprime market to the rest of the economy or to the financial system.[53]
> —BEN BERNANKE (b. 1953), chairman of the Federal Reserve,
>   2006–14

However, Stein's law applied, i.e., something that cannot go on forever won't and didn't. When the violins are playing, skepticism should trump, as mentioned earlier. Furthermore, if something is too good to be true, Ian Morley's first law for clients applies. (Ian Morley was the founding chairman of the Alternative Investment Management Association, AIMA, the global trade association for the hedge fund industry.)

> If it sounds too good to be true, you can bet your bottom dollar that it probably is.[54]
> —IAN MORLEY (b. 1951), chairman, Wentworth Hall
>   Consultancy, the first law for clients

There is an epigram saying exactly that:

> Too much of a good thing is just that.
> —Epigram

Contrarianism does not necessarily mean going against the crowd. Most people do not touch a hot stove. There is a reason for this. It is hot, risky, and devoid of reason. Doing the opposite from the crowd for the sake of doing the opposite of the crowd only works in exceptional circumstances. As Peter Thiel, cofounder of PayPal and Facebook's first investor, put it:

> The most contrarian thing of all is not to oppose the crowd but to think for yourself.[55]
> —PETER THIEL (b. 1967), American entrepreneur

Independent thought was too a cardinal rule for Benjamin Graham, born Benjamin Grossbaum, father of modern security analysis and value investing, who translated Homer into Latin and Virgil into Greek for fun:

> There are two requirements for success in Wall Street. One, you have to think correctly; and secondly, you have to think independently.[56]
> —BENJAMIN GRAHAM (1894–1976), London-born American investment manager

One exceptional circumstance is mass ignorance. Ignorance—and I am sure about this—is never advisable in the discipline of assessing risk and, therefore, long-term capital preservation.

> When everybody ignores a vital subject, it is likely to be important to everybody.[57]
> —HUMPHREY B. NEILL (1895–1977), author of The Art of Contrary Thinking

One final aspect of contrarianism is that it is easier said than done. Going against the mainstream is not for everyone. As Stanley Druckenmiller, an American hedge fund manager and Soros's Quantum Fund portfolio manager, put it:

> It takes courage to be a pig.[58]
> —STANLEY DRUCKENMILLER (b. 1953), American investor

Allow me to summarize.

Bottom Line

The pursuit of worldly wisdom is laudable but difficult, fraught with potholes, and time-consuming. Avoiding folly is easier. Wisdom is scarce; folly is not. One central takeaway of this book is to spot folly in others and avoid one's own. Avoiding folly *is* applied wisdom.

If something cannot go on forever, it will stop. Being skeptical of current investor behavior and the ensuing trend is all very well, but swimming against the current has widow-making potential.

Contrarianism is an attitude, a healthy way to gain perspective, not an investment axiom. There are times when it makes sense to join the crowd. Contrarianism can be both the key to success, as well as a widow maker. Being simply different is not enough. Thinking independently is a good starting point though.

There is wisdom in crowds. The public is often right during the trend. However, sometimes one ought to buy when the cannons are thundering and sell when the violins are playing, that is, do the opposite of the crowd. And, yes, it is easier said than done.

———

Joining the crowd or going against the crowd can both fail, as can everything else. It is an iron law, as discussed in the next chapter.

THE IRON LAW OF FAILURE

When circumstances change,
I change my mind—what do you do?
—John Maynard Keynes

The iron law of failure states that in the end, everything fails. There is gravitational pull to becoming toast. The universe, your government, your life, your toaster, etc. all will fail eventually. The term and law were coined by British author and economist Paul Ormerod. One key insight of the law is that it takes some of the uncertainty out of the equation: there is no uncertainty about the *if*, only about the *when.*

Circumstances change. Changing circumstances can be analyzed as to whether they are bringing a system or entity closer to failure or moving it away from failure. Paying attention to changing circumstances is paramount in the game of survival, followed by adapting to it.

Some man-made systems are chaotic, meaning that a small disturbance can have a large impact. If the wing flap of a butterfly in the Amazon can cause a tornado in Texas or the nose of an Egyptian goddess can change world history, forecasting outcomes in a chaotic system is foolhardy.

Failure can be good because there is learning. Survival, and therefore risk management, is key. Otherwise there is just death, rather than learning.

Fear of failure can be a good thing too. Both Mike Tyson and Leonardo da Vinci thought so. The key is to remain cool.

Blissful Ignorance and the Butterfly Effect

Cyborgs and Global Cooling

Everything fails. The known universe started a couple of billion years ago with the big bang and will probably end in a couple of billion years, a phenomenon called the big crunch. This is not a pessimistic assessment, even though Stephen Hawking was once asked in the Far East not to mention the big crunch because of the effect it might have on the stock market. (The market crashed anyhow.)[59] The big crunch being a couple of billion years out, there is plenty of time to enjoy oneself in the interim.

Our sun was born 4.6 billion years ago and will eventually run out of energy and start to turn into a red giant roughly five billion years from now. Given that Andromeda will collide with our own galaxy in around four billion years, our sun blowing up might actually not be such a big deal. While computer simulations of Andromeda bumping into "us" are quite fascinating to watch, the cosmic timescales are irrelevant for our purposes. But failure isn't.

Will Durant, who together with his wife popularized both history and philosophy between 1935 and 1975, once said:

> *Civilization is an interlude between ice ages.*[60]
> —WILL DURANT *(1885–1981), American writer, historian,*
>   *and philosopher*

Fortunately, our planet is heating up. Thanks to global warming, the next ice age is not in Homo sapiens' immediate future. All the predictions as to a new ice age just being around the corner by atmospheric physicists in the 1970s were wrong, fortunately.

Ice ages are not particularly friendly for complex life forms. "Too cold" is much worse than "too warm" both from a humanitarian as well as a biodiversity perspective. However, both the cosmological as well as the earthly geological timescale are not relevant for applying wisdom and avoiding folly in financial matters. Whether we will be finished off by cyborgs long before the next cosmological or geological catastrophe, an idea that both Stephen Hawking and James Lovelock of GAIA fame entertained, is open to debate. (Fun fact: James Lovelock [b. 1919] once held Stephen Hawking [1942–2018] in his arms when Stephen was a baby and James Lovelock was visiting the Hawkings.) The point here is that there is a law that ties together the long term and the short term: failure.

Excellence and Failure

Most empires and most businesses fail.[61] Extinction is common in politics, business, and life. Ninety-nine point ninety-nine percent of all biological species that have ever existed are now extinct. On a somewhat shorter timescale, empires come and go. On an even shorter timescale, roughly 80 percent of businesses do not survive beyond the first year. Between 1900 and 1920 there were almost two thousand car companies. Most of them are gone. Most of the firms in Tom Peters's *In Search of Excellence* from the 1980s have failed too by now. They went Kodak. British economist Paul Ormerod, in a very commendable book called *Why Most Things Fail*, calls this the iron law of failure:

> *The Iron Law of Failure appears to extend from the world of biology into human activities, into social and economic organisations. The precise mathematical relationship, which describes the link between the frequency and size of the extinction of companies, for example, is virtually identical to that which describes the extinction of biological species in the fossil record. Only the timescales differ.*[62]
>
> —PAUL ORMEROD *(b. 1950), British economist*

As Jim Rogers, cofounder of the Quantum Fund with George Soros in the 1970s, put it in the afterword to his bestselling *Investment Biker*, a book on his 65,067-mile motor bike tour around the world from March 1990 to August 1992:

> *If there's one thing I've learned in going around the world, it's that societies become rich, swagger around for a few years, decades, or centuries, and then their hour is done.*[63]
> —JIM ROGERS *(b. 1942), American investment biker and adventure capitalist*

Failure is, of course, not a new concept. Gustave Le Bon, who we met in chapter one in relation to the hipster effect, writing in 1895, ends his classic book on a cheerful note:

> *To pass in pursuit of an ideal from the barbarous to the civilized state, and then, when this ideal has lost its virtue, to decline and die, such is the cycle of the life of a people.*[64]
> —GUSTAVE LE *Bon (1841–1931), French polymath*

In essence, Stein's law from chapter one applies. What cannot go on forever, won't. The parallels between species, people, solar systems, firms, governments, political unions, reserve currencies, etc., are striking in terms of failure. They are all complex entities that try to survive in dynamic environments, which evolve over time but eventually fail.

Despite striking parallels between the social and economic world and the world of biology, there is a fundamental difference between the two. Ormerod writes: "The process of evolution in biological species cannot be planned. Species cannot act with the intent of increasing their fitness to survive. In contrast, in human society, individuals, firms and governments all strive consciously to devise successful strategies for survival. They adapt these strategies over time to avoid failure and alter their plans as circumstances change."[65]

John Maynard Keynes made the point most succinctly. The following is one of my top ten quotations of all time:

> *When circumstances change, I change my mind—what do you do?*[66]
> —JOHN MAYNARD KEYNES *(1883–1946), British economist*

Being Wrong and Staying Wrong

Dennis Gartman, a former trader and editor of the *Gartman Letter*, used to publish his most important trading rules every year. As far as I can tell, the rule from Keynes was nearly always on the list. Responding to change is key. (What change to overlook is key too. Managing wealth and risk would be too easy otherwise.) The practical relevance is that if circumstances change, so does one's investment thesis. If it does, it is best to reconsider one's risk and, potentially, reposition one's portfolio accordingly. This is how one writer put it when reminiscing about one famous stock operator:

> *I cannot fear to be wrong because I never think I am wrong until I am proven wrong.*[67]
> —EDWIN LEFÈVRE *(1871–1943), American journalist and writer*

The Keynes quotation says one ought to respond to changing circumstances before the iron law of failure applies. However, there are limits to planning. An early critic of conventional economic analysis was Austrian economist Friedrich August von Hayek, cowinner of the 1974 Nobel Memorial Prize in Economic Sciences.

> *Human reason can neither predict nor deliberately shape its own future. Its advances consist in finding out where it has been wrong.*[68]
> —F. A. HAYEK *(1899–1992), Austrian economist*

While most twentieth-century proponents of the dismal science suggest economics should be conducted in a similar fashion to physics, where theories depict mechanical systems and mathematics can precisely describe these systems, Hayek's views were much more rooted in biology. He believed individual behavior is not fixed like a screw or cog in a machine, but evolves in response to the behavior of others.

According to Paul Ormerod, Hayek, unlike most twentieth-century economists, understood and admired the achievements of other intellectual disciplines, especially anthropology. The complex interactions between individuals, in Hayek's view, give rise to inherent limits to knowledge of how systems behave at the aggregate level. No matter how smart the planner or how much information he gathers, there are inescapable limits to how much can be known about the systems.

The limits of knowledge were not lost on Bruce Lee:

> *Knowledge will give you power, but character respect.*[69]
> —BRUCE LEE *(1940–73), Hong Kong and American martial artist*

Whether Bruce Lee, who had a philosophical bent, was paraphrasing Francis Bacon, I do not know:

> *The philosopher Francis Bacon once said that knowledge is power. And that's true. But wisdom is perspective. And that's even more important than power.*[70]
> —THOMAS MORRIS *(b. 1952), American philosopher and author of* Philosophy for Dummies

Accidents and Cleopatra's Nose

In a book called *Normal Accidents*, sociologist Charles Perrow examines failures of man-made systems (power plants, airplanes, etc.). He makes the point that it is human nature to find someone to blame for an accident. We want to know the "cause." However, Perrow argues that the cause of an accident of a man-made system is to be found in the complexity of the system.

> *The odd term <u>normal accident</u> is meant to signal that, given the system characteristics, multiple and unexpected interactions of failures are inevitable.*[71]
> —CHARLES PERROW *(1925–2019), American sociologist*

An accident that results in a catastrophe is often a series of small events that, viewed by themselves, seem trivial. It is the interaction of multiple failures that can explain the accident.[72] Patient accident reconstruction often reveals the banality and triviality behind most catastrophes. In other words, great events can have small beginnings.

Chaos theory suggests, among other things, that meaningful events, accidents, disturbances, etc., can have a trivial beginning. This has been known for a while:

> *The beginnings of all things are small.*[73]
> —CICERO *(106–43 BC), Roman politician, orator, and*
>   *philosopher*

In the practitioner's literature, it is argued that, for example, the flatulence of a butterfly in the Amazon can cause a tornado in Texas. (In the academic literature, it is a butterfly's wing flap that causes the disturbance in Texas.) Cleopatra's nose was trivial; the actions taken by Julius Caesar and Mark Antony to win her over were not.

> *Cleopatra's nose, had it been shorter, the whole face of the world*
> *would have changed.*[74]
> —BLAISE PASCAL *(1623–62), French mathematician*

The idea of chaos theory suggests that what appears to be an overly complex, turbulent system (origins of life on Earth, weather, financial markets, etc.) can begin with simple components (amino acids, water, day traders, etc.), operating under a few simple rules (photosynthesis, evaporation, buy low/sell high, etc.). One of the characteristics of such a system is that a small change in the initial conditions, often too small to measure, can ultimately lead to radically different outcome or behavior.

Sensitivity to initial conditions is popularly known as the butterfly effect, so-called because of the title of a paper given by Edward Lorenz, the American mathematician, meteorologist, and pioneer of chaos theory, in 1972 to the American Association for the Advancement of Science, in Washington, DC, entitled "Predictability: Does the Flap of a Butterfly's Wings in Brazil Set Off a Tornado in Texas?" The flapping wing represents a small change in the initial condition of the system, which can cause a chain of events leading to large-scale phenomena. Had the butterfly not flapped its wings, the trajectory of the system might have been vastly different.

The butterfly effect is very much applicable to financial systems. Richard Bookstaber, who had chief risk officer roles on both the buy-side at

Moore Capital and Bridgewater, and on the sell-side at Morgan Stanley and Salomon, and from 2009 to 2015 also served in the public sector at the SEC and the US Treasury, writing on systemic risk in a book published prior to the 2008 financial crisis, put it simply:

> *Systems with high levels of interactive complexity are subject to failures that seem to come out of nowhere or that appear unfathomably improbable.*[75]
> —RICHARD BOOKSTABER *(b. 1950), American risk manager and risk researcher*

Markets and economies are systems with high levels of interactive complexity. Next time you hear someone predict the stock market, interest rates, or inflation one year hence, you now know how seriously to take the forecast(er).

The Devil and the Details

Big-picture thinking is all very laudable and grand, but the devil is in the details. However, when spending all one's energy on the details, there is the risk of missing the big picture, as in not seeing the wood for the trees. Andrew Haldane from the Bank of England, who in 2014 was named among the one hundred most influential people by *Time* magazine, summed it up well in a 2012 Jackson Hole speech with the wonderful apt title "The Dog and the Frisbee," and subtitle of "Ignorance is Bliss":[76]

> *The general message here is that the more complex the environment, the greater the perils of complex control. The optimal response to a complex environment is often not a fully state-contingent rule. Rather, it is to simplify and streamline. In complex environments, decision rules based on one, or a few, good reasons can trump sophisticated alternatives. Less may be more.*[77]
> —ANDREW G. HALDANE *(b. 1967), chief economist at the Bank of England*

In biology, we know extinction will occur in the future. We can elaborate on extinction's probabilities. However, we do not know which species are going to become extinct and when. I believe this is applicable to finance. We know that there will be failure, collapse, market mayhem, and wealth destruction in the future. We can also assess probabilities. However, we cannot pinpoint the next failure precisely. We can avoid errors by becoming savvier. That said, avoiding folly is a survival technique. Ayn Rand, author of *Atlas Shrugged*, founder of Objectivism, enthusiastic stamp collector, and long-term friend of Alan Greenspan, has some advice regarding avoiding folly:

> *You can avoid reality, but you cannot avoid the consequences of avoiding reality.*[78]
> —AYN RAND *(1905–82), Russian American novelist and philosopher*

Failure and survival are two sides of the same coin. Who will survive? It is not entirely random as to who survives in stressful situations or hostile environments and who does not. In mountaineering, it is not the best climbers who survive an accident but those who are best prepared and have no mismatch between perceived risk and true risk.

Avoiding reality is folly in mountaineering and elsewhere. Chance, as nearly everywhere else in the universe and human affairs, also plays a role. Louis Pasteur, whose scientific breakthroughs in vaccination and disease prevention reduced human suffering on an astronomical scale, put it well:

> *Chance favours only the prepared mind.*[79]
> —LOUIS PASTEUR *(1822–95), French chemist and microbiologist*

Readiness also holds true for any economic entity, company, asset manager, bank, etc. Any institution can get into dire straits under stress (or the other way around; get under stress in dire straits) or have the market "turn against them," wherein the environment becomes hostile. Institutions can also either fail or endure, but those that have an edge in aligning true risk with perceived risk may improve their chances of survival. Those with an edge have the optionality. The conservationist behind the Svalbard Global Seed Vault in Norway, a vault to preserve a wide variety of plant seeds from large-scale disaster, most likely understands options:

*In the game of life, less diversity means fewer options for change.
Wild or domesticated, panda or pea, adaptation is the require-
ment for survival.*[80]
—CARY FOWLER *(b. 1949), American agriculturalist*

Evolution and Survival

Stress and IQ Reduction

Aviation is an area of study where survival is concerned. Author and
scholar Laurence Gonzales, who spent his whole life seeking risk and
thinking and writing about survival, starts his praiseworthy book on the
subject by telling the story of his father who, at the end of World War II,
was shot down when piloting a B-17 over Dusseldorf. Somehow his father
survived the crash from twenty-seven thousand feet, while all other crew
members did not. Heavily injured, he watched a local peasant walk up to
the window, point a pistol at his head, and pull the trigger. Fortunately,
the gun malfunctioned. What are the chances? As Aristotle might have
said on the occasion:

> *Part of probability is that the improbable can occur.*[81]
> —ARISTOTLE *(384–322 BC), Greek philosopher*

In aviation, one often hears flight instructors say that, once airborne, a
pilot's IQ is halved. The logic of this notion is that the human brain, from
an evolutionary perspective, is not "designed" (poor choice of words, I
know) to deal with some of the modern-day vagaries. To put it differently, the time for the species—in this case, us—was too short to adapt
to the new environment (i.e., modernity). In hang gliding, for example,
one needs to land *into* the wind. If the pilot lands *with* the wind, i.e., the
wind coming from the rear instead of the front, the speed of the glider
is added to the wind instead of subtracted, which nearly always results
in an experience that is unpleasant and embarrassing. Oscar Wilde's wit
captures hang-gliding-landing accidents well:

> *Experience is the name that everyone gives to their mistakes.*[82]
> —OSCAR WILDE *(1854–1900), Irish author*

Wind direction is normally marked by a windsock in the landing zone. The windsock points in the opposite direction from where the wind comes. The pilot needs to fly a rectangle over the landing zone where the actual landing happens, *into* the wind. The speed of the glider is thus reduced by the wind. Given that the pilot needs to deal with three dimensions (for which evolution did not have enough time prepare the human brain yet) and needs to focus on the landing procedure, it can happen that the pilot sometimes misinterprets the direction of the windsock and lands *with* the wind instead of *into* the wind.

Interpreting from where the wind comes by observing a windsock under *normal* circumstances is trivial. However, under the *stress* of landing, the obvious can become fuzzy—hence the aphorism of the pilot not having his full IQ at his disposal. I was a hobby hang-gliding pilot in my early twenties. Suffice to say, I learned the above the hard way:

> *If you hold a cat by the tail, you learn things that cannot be learned in any other way.*[83]
> —MARK TWAIN *(1835–1910), American author*

Or, as the author of the all-time classic *A Random Walk Down Wall Street* put it in relation to investing in the stock market:

> *Some things in life can never fully be appreciated or understood by a virgin.*[84]
> —BURTON G. MALKIEL *(b. 1932), American economist*

Emotions and Moods

Under stress, mammalian emotions and savannah instincts take over. Stress releases cortisol into the blood. It invades the hippocampus and interferes with its work. Stress causes most people to focus narrowly on the thing that they consider most important, and it may be the wrong thing. Under extreme stress, the visual field narrows. This reaction is referred to as tunnel vision.

Laurence Gonzales in *Deep Survival* states that it has happened numerous times that airline pilots were ordered to abort landing and simply did not hear the warning from the tower or did not see the snowplow in the middle of the runway. Tunnel vision is one of the reasons why commercial airlines have a copilot.

Under stress, emotion takes over from the thinking part of the brain, the neocortex, to affect an instinctive set of responses necessary for survival. This has been referred to as the "hostile takeover of consciousness by emotion."[85] The young chronicler of humankind's brief history, the author of *Sapiens*, brings it to the point well:

> If the feelings of some ancient ancestor made a mistake, the genes shaping these feelings did not pass on to the next generation. Feelings are thus not the opposite of rationality—they embody evolutionary rationality.[86]
> —YUVAL NOAH HARARI (b. 1976), Israeli historian and author

Emotions are genetic survival mechanisms, but they do not always work for the benefit of the individual. They work across many trials to keep the species alive. The individual may live or die, but over a few million years, more mammals lived than died by letting emotion take over, and so emotion was selected as a stress response for survival. If I had to summarize Morgan Housel's book *The Psychology of Money* in a single word, it would be "survival."

> If I had to summarize money success in a single word it would be "survival."[87]
> —MORGAN HOUSEL (b. 1983), American columnist and author

Frank Lowy, who survived the ghetto in Hungary during World War II and a British detention camp in Cyprus when picked up en route, heading for Palestine, knew what he was talking about:

> The human being is very resourceful. When you fight for survival, you don't think much; you just do. If you think too much, you sink.[88]
> —FRANK LOWY (b. 1930), Czechoslovak-born Australian Israeli stuntman and businessman

There is a vast amount of empirical financial research pointing out that unprofessional investors have far poorer performance than professional investors. The key reason is emotions. Professional investors are often aware of the behavioral phenomena of being overconfident and thereby can adjust their behavior accordingly. The biggest mistake by nonprofessional investors is cutting profits short and not taking losses early:

> *The majority of unskilled investors stubbornly hold onto their losses when the losses are small and reasonable. They could get out cheaply, but being emotionally involved and human, they keep waiting and hoping until their loss gets much bigger and costs them dearly.*[89]
> —WILLIAM O'NEIL *(b. 1933), American investor*

Moods are contagious, and the emotional states involved with smiling, humor, and laughter are among the most contagious of all. Laughter does not take conscious thought. Laughter stimulates the left prefrontal cortex, an area in the brain that helps us to feel good and to be motivated. There is evidence that laughter can send chemical signals to actively inhibit the firing of nerves in parts of the brain, thereby dampening fear. Investors ordinarily do not share a laugh when their portfolios start the year with a 20 percent loss. They should. Having a good laugh is a survival technique, at least according to business management book writer Tom Peters, who has been in the business of searching for excellence for a long while.

> *In order to survive in these wild times, you're going to make a total fool of yourself with incredible regularity. If you can't laugh about it, then you are doomed.*[90]
> —TOM PETERS *(b. 1942), American business writer*

Fear and Coolness

Only in recent years has neuroscience begun to understand the detailed physiology of emotional states, such as fear. The neocortex is responsible for your IQ, your conscious decisions, your analytical abilities. But the amygdale stand as sort of a watchdog for the organism.[91] It is not a lack of fear that separates elite performers from the rest of us. They are afraid, too, but are not consumed by it. They manage fear. They use it to focus on taking correct action. Fear is both good and bad:

> *Fear is your best friend or your worst enemy. It's like fire. If you can control it, it can cook for you, it can heat your house. If you can't control it, it will burn everything around you and destroy you. If you can control your fear, it makes you more alert, like a deer coming across the lawn.*[92]
> —MIKE TYSON *(b. 1966), American boxer*

Leonardo da Vinci said pretty much the same thing. Fear is one of nature's risk management devices:

> *Just as courage imperils life, fear protects it.*[93]
> —LEONARDO DA VINCI *(1452–1519), Italian polymath*

Fear is universal and unavoidable, as General "Bandito" Patton might have said at this point:

> *If we take the generally accepted definition of bravery as a quality that knows no fear, I have never seen a brave man. All men are frightened. The more intelligent they are, the more they are frightened.*[94]
> —GEORGE S. PATTON *(1885–1945), American general*

Translating this into finance, too intelligent a person might be too risk-averse, and therefore somewhat unqualified to take the necessary risks that are a prerequisite for returns. As Warren Buffett put it, one need not be a genius to do well in finance:

> *Successful investing requires a quality of temperament, not a high IQ. You need an IQ of 125 tops . . . and you must be able to think for yourself.*[95]
> —WARREN BUFFETT *(b. 1930), chairman, CEO, and largest shareholder of Berkshire Hathaway*

One of the lessons Gonzales suggests from studying survival in aviation and extreme sports is to remain calm under stress (i.e., not to panic).

Not panicking is easier said than done. Because emotions are called "hot cognitions," not panicking is known as "being cool."

Bertrand Russell, who was an active pacifist during World War I and was dismissed from his lecturer job at Trinity College, Cambridge, due to his beliefs, on the relationship between knowledge and emotions:

> *The degree of one's emotions varies inversely with one's knowledge of the facts—the less you know, the hotter you get.*[96]
> —BERTRAND RUSSELL *(1872–1970), British philosopher*

"Cool" as a slang expression goes back to the 1800s, but its contemporary sense originated with African American jazz musicians in the 1940s. Jazz was "cool" compared with the hot, emotional bebop it had begun to overshadow. "Being cool" means to remain calm, to channel emotions, and to be able to turn fear into focus.

Failure and Idiocy

Hubris and Nonsurvival

The ability to concentrate one's attention on the matter at hand is a prerequisite for a survival strategy in a hostile environment or when under stress. Erasmus, the Dutch scholarly reformer, who sought refuge in Basel, Switzerland, where he was free to continue to write satire of the Roman Catholic Church, had some good advice when under stress:

> *Keep cool.*[97]
> —ERASMUS *(ca. 1466–1536), Dutch humanist, theologian, and philosopher, in a letter to Luther*

This was surprisingly good advice then, and still is. While humor, keeping cool, and controlled fear are good, hubris is not. Hubris was a human trait well known to the ancient Greeks, and it is one that many financial professionals can relate to. To Louis Moore Bacon (b. 1956), an American hedge fund manager, hubris is one of five warning signs when analyzing a manager.[98] Turnaround artist Albert J. Dunlap found a way to spot hubris in corporations:

> *[T]he success of a corporation is inversely proportional to the size and opulence of its headquarters.*[99]
> —ALBERT J. DUNLAP *(1937–2019), American business executive*

Many a financial institution's nonsurvival is attributed to hubris. How to avoid hubris? Become a Stoic philosopher:

> *What is the first business of one who practices philosophy? To get rid of self-conceit. For it is impossible for anyone to begin to learn that which he thinks he already knows.*[100]
> —EPICTETUS *(ca. AD 55–ca. 135), Greek Stoic philosopher*

As much as I like quoting philosophers, there is an element of risk in becoming one. Intellectual overconfidence and self-conceit are not entirely unheard of in finance and elsewhere. There is an element of risk when quoting philosophers, too, especially as I do, when quoting out of original context and applying to something else, finance and risk management in my case. Here is one way of putting it. It is from one of my all-time favorite films, *A Fish Called Wanda*:

Otto: "Apes don't read philosophy."

Wanda: "Yes they do, Otto, they just don't understand it."

Wanda, hilariously well performed by two-time Golden Globe–winning and Emmy Award–nominated Jamie Lee Curtis, Tony Curtis's daughter, then goes on:

> *Let me correct you on a few things. Aristotle was not Belgian. The central message of Buddhism is not "Every Man for Himself." And the London Underground is not a political movement. Those are all mistakes, Otto.*[101]
> —JAMIE LEE CURTIS *(b. 1958), American actress and writer of books for children, as Wanda*

Ignorance and Death

Gonzales tells the story of a US Army Ranger, arguably someone well trained for survival in hostile environments, who took a guided commercial rafting trip, fell off the boat, and drowned in shallow water. The ranger refused rescue. (Army Rangers fail the training program if rescued; their credo is "death before dishonor.") He floated calmly downstream. He felt he was in no real danger because of all the training he had undergone in much worse conditions. Then he arrived at a place where a big rock blocked the middle of the current. He was sucked under, pinned, and drowned. The official report said, "The guest clearly did not take the situation seriously."[102] This was brought to the point well by Minna Antrim, author of *Don'ts for Girls: A Manual of Mistakes*:

> *Experience is a good teacher, but she sends in terrific bills.*[103]
> —MINNA ANTRIM *(1861–1950), American writer*

Ueli Steck died aged forty on April 30, 2017. Ueli Steck was a Swiss extreme rock climber, a self-acclaimed "control freak," lauded for his speed and innovation, and nicknamed "Swiss Machine" for he did not actually climb mountains; he "sprinted" them, often alone. To nonmountaineers he was suicidal, as BASE jumpers or free solo climbers are often perceived.

In an interview in 2013, after a solo speed climb up Annapurna, the tenth highest mountain in the world, the sympathetic and humble Steck said that he consciously took risks of dying. He barely survived his first attempt up Annapurna in 2007, where he got hit by a stone and fell two hundred meters. Although married, he consciously, reasonably, commendably, and probably presciently did not reproduce. (His wife, a passionate rock mountaineer, too, nearly died during a "casual" local Sunday hike they took together in 2010. She slipped and fell thirty meters while overtaking other, more risk-averse hikers.) It is not just nonmountaineers who "perceive" the risk to be terminal; mountaineers know it too:

> *Life and death are part of the rope team.*[104]
> —*Mountaineering wisdom/French saying*

Walking on thin ice is risky; literally.

Walking on thin ice is always risky.[105]
—David Attenborough *(b. 1926), English naturalist and*
  broadcaster

Reinhold Messner, a surviving mountain adventurer who is famous for being the first man to climb Mount Everest with no supplemental oxygen, and who lost a brother during his first major Himalayan climb in 1970, keeps track of famous deaths. At the entrance of his museum, he maintains a plaque with a list of top mountaineers, "the rock and ice stars," who managed to turn seventy, i.e., survived. Messner says that over the past two hundred years, roughly half of the top mountain climbers have died in the mountains and did not reach the age of seventy. Messner argues luck is part of the game:

The real art [in rock climbing] is to survive. To survive we all
need a bit of luck though.[106]
—Reinhold Messner *(b. 1944), German-speaking Italian*
  mountaineer

Rock climbing, then, is quite different from nature. In nature, it is the toughest snow leopards that survive high altitude, not luck.

Only the toughest can survive among the savage beauty of the
world's highest mountains.[107]
—David Attenborough *(b. 1926), English writer, producer,*
  and director

The practical relevance here is that Steck did not die on a mission but during preparation for a mission. His next mission was running up Mount Everest, and then he proceeded with a traverse to the peak of Lhotse, the world's fourth-highest mountain, all without supplemental oxygen. This planned endeavor, of course, makes perfect sense to nearly anyone.

He fell a thousand meters during a solo but routine exploration tour, most likely underestimating risk. (He was alone, his partner staying at the base because of frostbite that day, so "bad luck" was involved too.) Reinhold Messner, who knows the place where Steck died, said that a small stone falling on your hand is enough to kill you. This means the risk-taker is exposed to an entirely trivial and noncontrollable occurrence. Death, therefore, is a macabre form of being "fooled by randomness." Here is how one BASE (B = Building, A = Antenna, S = Span, E = Earth) jumper put it:

> *It's all about the taste of fear and lack of control. I love it.*[108]
> —PAUL FORTUN *(b. 1968), Norwegian BASE jumper and
>   base-jumping event organizer*

Micro Risks and MicroMorts

There is a book called *The Norm Chronicles,* and it includes stories and numbers about danger. The authors, a journalist and a statistician, use a measure called a MicroMort, a unit that allows for comparing different dangers. The word is derived from the term *micro* risk, i.e., very low-probability risks like breaking your neck while showering, being struck by lightning, drowning in a beer flood, falling off a bridge and being sniped midway, etc., "Mort" means death in French.

One MicroMort is roughly the probability of a normal person in a normal country experiencing a nonnatural death during a normal day by just going about their normal business. It is about a one-in-a-million chance, i.e., roughly the same probability of tossing twenty coins into the air and having all of them fall heads, facing up. (Or playing Russian roulette seventy-six times in a row and still remaining standing.)

By using extensive statistics, the two authors can quantify and compare dangers. For example, one MicroMort is roughly like riding a motorbike for seven miles (in the UK), driving a car for three hundred and thirty-three miles, flying commercial for seventy-five hundred miles, or being hit by an asteroid during a lifetime. Scuba diving is about five MicroMorts per dive; skydiving around ten per jump, and base-jumping is around four hundred and thirty MicroMorts per jump.

Running a marathon is around seven MicroMorts. (After all, its founder, Pheidippides, dropped dead after running twenty-six miles to announce victory at the Battle of Marathon.) Your risk of being accidentally killed in a (UK) hospital due to an avoidable safety lapse is about seventy-six MicroMorts per day, i.e., roughly the same as seven to eight skydiving jumps. The funny thing, therefore, is that if you break your leg during a skydiving jump and are brought to the hospital, your risk of dying increases by a factor of fifty.[109]

Giving birth in the UK is about one hundred and twenty MicroMorts per birth for the mother, and much safer than elsewhere. (For the baby, it is about forty-three hundred MicroMorts in the UK, and forty thousand MicroMorts globally, per birth.) Serving in Afghanistan at peak risk period is forty-seven MicroMorts per day, which compares to around twenty-five thousand MicroMorts of flying a bomber command in the Second World War, per mission.

Mountaineering above seven thousand meters is about forty-three thousand MicroMorts per climb, i.e., a bit like playing Russian roulette with a twenty-three-chamber gun once. One of many aspects about danger the two authors highlight is that, for example, in skydiving, the probability of a novice to the sport dying is smaller than that of the expert. As in many other fields, there is less hubris among nonexperts. The nonexperts are more aware of their own ignorance than are the experienced macho daredevils.

At what level risk-taking becomes suicidal or idiotic is difficult to judge and subjective. The authors wrote in 2013:

> Taking sky-diving, scuba-diving, marathon-running and other moderately extreme sports, there seems to be some natural level of risk—up to around 10 MicroMorts—that most participants are prepared to accept while remaining reasonably sensible. This does not include base-jumping or climbing to high altitudes.[110]
>
> —MICHAEL BLASTLAND and DAVID SPIEGELHALTER

With respect to risk-taking and mountaineering, I believe the following sums up the situation well:

> To those who are enthralled by mountains, their wonder is beyond all dispute. To those who are not, their allure is a kind of madness.[111]
>
> —ROBERT MACFARLANE (b. 1976), British writer

Elite Training and the Turkey Problem

The takeaway of the ranger and Swiss Machine stories is twofold. First, elite and extensive training can cause overconfidence, resulting in an underestimation of risk. In the case of the Army Ranger, this was clearly the case. Rumor has it that mountaineering legend Reinhold Messner was returning late to his castle in the Dolomites from a social occasion in 1995, could not find his house keys, climbed over the wall, fell, and broke his heels. Other examples include mountain climbers who climbed in the Himalayas yet died at their local beginners' mountain that they thought they knew well, thereby underestimating risk.

If you are alive today, you survived all your risk-taking. Nassim Taleb calls this the turkey problem: a turkey might think it is a great survivor after waking up every morning and being fed. And then comes Thanksgiving. A turkey has it all: overconfidence, ignorance, risk-delusional, hubris, etc. It does not take too much imagination to apply this to mountaineering and finance. Reinhold Messner phrased the overconfidence of extreme mountain climbers, of which he, at the time of writing, is a surviving specimen, as follows:

> We always go with the happy camper feeling. We think we are invulnerable. This, of course, is completely naive and false.[112]
> —REINHOLD MESSNER (b. 1944), German-speaking Italian mountaineer and author

Second, experience is certainly good. Most professionals with experience and training know that they have experience and training, which inflates confidence. This self-confidence is beneficial when the experience and training apply to the current environment. However, experience and training can turn into ignorance when circumstances change, and the experience and training do not apply anymore. It can happen to all of us. This is only one way of putting it:

> I have great faith in fools—self-confidence, my friends call it.[113]
> —EDGAR ALLAN POE (1809–49), American writer

Changing environments can cause a mismatch between true risk and perceived risk and impact one's abilities to deal with it. As Will Rogers put it:

> You know everybody is ignorant, only on different subjects.[114]
> —WILL ROGERS (1879–1935), American humorist

Failure is grossly underappreciated, though, despite the iron law of failure being solid.

Mistakes and Success

In a sense, and misquoting Gordon Gekko, failure is good. Failure, survived failure, that is, is a great tutor. It is also what a great tutor tries to pass on:

> Pass on what you have learned. Strength, mastery. But weakness, folly, failure also. Yes, failure most of all. The greatest teacher, failure is.[115]
> —YODA, grand master of the Jedi Order

Failure is embarrassing. That is one reason why it is a great tutor. America has an advantage over other societies regarding failure. It is sort of okay if you fail. At least you tried. In Japan, for example, failure is treated differently. In earlier times, *seppuku* was one option to restore honor. Even today there are ritualized apologies and deep bowing from company executives when something goes wrong. The reason "failure is good," a pun on Gordon Gekko's famous line, is because of the learning effect it has. However, one prerequisite to failure having a learning effect is survival. It is a Japanese martial artist who succinctly made the point of failure being good:

> Failure is the key to success; each mistake teaches us something.[116]
> —MORIHEI UESHIBA (1883–1969), Japanese martial artist

There is no progress without trial and error:

Error is the price we pay for progress.[117]
—ALFRED NORTH WHITEHEAD *(1861–1947), British mathematician*

Failure and surrender are two different things. At one level, failure is good:

Strength does not come from winning. Your struggles develop your strengths. When you go through hardships and decide not to surrender, that is strength.[118]
—ARNOLD SCHWARZENEGGER *(b. 1947), Austrian-born American bodybuilder, actor, and politician*

This wisdom, i.e., the idea that failure is key to success, was applied to finance by Paul Tudor Jones, a hedge fund manager not necessarily famous for his failures:

One learns most from mistakes, not successes.[119]
—PAUL TUDOR JONES *(b. 1954), American hedge fund manager*

Bottom Line

In the end, everything fails. Being wrong is bad, but staying wrong is worse.

If an Egyptian queen's nose can have an impact on world affairs and a sunny day in Brazil can cause destruction in Texas, paying attention to forecasts might be pure folly.

Overconfidence can kill, literally. Survivors can control fear and remain cool when under duress. Self-confidence is beneficial when the experience and training apply to the current environment. However, experience and training can turn into ignorance and hubris when circumstances change.

———

In the end, failure is unavoidable. However, keeping things simple might delay the end a bit.

THE SIMPLICITY PRINCIPLE

Simplicity is the ultimate sophistication.
—Leonardo da Vinci

Risk illiteracy can kill. Often simple rules of thumb and checklists are the key that can be applied quickly and effectively when failure lurks.

An error culture is of paramount importance when dealing with failure. Nonfatal failure is a learning experience. Both Muhammad Ali and Confucius were on the same page in this regard.

A bull market is random market movement, causing the average investor to mistake himself for a financial genius. Stay humble when winning. Genius comes before the fall.

Aesop said you should not cry over spilled milk. He was wrong. You should. Learn by failing, or you fail to learn. Make a fuss of the spilled milk. There is no learning, and therefore no "applied wisdom" otherwise. Learning from mistakes is not the same as throwing good money after bad. Learning has upside optionality.

What do Leonardo da Vinci, Marilyn Monroe, and Voltaire have in common? KISS: keep it simple, stupid. Knowledge is a process of piling up facts; wisdom lies in their simplification.

The last duty of a central banker is to tell the public the truth. BS ought to manipulate the investor. The amount of energy needed to refute BS is larger than to produce it.

Error Culture and Spilled Milk

Ignorance of Ignorance and Sunk Costs

New York, January 15, 2009: US Airways flight 1549, with one hundred and fifty-five people on board, takes off from LaGuardia Airport at 3:26 p.m. Two minutes later a flock of Canada geese collides with the plane's two engines and kills both—the engines and the geese. Four minutes later Captain Chesley Sullenberger lands the plane on the Hudson River. What saved the lives of one hundred and fifty passengers and five crew members was, among other things, checklists. In the four minutes in between being hit by the geese and landing the plane safely on the Hudson River, there was good decision-making, i.e., the risk management procedure worked. Checklists played a central role. Gerd Gigerenzer, author of the very commendable book titled *Risk Savvy*, summarized the miracle as follows:

> *It was the combination of teamwork, checklists, and smart rules of thumb that made the miracle possible.*[120]
> —GERD GIGERENZER *(b. 1947), German psychologist and author*

The first rule of thumb, or heuristic, Captain Sullenberger used when the geese killed both engines was the gaze heuristic. (Fix your gaze on an object, and adjust your speed so that the angle of gaze remains constant). Dogs use it to catch Frisbees. Pilots are trained to use the heuristic too. In the case of US 1549, it allowed the pilots to decide fast that flying back to LaGuardia was not an option. Again, Gigerenzer, who argues complex problems do not require complex solutions, sums it up well:

> Intelligent decision making entails knowing what tool to use for what problem. Intelligence is not an abstract number such as an IQ, but similar to a carpenter's tacit knowledge about using appropriate tools. . . . Experts often search for less information than novices do, using heuristics instead. . . . The important point is that ignoring information can lead to better, faster, and safer decisions.[121]
> —GERD GIGERENZER, director at the Max Planck Institute for Human Development

One aspect of this comparison is related to skin in the game. Pilots have skin in the game. In commercial aviation, pilots are not allowed to have parachutes on board, for obvious reasons. Medical staffers have no or much less skin in the game. Doctors, according to Gigerenzer, who works with doctors in a consulting capacity, can have highly inflated egos. They are well trained. The extensive training can cause the ego to inflate and end up as overconfidence. Gigerenzer in *Risk Savvy* tells some interesting stories of how doctors, who are among the well-respected professionals in nearly any society, can be extremely risk illiterate.

Failure and Persistence

It goes without saying that the learning-from-mistakes idea goes far beyond the realms of finance. It is probably a truism with very wide application. Survival is nature's number one rule. Adapting to changing circumstances is the key survival strategy. Learning from nonfinal mistakes plays a key part. (Dying from one's mistakes also has a learning effect; it is just that the lessons are not applicable.) Michael Jordan, the billionaire athlete who has a fear of water, on the topic:

> I've missed more than 9000 shots in my career. I've lost almost 300 games. 26 times, I've been trusted to take the game winning

shot and missed. I've failed over and over and over again in my
life. And that is why I succeed.[122]
—MICHAEL JORDAN *(b. 1963), American basketball player*

The relaxed American attitude toward failure—sometimes referred to as an "error culture"—and inherent optimism is captured well in the following quotation.

Fail early, fail often and fail forward. . . . You fail your way to
the top.[123]
—WILL SMITH *(b. 1968), American actor*

Dishonor from failure is limited, and self-sacrifice is not required for atonement. Failure is progress:

Even if you fall on your face, you're still moving forward.
—VICTOR KIAM *(1926–2001), American entrepreneur*

It is persistence that matters to great achievers:

Do not judge me by my successes, judge me by how many times
I fell down and got back up again.[124]
—NELSON MANDELA *(1918–2013), South African politician*
    and anti-apartheid revolutionary

Life, including investment life, sometimes punches one metaphorically in the face. So what? Failure that one survives is often not all bad. The failure of learning from failure is wrong. The idea of not staying down is old. It is even a Japanese proverb:

Nana korobi ya oki. (Fall seven times, stand up eight.)
—*Japanese proverb*

Ali and Confucianism

The idea of learning from failure was not lost on Confucius:

Our greatest glory is not in never falling, but in rising every time
we fall.[125]
—CONFUCIUS *(551–479 BC), Chinese philosopher*

Cassius Marcellus Clay Jr. was quoting Confucius then:

> *Inside of a ring or out, ain't nothing wrong with going down. It's*
> *staying down that's wrong.*[126]
> —MUHAMMAD ALI (1942–2016), American boxer

The earlier mention of *seppuku* after a failure is only one trivial part of Japanese culture. Resilience, perseverance, and the endurance of pain are much more important characteristics of complex Japanese culture. Not only is self-sacrifice not required; extraordinary insight, skill, and intelligence might not be required either. In a chapter called "How to Be Stupid," Nassim Taleb says what is required:

> *If you "have optionality," you don't have much need for what*
> *is commonly called intelligence, knowledge, insight, skills, and*
> *these complicated things that take place in our brain cells. For*
> *you don't have to be right that often. All you need is the wis-*
> *dom to <u>not do</u> unintelligent things to hurt yourself (some acts of*
> *omission) and recognize favorable outcomes when they occur.*[127]
> —NASSIM NICHOLAS TALEB (b. 1960), Lebanese American
>   risk analyst and author

This is the avoiding folly idea; the Obama Doctrine, discussed in chapter one. (I will address optionality in more detail a bit later in the book.) The applicability of this *nana-korobi-ya-oki* wisdom was described well by George Soros, who has been learning the craft that is investment management for roughly six decades and was the *Financial Times's* "person of the year" in 2018.

> *Once we realize that imperfect understanding is the human*
> *condition, there is no shame in being wrong, only in failing to*
> *correct our mistakes.*[128]
> —GEORGE SOROS (b. 1930), Hungarian-born American
>   hedge fund manager

There is no folly in being wrong and taking a punch. The folly is staying wrong and watching the losses grow, or worse, adding to a losing position. Remember:

A step backward after making a wrong turn, is a step in the right
direction.[129]
—KURT VONNEGUT *(1922–2007), American writer*

There is a saying that one ought not to throw good money after bad; a saying that appears in many lists of investors' "golden rules." In the early part of his career, Paul Tudor Jones, the American hedge fund manager, kept a handwritten note on his office wall behind his desk, a reminder of the saying:

Losers average losers.
—PAUL TUDOR JONES *(b. 1954), founder of Robin Hood*
Foundation

The term "average" means averaging down, i.e., reducing the entry level by adding to the losing position at a lower price. For example, a hypothetical investor who had bought Valeant Pharmaceuticals at $200 could have reduced his initial entry price by 25 percent when doubling his position when the stock fell to $100.

By the time a $200 stock hit $100, or a bit earlier, ideally the investor should have realized that his investment thesis was wrong. Averaging down does not change the initial investment thesis, and the averaging down is probably closer to investor hubris than investment wisdom. (That said, there are exceptions to almost any rule.)

Another prominent example is Enron. Once the stock had halved, one ought not to have doubled the position, even if the stock had been endorsed by the president. Losers averaging losers is also part of poker wisdom.

Positive and Negative Error Culture

According to the Bureau of Aircraft Accidents' archives, the average annual death toll from commercial aviation accidents per year globally is one thousand twenty-two deaths.[130] The one thousand twenty-two deaths from commercial airline accidents compare to one hundred and sixty-one thousand five hundred deaths from avoidable errors in US hospitals alone per year.[131]

Gigerenzer distinguishes between positive and negative error cultures. A positive error culture learns from past mistakes while a negative error culture does not. The contrast between commercial aviation and hospitals is quite extreme. The commercial aviation industry is an extreme example of a positive error culture, while hospitals are an extreme example of a negative error culture. The following one-liner is a good summary of Gigerenzer's findings:

> *If we had the safety culture of a hospital, we would crash two planes a day.*[132]
> —*Head of risk management of an international airline*

Checklists can alleviate risk illiteracy, laxity, and overconfidence. Commercial airline pilots have checklists, hospitals to a much lesser degree. And if they do have checklists, they are not followed, either due to time pressure, laxity, or the ego of the medical staff. Case in point of a hospital's checklist:

Doctors are supposed to:

1. wash their hands with soap;
2. clean the patient's skin with chlorhexidine antiseptic;
3. put sterile sheets over the entire patient;
4. wear a sterile mask, hat, gown, and gloves; and
5. put a sterile dressing over the catheter site once the line is in.

According to research cited in Gigerenzer's *Risk Savvy*, at least one step is skipped for around a third of all patients. A checklist allows for a positive error culture.

In commercial aviation every single error is analyzed and shared with peers. It is central for the commercial aviation industry that these errors are not repeated. If a short circuit of the onboard coffee machine caused a cable fire in the cockpit that brought down a plane, this never ought to happen again. The failure, i.e., the causal links, will enter a new safety rule or maintenance checklist. This is the reason why the pieces of a crashed plane are painstakingly put back together after the crash: to learn from what went wrong. We err and learn:

We are human. We fail. And, crucially, we keep learning.[133]
—RICHARD BRANSON *(b. 1950), English serial entrepreneur*

It is for this reason that I introduced checklists into my risk management research a couple of years ago. It institutionalizes a positive error culture. I probably got the idea from Charlie Munger:

> *How can smart people so often be wrong? They don't do what I'm telling you to do: use a checklist to be sure you get all the main models and use them together in a multimodular way.*[134]
> —CHARLIE MUNGER *(b. 1924), American investor and vice chairman of Berkshire Hathaway*

A checklist allows for a positive error culture. Akin to learning from past errors, a checklist in relation to risk management in finance institutionalizes past warning signals. It allows for more discipline and more efficiency in asset allocation, portfolio rebalancing, and risk management.

Learning and Doing

Mistakes and Optionality

One of the disadvantages of learning by making mistakes is the cost associated with the mistakes. Common sense suggests, and probably most philosophers agree, that it is far better to watch someone burn his hands on a hot stove than learn the lesson the hard way. Learning by doing was not Germany's Iron Chancellor's motto:

> *You are all idiots to believe that you can learn from your experience. I prefer to learn from the mistakes of others to avoid own mistakes.*[135]
> —OTTO VON BISMARCK *(1815–98), Prussian statesman*

The argument to learn from others is obviously a powerful one. Eleanor Roosevelt also thought one ought to learn from the mistakes of others, as there is no time to make them all yourself. Not only is it advantageous to learn from others, but the best lessons of financial history are also provided by fools:

> The best lessons come from stupid people.[136]
> —RUSSELL NAPIER *(b. 1964), British financial market historian*

According to *Poor Richard's Almanack*, your author, sadly, is a fool:

> Wise Men learn by other's harms;
> Fools by their own.[137]
> —BENJAMIN FRANKLIN *(1706–90), American polymath*

The idea of learning from the mistakes of others is somewhat obvious and is probably as old as civilization:

> The best plan is to profit by the folly of others.[138]
> —PLINY THE ELDER (AD *23–79), Roman philosopher*

Pliny the Elder, who, according to Pliny the Younger, his nephew, was the luckiest of men because he wrote good books worth reading, possibly got it from Aesop:

> Better be wise by the misfortunes of others than by your own.[139]
> —AESOP *(ca. 620–564* BC*), Greek fabulist*

Learning from others is laudable. However, I am not convinced that's how it works. Douglas Adams, who claimed he was the first person in the United Kingdom to buy an Apple Macintosh computer, saw it differently:

> [H]uman beings, who are almost unique in having the ability to learn from the experience of others, are also remarkable for their apparent disinclination to do so.[140]
> —DOUGLAS ADAMS *(1952–2001), English humorist and science fiction novelist*

There is an element of skepticism about learning from others. I have been investing since I was around seventeen years old. When I was seventeen, I knew everything. Based on the following definition, I was a poet then:

Science is for those who learn;
poetry, for those who know.[141]
—JOSEPH ROUX *(1834–1905), French Catholic parish priest,*
poet, and philologist

Not only is there evidence that we do not learn from others, but there is also evidence that we do not learn from mistakes. A case in point is the two space shuttle accidents in 1986 and 2003. In the 1986 accident it was a faulty seal that cracked during winter. As the seals had cracked in a previous mission, the staff assumed it was safe. This was a mistake, as one member of the commission to investigate the accident, with a one hundred and twenty-five IQ, put it:

When playing Russian roulette, the fact that the first shot got off
safely is little comfort for the next.[142]
—RICHARD FEYNMAN *(1918–88), American physicist*

In the 2003 disaster it was foam insulation that broke off an external tank that caused the accident. This, too, had happened before but was considered safe as nothing had happened. Nonlearning is not limited to governmental bureaucracies but, according to Catherine Tinsley, a professor of management at Georgetown University, who studies disasters and decision-making under risk and uncertainty, applies to the corporate world too:

Multiple near misses preceded (and foreshadowed) every disas-
ter and business crisis we studied, and most of the misses were
ignored or misread.[143]
—CATHERINE TINSLEY *(b. 1964), American management*
professor and risk analyst

Genius and Failure
By October 1987 I was twenty years old and already had built up a healthy ego; after all, I was making money. However, an alternative definition of an equity bull market applied; one, that I was not aware of at the time:

*Bull market, def.: a random market movement causing the aver-
age investor to mistake himself for a financial genius.*[144]
—*Alternative definition of an equity bull market*

I had gotten the curiosity bit and the learning-by-doing right, but not
the intellectual humility. Bernard Baruch's advice would have been helpful
prior to October 1987.

Become more humble as the market goes your way.[145]
—BERNARD BARUCH *(1870–1965), American financier and
stock market speculator*

In the ominous week of October 1987, the week of the crash, I was
doing, somewhat ironically, survival training during my mandatory military service. This means I was running around with a big and heavy
gun—in 1987 the Swiss Army still had the 1957 version, which, by today's
standards, was more a machine gun than an assault rifle—in a Swiss forest,
all week, wearing perma-damp combat gear and obligatory camouflage
face paint, with no access to outside information. On Friday of that week,
around midnight—for some reason I remember this well—we returned
to camp after a long, mountainous, blister-inducing march. It was then
where I learned of the market falling by 20 percent and my stocks falling
closer to 50 percent. I was neither bemused nor thinking of Yoda's wisdom
at the time.

Do, or do not. There is no try.[146]
—YODA

Galbraith's wisdom was certainly applicable:

Financial genius is before the fall.[147]
—JOHN KENNETH GALBRAITH *(1908–2006), Canadian
American economist*

However, losing 50 percent was—on an entirely different level—
wonderful. And efficient:

[B]eing broke is a very efficient educational agency.[148]
—EDWIN LEFÈVRE *(1871–1943), American journalist and*
   writer

"Wonderful and efficient," with the benefit of a long period of hindsight, that is. Why? Because by 2000 I already had touched that proverbial hot stove; peed on the electric fence, as Will Rogers will say in chapter five. Pestalozzi was right:

Das Leben bildet. (Life forms or it is life itself that educates.)[149]
—JOHANN HEINRICH PESTALOZZI *(1746–1827), Swiss*
   educational reformer

As valuable and intelligent as the Obama Doctrine ("Don't do stupid shit") from chapter one is, missteps are unavoidable:

We all step in shit from time to time. . . . Stepping in shit is inevitable, so let's either see it as good luck, or figure out how to do it less often.[150]
—MATTHEW MCCONAUGHEY *(b. 1969), American actor*

During the Bitcoin bull phase of 2017, regulators and other governmental entities were falling over themselves to ban or limit trading in Bitcoin for various reasons. One reason was that Bitcoin, to one famous economist with an Italian accent, the "mother and father of all bubbles," is used for illicit activity, and therefore it is a fraud. According to this logic, all fiat money is also a fraud because US dollars, euros, etc., are also used for illicit activity. Another reason for a potential ban was investor protection, as cryptocurrencies are extraordinarily volatile. This is counterproductive because it deprives risk-taking, cryptocurrency-trading young people from learning a lesson:

Risks, I like to say, always pay off. You learn what to do, or what not to do.[151]
—JONAS SALK *(1914–95), American medical researcher and*
   virologist

Sunk Cost and Spilled Milk

Interestingly, in the late 1990s, it was those who were roughly ten years younger than I who were loading up on the dogfood.coms of the time. I had learned my lesson and was investing asymmetrically by then, i.e., making money when right; sustaining minuscule, predeterminable losses when wrong.[152] The idea of "asymmetric returns," the title of my three hundred and thirty-six-page second book, was summarized in one sentence well by Stanley Druckenmiller:

> I've learned many things from him [George Soros], but perhaps the most significant is that it's not whether you're right or wrong that's important, but how much money you make when you're right and how much money you lose when you're wrong.[153]
> —STANLEY DRUCKENMILLER *(b. 1953), American hedge fund manager*

(I came across this quotation after writing the three hundred and thirty-six pages.) The positive aspect of losing money, the benefits of failure, was pointed out aptly by creativity theorist Roger von Oech:

> Remember the two benefits of failure. First, if you do fail, you learn what doesn't work, and second, the failure gives you the opportunity to try a new approach.[154]
> —ROGER VON OECH *(b. 1948), American author and speaker*

Aesop, from whom the dictum "don't cry over spilled milk" originates, was wrong.[155] Jeremy Grantham, cofounder and chief investment strategist of Boston-based Grantham, Mayo, & van Otterloo (GMO), was right:

> Always cry over spilt milk.[156]
> —JEREMY GRANTHAM *(b. 1938), British investor*

If you do not make a fuss about past mistakes, there is no learning. The don't-cry-over-spilled-milk idea is related to the let-bygones-be-bygones dictum applied to economics and business administration:

> Sunk costs are sunk.
> —Saying

Sunk costs are indeed sunk. You cannot put the toothpaste back in the tube. Many investors and poker players know this:

> *Don't throw good money after bad.*
> —*Saying*

However, that is not the end of the story. The sunk cost can be viewed as an option with a potential future, a higher payoff. If there is no learning from the cost, there is no learning, i.e., the option was just a cost with no payoff. In that case, then, yes, one ought to let bygones be bygones. However, if the investor, entrepreneur, or poker player learned something from the mistake, the future payoff could be, potentially, multiples from the initial cost. That is the reason one ought to cry over spilled milk; the "fuss-making" creates an option. Learning by doing is a survival technique:

> *Learn by failing, or you fail to learn.*[157]
> —GERD GIGERENZER *(b. 1947), German psychologist*

Experience and Fees

Learning by doing, i.e., losing money to gain experience, can be expensive though. It is best to do it early in life; for example, when you are a "PhD," where "PhD" stands for "poor, hungry, and devoted." One of my favorite quotes in this regard is from Robert Orben, an American magician and comedy writer; it is often attributed to Harvard president Derek Bok, who used the quote, but he did not originate it.

> *If you think education is expensive, try ignorance.*[158]
> —ROBERT ORBEN *(b. 1927), American comedy writer and
>   author*

Learning by doing requires not giving up, as Winston Churchill or Abraham Lincoln might have never said, but could have:

> *Success is going from failure to failure without a loss of
> enthusiasm.*[159]
> —*Anonymous*

The learning-by-doing dictum might even be divine:

> *When God made man, she was practicing.*[160]
> —RITA MAE BROWN *(b. 1944), American writer*

Mark Twain might also have supported learning by doing; as he probably never said, but could have:

> *Don't let schooling interfere with your education.*[161]
> —GRANT ALLEN *(1848–99), Canadian writer*

I think the last word on the subject goes to Aristotle, who hit the proverbial nail on its head a long time ago:

> *For the things we have to learn before we can do, we learn by doing them.*[162]
> —ARISTOTLE *(384–322 BC), Greek philosopher*

The idea of learning by doing is not new then. KISS helps.

KISS Principle and Occam's Razor

Marilyn Monroe and Simplicity

One way to avoid failure and help learning is to keep things simple. The simplicity principle, traditionally referred to as Occam's razor, is the idea that simpler explanations of observations should be preferred to more complex ones. In this regard, the KISS idea is applicable. KISS is an acronym for "keep it simple, stupid," a design principle noted by the US Navy in 1960. The KISS principle states that most systems work best if they are kept simple rather than made complicated; therefore, simplicity should be a key goal in design, and unnecessary complexity should be avoided.[163] One of my all-time favorite quotes is from Leonardo da Vinci, despite the caveat in the endnote:

> *Simplicity is the ultimate sophistication.*[164]
> —LEONARDO DA VINCI *(1452–1519), Italian polymath*

What do the quoted Renaissance Man and Marilyn Monroe have in common? Keeping it simple:

> *What do I wear in bed? Why Chanel No. 5, of course.*[165]
> —MARILYN MONROE *(1926–62), American actress*

This was also Voltaire's motto; not wearing Chanel No. 5 in bed, but simplicity:

> *My motto is "to the point."*[166]
> —VOLTAIRE *(1694–1778), French philosopher*

KISS is related to wisdom:

> *Knowledge is a process of piling up facts,*
> *wisdom lies in their simplification.*[167]
> —MARTIN HENRY FISCHER *(1879–1962), German-born*
>   *American physician and author*

Simplicity also made it into a proverb.

> *Brevity is the soul of wit.*[168]
> —*Proverb*

KISS, when applicable to finance, is most likely a balancing act between the big picture and finding ever-more granular data. Three of the thirteen points of my firm's investment philosophy are the following:

> *Knowledge, understanding, insight, perspective, and, ideally,*
> *applied wisdom improve the quality of investment decisions;*
> *more granular data does not.*
>
> *When it comes to understanding, most of the detail simply*
> *does not matter. Common sense trumps minutiae.*
>
> *Yes, the devil is in the details. But if you get the big picture*
> *wrong, you need not worry about detail.*[169]
> —*Part of IR&M's investment philosophy*

There are exceptions to everything, also to the bullet points above. However, there are times when simplicity can trump minutiae:

*Simplicity, concentration, and economy of time and effort have
been the distinguishing features of the great players' methods,
while others lost their way to glory by wandering in a maze of
details.*[170]
—TOMMY ARMOUR *(1896–1968), Edinburgh-born American
golfer*

There are times, of course, where being overly relaxed with details has
its limitations:

*I took a course in speed reading, learning to read straight down
the middle of the page, and I was able to go through* War and
Peace *in 20 minutes. It's about Russia.*[171]
—WOODY ALLEN *(b. 1935), American actor and filmmaker*

Sincerity and Elegance
Ignoring detail is, like many concepts touched upon in this book, easier
said than done. The key to the kingdom is what to overlook:

The art of being wise is the art of knowing what to overlook.[172]
—WILLIAM JAMES *(1842–1910), American psychologist*

Leo Tolstoy, to many the greatest writer ever, on simplicity:

*[T]here is no greatness where there is not simplicity, goodness,
and truth.*[173]
—LEO TOLSTOY *(1828–1910), Russian writer*

As I will point out later, complexity can be a form of deception, certainly in the field of finance. There is a connection between simplicity
and honesty. Tolstoy, who created a seemingly endless list of rules by
which he aspired to live, inspired in part by the thirteen virtues Benjamin
Franklin spelled out in his autobiography, was not the first to think along
those lines:

*Simplicity and sincerity generally go hand in hand, as both pro-
ceed from love of truth.*[174]
—MARY WOLLSTONECRAFT *(1759–97), English writer and
women's rights activist*

The idea of seeking simplicity has been translated into investment parlance by many investors, including Warren Buffett:

> *We don't like things you have to carry out to 3 decimal places. If someone weighed somewhere between 300–350 pounds, I wouldn't need precision—I would know they were fat.*[175]
> —WARREN BUFFETT *(b. 1930), American investor*

Peter Lynch, of Magellan and stock-picking fame, was also thinking along those lines:

> *Never invest in an idea you can't illustrate with a crayon.*[176]
> —PETER LYNCH *(b. 1944), American investment manager*

I believe a lot of what is applicable in investment management is also often true in trading, and vice versa, even if the two disciplines differ. As Dennis Gartman once put it:

> *We have long said that keeping things simple is, far more often than not, the better part of trading valor. Confusion, as we have said countless times, breeds contempt. Confusion is often the last redoubt of the high minded, the intelligentsia and academia. We prefer the simplicity of Audrey Hepburn's simple black dress to the egregious tastelessness of designs by modern day designing madmen.*[177]
> —DENNIS GARTMAN *(b. 1950), American investment newsletter writer*

At least one fashion icon agrees with Mr. Gartman:

> *Simplicity is the keynote of all true elegance.*[178]
> —COCO CHANEL *(1883–1971), French fashion designer and businesswoman*

Simplicity and Distrust

Occam's razor is loosely related to avoiding calculating financial ratios to three decimal places and Audrey Hepburn's simple black dress. When solving a problem, Occam's razor is often perceived as the simplest solution being the best one.

Occam's razor, also called the law of parsimony, is named after William of Ockham, a Franciscan philosopher, theologian, and political writer in the fourteenth century. There is a debate as to what exactly William of Ockham said and when, or whether he applied this principle to his work or not. Occam's razor is sometimes also called the principle of simplicity or simplicity principle. A layman's formulation of Occam's razor is "the simplest explanation is usually the correct one." As Agatha Christie's Monsieur Poirot would have it:

> *You gave too much rein to your imagination. Imagination is a good servant, and a bad master. The simplest explanation is always the most likely.*[179]
> —Hercule Poirot *(ca. 1854/73–1949), fictional Belgian detective*

As with nearly anything in life, an idea can be taken too far:

> *My experience tells me that in this complicated world the simplest explanation is usually dead wrong. But I've noticed that the simplest explanation usually sounds right and is far more convincing than any complicated explanation could hope to be.*[180]
> —Scott Adams *(b. 1957), American cartoonist and writer*

Occam's razor does not imply the simpler solution is better; it implies the simple solution is simpler. Seeking simplicity for simplicity's sake is too simplistic; this from the author of *Simplicity*:

> *Simplicity before understanding is simplistic,*
> *simplicity after understanding is simple.*[181]
> —Edward de Bono *(1933–2021), Maltese physician, author, and consultant*

I believe the bottom line on simplicity is the following:

> *Seek simplicity and distrust it.*[182]
> —Alfred North Whitehead *(1891–1947), English mathematician and philosopher*

One practical application of distrust is spotting BS.

Pinocchio and the BS Asymmetry Principle

Lie-watching and Bamboozlement
There is a hobby called "bird-watching," which, well, is pretty much about what it says; namely watching birds, i.e., warm-blooded egg-laying vertebrates characterized by feathers and forelimbs modified as wings. When markets behave in a disorderly fashion, it is not always because of market participants being irrational or anything like that. Sometimes the market just sees the train wreck unfolding in slow motion and acts accordingly.

Politicians and politically incentivized government officials, e.g., regulators, central bank staff, etc., have a strong incentive to calm markets. They step in, and, well, among other things, lie. It is important that investors take note. I hereby recommend "lie-watching," not as a hobby but as a commercial endeavor, risk assessment tool, and survival technique. Alan Blinder, a former Federal Reserve Board vice chairman, who in 2008 thought that Minsky (stability begets instability) was right and excessive complexity was dangerous, is often quoted to have said the following:

> *The last duty of a central banker is to tell the public the truth.*[183]
> —ALAN BLINDER *(b. 1945), American economist and former
> Federal Reserve Board vice chairman*

Fake news (and fake quotes) and alternative truths are nothing new. One of the lessons of history is that being bamboozled, a sophisticated scientific term, is not good:

> *One of the saddest lessons of history is this: If we've been bamboozled long enough, we tend to reject any evidence of the bamboozle. We're no longer interested in finding out the truth. The bamboozle has captured us. It's simply too painful to acknowledge, even to ourselves, that we've been taken. Once*

*you give a charlatan power over you, you almost never get it
back.*[184]
—CARL SAGAN *(1934–96), American astronomer and science
popularizer*

In politics, lying is the rule, not the exception. Jovial Jean-Claude
Juncker, a European politician whose drinking habits are legendary, was
stating the obvious when he said:

When it becomes serious, you have to lie.[185]
—JEAN-CLAUDE JUNCKER *(b. 1954), Luxembourgish
politician and former EC President*

Juncker knows his *Prince*:

A prince never lacks legitimate reasons to break his promise.[186]
—NICCOLÒ MACHIAVELLI *(1469–1527), Italian political
philosopher*

In relation to Juncker's remark: it is always serious. Donald Trump just
lifted the lying to a new level. However, in defense of Mr. Trump, there
are two types of truths:

*There are two kinds of truth. There are real truths, and there are
made-up truths.*[187]
—MARION BARRY *(1936–2014), American politician, former
mayor of Washington, DC*

The truth is laudable. The truth is to a lie what *La La Land* is to *The
Exorcist*; or, as Leonardo da Vinci put it:

*Beyond a doubt truth bears the same relation to falsehood as
light to darkness.*[188]
—LEONARDO DA VINCI *(1452–1519), Italian polymath*

Lies and Baloney Detection

There is an important difference between lying and bullshitting. As one famous authority on BS and author of one scholarly work on the subject—*On Bullshit*—put it:

> *Liars attempt to conceal the truth by substituting the truth with something that isn't true. Bullshitting is not a matter to conceal the truth. It's a matter of manipulating the listener. If the truth will do, then that's fine. If the truth won't do, then that's also fine. The bullshitter is indifferent to the truth in which the liar is not.*[189]
>
> —HARRY FRANKFURT *(b. 1929), American philosopher and founder of the theory of bullshit*

Vox news called Donald Trump the bullshitter-in-chief based on the work of Harry Frankfurt.[190] The argument was applying the theory of bullshit: "Trump, more often than not, isn't interested in convincing anyone of anything. He's a bullshitter who simply doesn't care." However, the caricature that went with the article shows Trump with a long red nose. (Pinocchio did not get a long red nose from bullshitting.)

The term "bull," meaning nonsense, falsehood, to befool, mock, cheat, among other things, dates from the seventeenth century, while the term "bullshit"—also known as bollocks in the UK and Ireland and often shortened to "BS"—was used as early as 1915 in American slang and came into popular usage only during World War II. The word "bull" itself may have derived from the Old French "boul," meaning fraud, deceit, or trickery.

Some people's motto, in politics, finance, and elsewhere, was captured well with the following:

> *If you can't dazzle them with brilliance, baffle them with bullshit.*[191]
>
> —W. C. FIELDS *(1880-1946), American comedian and writer*

A bullshitter is not necessarily an idiot. It could well be that it is the receiver of the BS who cannot spot the BS that is the idiot. For instance, if a politician boasts wrongly that he had the largest inauguration crowd ever, it could well be a tactical move to dazzle the politician's constituency. In this entirely hypothetical case, it is the baffled constituency who believe the BS and who succumb to idiocy. The funny thing is the following: the critics who call the bullshitter an idiot are potentially idiots, too, because they cannot see the bullshitter's political incentive to dazzle his constituency.

François-Marie Arouet, pen-named Voltaire, an advocate of freedom and famous for his wit, phrased the dazzling and baffling as follows:

> *Those who can make you believe absurdities, can make you commit atrocities.*[192]
> —VOLTAIRE *(1694–1778), French Enlightenment writer, historian, and philosopher*

Bullshitting, like wit, is also a survival technique:

> *I'm one of the world's great survivors. I'll always survive because I've the right combination of wit, grit and bullshit.*[193]
> —DON KING *(b. 1931), American boxing promoter*

Deception is not entirely unheard of in the field of finance. In the realm of investment management, math or science is often added to sell an idea or product:

> *The easiest way to be "superior" is to pretend to understand what others cannot understand. For that you need complexity.*[194]
> —EDWARD DE BONO *(1933–2021), Maltese physician, psychologist, author, inventor, and consultant*

A successful investor develops an overly sensitive BS detection-sensing system over time. It served Edward Thorp, the math professor who met Warren Buffett in 1968, has invested in Berkshire Hathaway since 1982, and spotted the Madoff fraud seventeen years before it blew up, well:

> *One of the things that's served me very well in life is have an extraordinary bullshit detector.*[195]
> —EDWARD THORP *(b. 1932), American mathematician, hedge fund pioneer, and author*

Untruth and Brandolini's Law

BS sensitivity is important when one wants to beat the market or the casinos, or, in Ed Thorp's case, both. The cost of being bullshitted to can be high. This has to do with the bullshit asymmetry principle, also known as Brandolini's law:

> *The amount of energy needed to refute bullshit is an order of magnitude bigger than to produce it.*[196]
> —ALBERTO BRANDOLINI, *Italian programmer and author*

Spotting the lie is at least as important as spotting BS. In a game of poker, you do not show your hand. Concealing the truth is part of the game. Under competition, transparency can be a negative. This is true in poker as well as in politics and in finance. The practical investment relevance is that the roles of the politicians and other elected and unelected government officials are becoming more and more relevant in influencing market prices and trends. There is more and more lying. It is, in Juncker's terms, always serious. Many politicians have adapted Quentin Crisp's credo:

> *The lie is the basic building block of good manners. That may seem mildly shocking to a moralist—but then what isn't?*[197]
> —QUENTIN CRISP *(1908–99), English writer*

We all lie. It's human. According to one estimate, 60 percent of people lie during a typical ten-minute conversation, and they average two to three lies during that short time frame.[198] People lie in everyday conversation to appear more likable and competent.

Spotting the lie is not just a profitable endeavor; it is a survival necessity. If it works for Ed Thorp, chances are it works for you too. Michael Crichton, the *Jurassic Park* author who in 2003 thought that environmentalism resembled a religion for urban atheists and who has a dinosaur named after him, *Crichtonsaurus*, also suggested lie-watching:

> *The greatest challenge facing mankind is the challenge of distinguishing reality from fantasy, truth from propaganda.*[199]
> —MICHAEL CRICHTON *(1942–2008), American author*

Separating truth from untruth is not a historical artifact but a contemporary risk management tool. By being able to identify propaganda and deceit, truth is revealed.

> *Propaganda is the art of persuading others of what you don't believe yourself.*
> —Ausonius *(310–395), Roman poet, and/or* Abba Eban
>   *(1915–2002), Israeli diplomat and politician*

Bottom Line

You do not know everything. Use a checklist. It allows for a positive error culture. Akin to learning from past errors, a checklist in relation to risk management in finance institutionalizes past warning signals. It allows for more discipline and more efficiency in asset allocation, portfolio rebalancing, and risk management.

Cry over spilled milk. Mistakes one survives have optionality.

Keep things simple. Wear No. 5 in bed. Seek simplicity and distrust it.

There is no shortage of BS in finance, as well as elsewhere. *Caveat emptor.*

Seeking simplicity is easier said than done. We err. We are human, and life is uncertain.

THE HUMAN UNCERTAINTY PRINCIPLE

Risk comes from not knowing what you're doing.
—Warren Buffett

Human involvement can make things complicated. Putting a man on the moon is simple. But imagine the moon had mood swings or was susceptible to fashion and would rotate around its axis based on its current feelings. Putting a man on the moon would be inordinately more difficult. Welcome to the social sciences.

When humans are involved, long-term success is difficult. Thinking otherwise is delusional. There is a thing called "delusion of lasting success."

Risk is exposure to change. And as Mr. Spock said, it would be illogical to think otherwise. This is true even when the math is irresistible, as, for example, a Hillary Clinton win in 2016.

There is also a delusion of rigorous research. It is better to be vaguely right than precisely wrong. We are far better at inventing tools than using them wisely.

Wealth preservation is difficult, and risk management is not a science. If this were untrue, Nobel laureates would be good at it. A fool with a tool is still a fool.

Boring is good. Good investing is boring.

Uncertainty and the Human Factor

Knightian Uncertainty and Risk

Werner Heisenberg (1901–76) was nominated for the Nobel Prize in Physics by Albert Einstein in 1928, an honor Heisenberg then was awarded in 1932. One of his achievements was to prove that things that were previously thought as being precisely determinable might not be as such. "Things" were more complicated, and measurements, therefore, more uncertain. One of his assertions was that there is a fundamental limit to the precision with which certain pairs of physical properties of a particle, known as complementary variables, such as position and momentum, can be known.

This idea is applicable to finance. When analyzing the economy, for example, we also examine the state of the economy, i.e., where we stand in, say, an economic expansion, as well as the dynamics, e.g., the "speed" of the expansion, the momentum. There is uncertainty on both measurements.

The "uncertainty principle," also known as "Heisenberg's uncertainty principle" today, is a term from quantum mechanics, quantum mechanics not being part of this book. Heisenberg's uncertainty principle was an important ingredient in George Soros's theory of reflexivity, which is, at least tangentially, part of this book. Mr. Soros adapted the term "human uncertainty principle," which is more applicable for our purposes. Especially the "human" in human uncertainty principle is important:

> *The human factor is always incalculable.*[200]
> —AGATHA CHRISTIE *(1890–1976), English crime novelist*

The context of the above quotation is as follows: "Any medical man who predicts exactly when a patient will die, or exactly how long he will live, is bound to make a fool of himself. The human factor is always incalculable." Replace "medical man" with "economist" and "patient" with "economic expansion," and the quotation is almost perfectly applicable to finance.

Knightian uncertainty has its origins in the 1930s, as outlined later. George Soros, who in 1996 donated funds to promote ballot initiatives in California and Arizona that eventually led to the legalization of medicinal marijuana, stumbled upon the idea when he was at the London School of Economics. His theory of reflexivity was first published in book form in 1987.

> *The major insight I gained from the theory of reflexivity and what I now call the human uncertainty principle is that all human constructs (concepts, business plans or institutional arrangements) are flawed. The flaws may be revealed only after the construct has come into existence.*[201]
> —GEORGE SOROS *(b. 1930), Hungarian-born American hedge fund manager*

In 2013 Mr. Soros referred to the human uncertainty principle and Knightian uncertainty synonymously, the latter being an important aspect of this chapter and this book. The Soros quotation above sits nicely with Paul Ormerod's iron law of failure, discussed in chapter two.

> *No matter how much information we gather, no matter how carefully we analyze it, a strategy of predict, plan and control will in general fail.*[202]
> —PAUL ORMEROD *(b. 1950), British economist*

Failure and the Delusion of Lasting Success
Failure destroys wealth. This means a long-term investor needs to, ideally, avoid failure, or, somewhat less ideally, survive it unharmed or little harmed, for operations and investment life to continue. There are few families and institutions that accumulate wealth and keep it for centuries. The reason why an accumulated pot of wealth does not last for centuries is because it is difficult to protect from failure, such as wars, hyperinflation,

expropriation, sticky authoritarian fingers, tyrants, revolutions, third-generation profligacy, fourth-generation idiocy, etc.

Staying in business is also difficult despite thousands of how-to business books suggesting otherwise. Those who claim it is easy are either talkers rather than doers, or people just manage to self-delude themselves. Phil Rosenzweig, a professor of strategy and international business at IMD in Lausanne and a best-selling author, calls this the delusion of lasting success:

> Almost all high-performing companies regress over time. The promise of a blueprint for lasting success is attractive but not realistic. . . . Lasting business success, it turns out, is largely a delusion.[203]
> —PHIL ROSENZWEIG (b. 1955), American business school professor and author

A forty-year bull market in government bonds in many industrialized economies, and an equally strong US equity market, albeit with interruptions, erased the empirical notion from public memory that wealth preservation is difficult. That is dangerous. The key discipline in the preservation of wealth is generally called "risk management." One way to put it is as follows:

> I'm always thinking about losing money as opposed to making money. Don't focus on making money, focus on protecting what you have.[204]
> —PAUL TUDOR JONES (b. 1954), American hedge fund manager

If there is wisdom from trading, betting games, and speculation that is applicable to avoiding folly, we will take it. The operative word from the term "applied wisdom" is *applied*. Paul Tudor Jones's insight, allegedly, was not lost on Mark Twain:

> I'm more concerned about the return _of_ my money than with the return _on_ my money.[205]
> —Anonymous, Mark Twain or Will Rogers

Safety and Morons

The definition of risk can result in materially different conclusions as to whether investment A is more or less risky than investment B. It is a matter of perspective. The late Professor Galbraith, ridiculed when predicting the 1987 crash based on historical precedent of speculative euphoria, was certainly on to something when he said:

> *There can be few fields of human endeavor in which history counts for so little as in the world of finance. Past experience, to the extent that it is part of memory at all, is dismissed as the primitive refuge of those who do not have the insight to appreciate the incredible wonders of the present.*[206]
> —JOHN KENNETH GALBRAITH *(1908–2006), Canadian American economist*

All investments are risky; it is obvious:

> *Risk, to state the obvious, is inherent in all business and financial activity.*[207]
> —ALAN GREENSPAN *(b. 1926), American economist and former chairman of the Fed*

All investments are speculative. As is so often the case when human action is involved, Ludwig von Mises—the son of a successful and respected engineer—already made the point a couple of decades ago:

> *There is no such thing as a nonspeculative investment. In a changing economy action always involves speculation. Investments may be good or bad, but they are always speculative. A radical change in conditions may render bad even investments commonly considered perfectly safe.*[208]
> —LUDWIG VON MISES *(1881–1973), Austrian School economist and author of* Human Action

Regarding new investments and new ideas in finance, it is Lord Bauer who hit the proverbial nail squarely on its head. According to Thomas Sowell, Peter Bauer insisted on talking sense, even when dangerous nonsense was at the height of its popularity.[209]

Peter Bauer, the penniless son of a Budapest bookie, was at the time of his death a fellow of the British Academy, professor emeritus at the London Business School of Economics, and the lifetime fellow of a Cambridge college. He saw England, as many refugees from Eastern Europe in the 1930s did, as a successful liberal society. England was a magnet for talent as much as German-speaking Europe was not at that time. However, after seeing that liberal society fall apart a couple of decades later, Bauer joined Lady Thatcher to restore that kind of "conservative liberalism" in the 1980s. The following quote belongs to the top ten pieces of wisdom in this book. It could well be the most-often used quotation in my research over the past thirty years or so.

> *A safe investment is an investment whose dangers are not at that moment apparent.*[210]
> —PETER THOMAS BAUER *(1915–2002), Austro-Hungarian British economist*

This idea was not lost on the writers of *Downton Abbey*, a British historical period drama television series, in relation to the *Titanic*.

> *Every mountain is "unclimbable" until someone climbs it.*
> *So, every ship is "unsinkable" until it sinks.*[211]
> —HUGH BONNEVILLE *(b. 1963), as Robert Crawley, Earl of Grantham*

I recommend Lord Bauer's one-liner as a healthy attitude in finance. It could also be phrased as follows:

> *There is no safety. Only varying states of risk. And failure.*[212]
> —LOIS McMASTER BUJOLD *(b. 1949), American fiction writer*

Legislation, regulation, and scholarly finance seek precision where there is uncertainty and transparency where there is ambiguity. Terms such as "unambiguous legislatorial drafting" or "transparent political solution" (or just "political solution") seem oxymoronic; like "political science" or "congressional ethics" or "exact estimate" or "United Nations" or "social security" or "airline food" or "debt ceiling" or "deficit-cutting plan" or—most importantly of all, arguably the mother of all oxymoronic terms in finance—"risk-free rate of return."

Stability and Exposure to Change

There are different definitions for uncertainty and risk. One colloquial "definition" of risk is having to sell when you do not want to. One of my favorite definitions for risk is the following:

> Risk, def.: exposure to change.[213]
> —O'Connor's definition for "risk" in the 1980s

Mark Twain's money is exposed to "change." Of course, he will get his money back. Well, unless things change; something could go wrong, i.e., fail. It would be unreasonable to think that circumstances cannot change; or, as Mr. Spock would have it, "illogical."

> It would be illogical to assume that all conditions remain stable.[214]
> —MR. SPOCK (2230–2387), Vulcan science officer

The definition of risk being exposure to change is amazingly simple and unscientific but immensely powerful and has stood the test of time. It makes sense to distinguish two terms: risk and uncertainty. These terms are often used interchangeably, which is fine for everyday use. However, in finance-speak there is a distinction that is truly relevant from a risk management point of view.

The term "uncertainty" can involve Klingons, while the term "risk" typically does not. We cannot quantify the probability of extraterrestrials listening to *Voyager's* Golden Record, finding us, and learning to appreciate Homo sapiens as a yummy delicacy to their diet. Uncertainty is not quantifiable.

In finance, the term *risk* is used as the trade-off for the expected return. Expected returns are guessable, i.e., one can make up a number and then call it a forecast; as in "expected return," and then go on and add the numerical value into an econometrical model. Risk needs to be quantifiable too; it would not fit into all the scientific models otherwise. However, this urge to quantify has caused a lot of damage and confusion.

Here another broad, nonscientific definition for "risk." It is rule number five of James Montier's seven immutable laws of investing. James Montier is a member of the asset allocation team of GMO, an asset management firm, and has authored many books related to finance, behavioral finance mainly.

> *Risk is the permanent loss of capital, never a number.*[215]
> —JAMES MONTIER *(b. 1971), British strategist and author*

Long-Term Capital Management (LTCM), a hedge fund that blew up in 1998, for example, learned this rule the hard way. This was the error in their line of thought:

> *Risk is a function of volatility. These things are quantifiable.*[216]
> —PETER ROSENTHAL, *LTCM's spokesman*

It turns out that "these things" are not as easily quantifiable. This is the reason why the distinction between risk and uncertainty is important. Investment life and wealth preservation would be much easier if "these things" were quantifiable. Barton Biggs put it well:

> *Quantitatively based solutions and asset allocation equations invariably fail as they are designed to capture what would have worked in the previous cycle whereas the next one remains a riddle wrapped in an enigma.*[217]
> —BARTON BIGGS *(1932–2012), American strategist and investor*

When dealing with uncertainty, a healthy dose of skepticism is warranted with regard to the applicability of math. Tanya Beder, an American financial professional and executive, named by *Euromoney* as one of the top fifty women in finance around the world, put it well in 1995:

> *[M]athematics is integral to finance, but finance does not always follow mathematics.*[218]
> —TANYA BEDER, *chairman & CEO of the SBCC Group*

Markets and Math

One of the problems with mathematics being an integral part of finance is the added complexity, especially for nonmathematicians. It is a different language for most of us. Take it from an admirer of Napoleon, who was awarded the Chevalier de la Légion d'Honneur by Napoleon in 1808, and who knew Latin, Greek, Hebrew, German, Italian, English, and French:

> *Mathematicians are like Frenchmen: whatever you say to them, they translate it into their own language, and forthwith it means something entirely different.*[219]
> —JOHANN WOLFGANG VON GOETHE *(1749–1832), German philosopher*

Often efficiency, abundant liquidity, and linearity are assumed in econometric modeling, but markets gap:

> *[F]inancial market history is characterized by discontinuities. . . . Real markets do not dance to a tidy mathematical tune. They change and evolve through time, and portfolio managers need skill and creativity to keep up.*[220]
> —DAVID HARDING *(b. 1961), British investment business founder*

One of the reasons for the 2008 financial crisis was a disconnect between the complexity of the risk exposures in, say, banks and the senior management, most of whom were nonmathematicians. While it is always attractive to blame those at the helm, they can only be partially blamed for the disconnect. It really was complicated. (And levering up balance-sheet-complexity twenty or thirty times was not very helpful in the end either.) As Albert Einstein, tongue firmly in cheek, I assume, put it:

> *Since the mathematicians have invaded the theory of relativity, I do not understand it myself anymore.*[221]
> —ALBERT EINSTEIN *(1879–1955), the Swiss patent office's most famous employee*

Replace "the theory of relativity" with "banking" in the quotation above, and you pretty much have the situation for most seasoned bankers, bank CEOs, and board members of large banks. Sometimes the math is irresistible though:

> *Don't worry. She'll win. The math is irresistible.*[222]
> —*Seasoned and well-connected Hillary Clinton supporter in 2016*

Life and Probability

It was Frank Knight (1885–1972), an American economist, who made this important distinction between "risk" and "uncertainty."[223] Risk describes situations where an explicit probability distribution of outcomes can be calculated, perhaps on the basis of actuarial data. In contrast, uncertainty describes situations where probabilities are unknown, and more importantly, where they are impossible to calculate with any confidence due to the uniqueness or specificity of the situation.

Scholars of academic finance often use games that involve dice or roulette or lottery tickets as examples for probabilities associated with risk. In all these cases the possible outcomes are known and quantifiable. If you throw two dice, there is a finite, calculable number of outcomes. The probability of throwing two fours is precisely $(1/6)^{\wedge 2}$. An earthquake occurring precisely while two fours are thrown is never part of the analysis. It should be. Weird things do happen every now and then in life, investments, and everything:

> *Life is a school of probability.*[224]
> —WALTER BAGEHOT *(1826–77), British journalist, businessman, and essayist*

Bagehot, an influential journalist and once editor of *The Economist*, a weekly magazine, was on the same page as Cicero, who is considered the greatest lawyer of antiquity; one with great respect for the lessons of history, who defended those unjustly accused by dictatorial leaders and brought down corrupt governments:

> *Probability is the very guide of life.*[225]
> —CICERO *(106–43 BC), Roman politician, orator, and philosopher*

Uncertainty, as outlined above, is sometimes referred to as "Knightian uncertainty," giving credit to Frank Knight, although Keynes was also thinking along similar lines around the same time in the early 1920s. Knight starts his 1921 book with the sentence: "There is little that is fundamentally new in this book." In a 2013 white paper, George Soros treats the terms "human uncertainty principle" and "Knightian uncertainty" synonymously, as already mentioned.

Two quants—well known for their skill of making quantitative finance somewhat more accessible for non-quants—refer to the uncertainty principle as the better explanation of market lunacy; better than theorems based on market efficiency.

> Markets are unpredictable not because they are efficient, but because of a financial version of the uncertainty principle ... markets are not determined by fundamental laws, deterministic or probabilistic.[226]
> —PAUL WILMOTT (b. 1959) and David Orrell (b. 1962), both
>   quants, authors, and consultants

Humans and the Delusion of Rigorous Research

Pseudo-precision and Chainsaws

One reason for man being at the top of the food chain is the invention and the use of tools. Inventing tools and using them wisely is not the same though:

> Humans were always far better at inventing tools than using them wisely.[227]
> —YUVAL NOAH HARARI (b. 1976), Israeli historian and
>   author

The use of tools can be dangerous. Economic or climate models can be faulty, potentially resulting in the user's overconfidence in the model.

Seeking ever more refinement of a model, and seeking precision where precision is inappropriate can be dangerous:

> *It is better to be vaguely right than exactly wrong.*[228]
> —CARVETH READ *(1848–1931), British philosopher and*
>   *logician*

In finance, quantitative analysis is a tool. In the hedge funds space, for example, some of the greatest success stories to date are "quant," while some of the most spectacular blowups were "quant" too. Here is one definition for a quant, i.e., an analyst/researcher in the field of quantitative finance:

> *Quants are the classical boffins, here outside of academia, who*
> *do the esoteric mathematics, write the computer code, quantify*
> *a bank or hedge fund's risk, and often design the algorithms*
> *that actually make the trades. As it has become cool to be a*
> *programming nerd, so it is cool to be a quant (the big salary*
> *helps).*[229]
> —PAUL WILMOTT *(b. 1959) and* DAVID ORRELL *(b. 1962),*
>   *both quants, authors, and consultants*

Quantitative analysis is a bit like a chainsaw: a highly efficient tool for those who are well trained in the tool; a potential source of self-mutilation for everyone else. Large banks employ many quants in their risk management departments. One reason was because the regulatory regime requires quantitative modeling, irrespective of whether it makes sense or not.

Quant-authors Wilmott and Orrell pointed out in 2017 that as the educational requirements for quants rose, "the commonsense requirements dwindled to near zero."[230] It turned out that not only were these quants not managing risk but measuring risk; they also were fooled by the idea that risk is something that one can measure down to three or four decimals. Phil Rosenzweig of halo-effect fame calls this the delusion of rigorous research:

If the data aren't of good quality, it doesn't matter how much
we have gathered or how sophisticated our research methods
appear to be.[231]
—PHIL ROSENZWEIG *(b. 1955), American business school*
professor and author

Dallas-based Ed Easterling, a fellow independent financial analyst, made the following appropriate point in 2006, in the context of hedge fund index tracker funds:

You can't program a computer with management skills from Jack
Welch's book and expect it to run General Electric.[232]
—ED EASTERLING *(b. 1959), founder of Crestmont Research*

Computers and Oracles
Another example of the conflict between doers and modelers is Clint Eastwood's film *Sully* about pilot Captain Chesley "Sully" Sullenberger and his copilot, who conducted an emergency landing in New York's Hudson River after US Airways Flight 1549 was struck by a flock of geese in January 2009. The whole film was about the modelers not understanding the doers' (Sully and his copilot Jeff Skiles) real-world perspective.

All models (theoretical calculations, simulations, etc.) indicated that Sully could have landed safely at a nearby airport. But once all factors were considered, toward the end of the film, it was clear to everyone that they couldn't. All the models missed the main point. The models were fancy, scientific, and convincing at first sight, but they still missed the main point, the human factor.

The nondoers did not understand the human uncertainty principle. The models did not reveal the truth; they did not represent reality well. They were not applicable in the real world. The practical relevance to investing and wealth preservation is that risk is managed in the real world, not the model world. Strong belief in models and precision can be delusional without the observer being aware of the delusion. It would not be a delusion otherwise.

No one, needless to say, who shares a delusion ever recognizes it as such.[233]
—SIGMUND FREUD *(1856–1939), Austrian neurologist and the founder of psychoanalysis*

The problem related to managing risk in finance is that most of the financial risk management literature is about risk *measurement*, not risk *management*. Risk measurement is done by the modelers. Risk management is done by the doers. There's a big difference between the two in relation to Flight 1549 and elsewhere. The late Peter Bernstein, who I owe greatly, not just for his insight, but also for his endorsements of my first two books, put it most brilliantly:

> *Nothing is more soothing or more persuasive than the computer screen, with its imposing arrays of numbers, glowing colors, and elegantly structured graphs. As we stare at the passing show, we become so absorbed that we tend to forget that the computer only answers questions, it does not ask them. Whenever we ignore that truth, the computer supports us in our conceptual errors. Those who live only by the numbers may find that the computer has simply replaced the oracles to whom people resorted in ancient times for guidance in risk management and decision-making.*[234]
> —PETER L. BERNSTEIN *(1919–2009), American financial historian and economist*

Pablo Picasso, a doer, would most certainly have agreed:

> *Computers are useless. They can only give you answers.*[235]
> —PABLO PICASSO *(1881–1973), Spanish painter*

Models and Missions

Economic modeling without thought is, well, thoughtless. There are many definitions for risk, as already alluded to. Since the financial crisis of 2008, we all know that it has truly little to do with VaR (value at risk) or tracking risk. (Tracking risk is a measure used to analyze the difference between an active manager's portfolio and the underlying benchmark of the portfolio.) The distinction between tracking risk, i.e., the possibility of underperforming a benchmark, and total risk, i.e., the possibility of losing a lot of money, is important. Warren Buffett's witty "definition" for risk is to the point:

> Risk comes from not knowing what you're doing.[236]
> —WARREN BUFFETT (b. 1930), American investor and
>   businessman

Warren Buffett's "definition" of risk is witty (as well as true, good advice, and relevant for both private as well as institutional investors). It is also good advice for all sports activities other than perhaps air karate. I believe Arthur Ash would agree with Mr. Buffett's recommendation:

> Either you understand your risk, or you don't play the game.[237]
> —ARTHUR ASHE (1943–93), American tennis player

One of my favorite definitions of risk, which considers the asymmetries, i.e., making the distinction between the "upside" and "downside," is the following:

> Risk is defined as permanent impairment of mission.[238]
> —TOWERS WATSON, international business consultant

This definition by an institutional consultant is unambiguous and is applicable to nearly everything. Applying it to private individuals, it means that slipping in the shower and breaking one's neck is a risk, while being stung by a bee is not. (Assuming one is not allergic, of course.) Applying the definition to a small bank means risk is defined as bankruptcy. (Applying the definition to a large bank means risk is defined as complete failure for the bank requiring a bailout, because large banks don't "fail"; they are too big to.) A bank exceeding the daily VaR by a couple of basis points is analogously equivalent to being stung by a bee. Applying the definition to pension funds, it means risk is defined as not being able to service one's current and/or future pensioners. And so on. Remember:

Risk means more things can happen than will happen.[239]
—ELROY DIMSON *(b. 1947), professor at the London Business School*

Dullness and Prosperity

Your author is Swiss. One of the many stereotypes of the Swiss is that they are perceived by the international non-Swiss community as dull. Or, as an English-speaking non-Swiss once put it to me: "The Swiss do not have a monopoly in the humor department." One Swiss satirist—"Swiss satirist" being an oxymoron to many non-Swiss—described the Swiss as follows:

> *The Swiss is never really funny and never really serious. This makes him pleasant-natured, amiable, congenial, and boring.[240]*
> —ANDREAS THIEL *(b. 1971), Swiss satirist*

One Switzerland-demystifier, Clare O'Dea in *The Naked Swiss*, traces the Swiss-are-dull idea to Fyodor Dostoyevsky, the Russian author who traveled Europe in 1862, including Switzerland, and thought that pan-slavism was a good idea, while capitalism wasn't. What most stereotypers do not know is that humor is actually and quite literally our middle name. "Witz" means joke in German and, literally, it's part of "S*witz*erland."

The Greek philosopher Posidonius (135–51 BC) described the "Swiss," the Helvetians that were a Celtic people who arrived between 200 and 100 BC, as "rich in gold but peaceful." The Celts were among the first people of Europe to work with iron. They also are credited with introducing money; the latter being something many can relate to Switzerland in one way or another.

One of the reasons the Swiss are (perceived) as dull—according to an article I came across many years ago—is that the Swiss never had victories on battlefields to speak of, never had colonies, never had social upheavals, never had social disasters. Swiss politicians go home after work, not to Macao. (Hence the big difference between Switzerland and China in Transparency International's Corruption Perceptions Index.)[241]

Peace and Distrust for Big Government

The Swiss, unlike their neighbors, don't even go on strike. The article went on to argue that periods of stress, such as war, for example, bring out the best in terms of human inventiveness and creativity. The article continued arguing that the works of Michelangelo, da Vinci, et al. fell into such stress periods. Because of the Swiss being so peaceful and dull, the article went on, the Swiss are extremely uncreative.[242]

The article, written prior to Roger Federer's ascent, went on arguing that apart from one famous psychiatrist and one only partly forgotten reformist theologian, the Swiss have no famous people; no poets, no composers, no philosophers, hardly any writers, and no painters of international acclaim to speak of. The only creative legacy from the Swiss to the world—per the mentioned article—is the cuckoo clock. (The cuckoo clock was invented in southern Germany, but never mind.) As Orson Welles's Harry Lime famously noted in the 1949 film *The Third Man*:

> [I]n Italy for 30 years under the Borgias they had warfare, terror, murder, and bloodshed, but they produced Michelangelo, Leonardo da Vinci, and the Renaissance. In Switzerland they had brotherly love—they had 500 years of democracy and peace, and what did that produce? The cuckoo clock.[243]
> —HARRY LIME, *The Third Man*

The last civil war in Switzerland in November 1847 was so peaceful that it lasted just three weeks and resulted in only around one hundred casualties. At that time, Switzerland was divided, under-industrialized, and poor. Switzerland's current peace and prosperity can partially be attributed to luck:

> The Swiss have an interesting army. Five hundred years without a war. Pretty impressive. Also pretty lucky for them. Ever see that little Swiss Army knife they have to fight with?
> —JERRY SEINFELD *(b. 1954), American comedian*

Mr. Seinfeld points to the reason why the Swiss most likely lost against Caesar at the Battle of Bibracte[244] in 58 BC and against Francois

I, the French king, in Marignano in 1515. (Fun fact: on the night of September 13, 1515, at Marignano, Swiss and French forces were forced to suspend hostilities because they couldn't see who was who. They slept alongside one another on the battlefield and continued fighting the next morning.)

Even if its army is under-armed and its citizens do not hold a monopoly in the humor department, Switzerland—by any standard—is also among the world's most prosperous nations. Has the reader ever thought that there might be a relationship between dullness and prosperity? Potentially there is. This is how Jeremy Bentham, who formulated the "greatest-happiness principle" that holds that, within reason, one must always act so as to produce the greatest aggregate happiness among all sentient beings, and who Karl Marx described as "the facile leather-tongued oracle of the ordinary bourgeois intelligence," put it:

> Wars and storms are best to read of, but peace and calms are better to endure.[245]
> —JEREMY BENTHAM (1748–1832), British philosopher

Oliver Stone's Gordon Gekko preferred "peace and calms" too. This is his response to the question where he puts *his* money:

> Me? Switzerland. Still the best. Got a healthy distrust for big government.[246]
> —GORDON GEKKO, fictional rogue financier

Boring and Good Investing

I herein argue that "boring is good." As a financial analyst for an investment bank in London, I first encountered hedge funds in the late 1990s based on the research I was doing then and started examining the hedge fund industry around the year 2000. One of hedge fund marketing's one-liners at the time was something along the lines of "we offer dull products." This was a tongue-in-cheek reference to the volatility of fund of hedge funds portfolios being low, i.e., bond-like. Hence the reference "boring is good," another pun on Gordon Gekko's most famous one-liner. Walter Bagehot thought boring was good too:

[D]ullness in matters of government is a good sign, and not a bad one—in particular, dullness in parliamentary government is a test of its excellence, an indication of its success. The truth is, all the best business is a little dull.[247]
—WALTER BAGEHOT *(1826–77), British journalist, businessman, and essayist*

In finance, there is a measure for the degree of dullness: the standard deviation of returns or—in its annualized form—the volatility. So, a fund of hedge funds could argue that if survival and sustainable compounding of capital (two elements that are arguably related) are major objectives, then large erratic swings on the downside are to be avoided. The bottom line of this analogy is the following. The Swiss—allegedly—are dull but somehow got compensated for their collective loss of sense of humor by creating an environment that allowed for a long-term and sustainable creation of prosperity that has been handed over from one generation to the next.[248] Boring works:

If investing is entertaining, if you're having fun, you're probably not making any money. Good investing is boring.[249]
—GEORGE SOROS *(b. 1930), American hedge fund manager and philanthropist*

Staying out of trouble might not be fascinating, but it makes sense from a wealth preservation perspective. In 1910, the market capitalization of Swiss stocks was smaller than that of UK stocks in Swiss Francs by a factor of 22.5 and smaller than Austria-Hungary by a factor of 3.8. By the end of 2020, Swiss market capitalization was still smaller than that of UK stocks. However, the factor was not 22.5 but 1.7, while Swiss market capitalization was fourteen times the market capitalization of Austria and Hungary combined.[250]

Lacking the ambition to build an empire might be dull (and might or might not rob its citizens of a sound sense of humor). However, dullness (read: stability, sustainability, and predictability) is potentially good when compounding capital on a sustainable basis is a major objective. Or as Oscar Wilde put it:

> *It is better to have a permanent income than to be fascinating.*[251]
> —OSCAR WILDE *(1854–1900), Irish author*

Boring works. Bagehot, quoted earlier, was right. As odd as it sounds, boring should be high on people's wish list:

> *Life in unhappy countries—Myanmar, Syria, Zimbabwe—is not*
> *boring, but much of the population desperately wishes it was.*[252]
> —JOHN KAY *(b. 1948), British economist*

Science and Wisdom

The observation that the mathematical rigor that makes sense when examining the motion of planets or molecules might not apply to some of the social sciences was either overlooked or consciously ignored. In his acceptance speech when picking up the Nobel Prize in 1974, Friedrich Hayek argued against the use of the tools of hard science in the social sciences. Hayek, author of *Road to Serfdom*, a book every investor, as of January 2021, should be familiar with, on the limits of planning under uncertainty:

> *The curious task of economics is to demonstrate to men how little*
> *they really know about what they imagine they can design.*[253]
> —F. A. HAYEK *(1899–1992), Austrian economist*

Potentially a case could be made that financial economics is not only in need of an overhaul with respect to finding new ways of explaining the Darwinian fight for survival under competition but also a simplification of the theories in order for them to be of value to practitioners making decisions under uncertainty. We ought to simplify, as already mentioned. Will Durant, American historian, and author of *The Story of Civilization*, on the limits of science:

> *Science gives us knowledge, but only philosophy can give us*
> *wisdom.*[254]
> —WILL DURANT *(1885–1981), American historian, writer,*
>   *and philosopher*

If you think this book is too philosophical and weak on mean-variance optimization, Brownian motions, and generalized autoregressive conditional heteroscedasticity models, please reread the quotation above, this time including the endnote. The word "philosophy" comes from the Ancient Greek *philosophia*, which literally means "love of wisdom." However, philosophy needs to be applicable to be useful. Lao-tzu's "A journey of a thousand miles begins with a single step" is wonderfully put, philosophically or poetically speaking. However, adding some realism makes the concept more applicable:

> *A journey of self-discovery starts with a single step. But so does falling down a flight of stairs.*[255]
> —KATHY LETTE *(b. 1958), Australian-British author*

Wisdom and the Knowledge Pyramid

This book's cover shows a sketch of a so-called *knowledge pyramid*. My firm's logo too represents a symbolized knowledge pyramid. The concept behind using a symbolized knowledge pyramid as my logo is that the lower part of the pyramid is easily obtainable, but it gets more difficult or expensive as you move up the pyramid. The knowledge pyramid I use has five layers, starting from the base: data, information, knowledge, understanding, and wisdom, or in the case of this book, applied wisdom.[256] (The operative word is "applied." There is a lot of wisdom in "an apple a day keeps the doctor away," but the proverb is not applicable to finance. It's applicable to *health* preservation, not *wealth* preservation. The causality between the two, I will skip for now.)

Understanding is rated higher than knowledge, which is rated higher than information, which is rated higher than just data. Knowledge is something you can easily look up. Understanding, you cannot look up; it is achieved by effort; thinking mostly. This is how Charles F. Kettering, an inventor who had one hundred and eighty-six patents to his name, phrased it:

You can be sincere and still be stupid. There is a great difference
between knowing a thing and understanding it. You can know
a lot about something and not really understand it.[257]
—CHARLES F. KETTERING *(1876–1958), American inventor,*
   engineer, and businessman

The distinction between knowledge and understanding is not new, of course. The idea that wisdom comes sequentially after acquiring knowledge can be traced:

Science is organized knowledge.
Wisdom is organized life.[258]
—IMMANUEL KANT *(1724–1804), German philosopher*

A great deal of damage has been done to the financial landscape by the regulatory bodies by requesting ever more granular data and thereby focusing entirely on the lower end of the knowledge pyramid. And there is little evidence that the matter is improving in that regard. Some of the new regulatory works are so complex and ambiguous that smaller companies will either not be able to cope or will cope at a prohibitive cost. The result is smaller entities throwing in the towel or merging into larger entities. The resultant clustering means less diversity and therefore a higher risk to the system as a whole. (In nature, biodiversity is a good thing. Take barracudas out of the Amazon, and a large part of the ecosystem collapses. The idea is applicable to socioeconomic systems. Ask China. They partly removed women from the gene pool via the one-child policy intervention and now have a large male population not able to find a mate.)

Fools and Heroes
There is probably a fine line between knowing a lot and deluding yourself. Hubris, a form of delusion, is not entirely unheard of in the field of economics and finance. The differentiation between book-smartness and street-smartness is extremely important. I believe this was put very appropriately a long time ago by Gustave Le Bon.

The conditions of success in life are the possession of judgment, experience, initiative, and character—qualities which are not bestowed by books. Books are dictionaries, which it is useful to consult, but of which it is perfectly useless to have lengthy portions in one's head.[259]
—GUSTAVE LE BON *(1841–1931), French polymath*

This last quotation is derived from Aristotle's *phronesis* from chapter one. One investment firm I came across once had a note on the door to its main meeting room that said: "leave your ego outside." The reason for this demand is that being misinformed or delusional can be expensive:

Don't be a hero. Don't have an ego. Always question yourself and your ability. Don't ever feel that you are very good. The second you do, you are dead.[260]
—PAUL TUDOR JONES *(b. 1954), American investor and philanthropist*

In the Great Recession and financial crisis of 2008, it became apparent that it is the decision makers who are the risk managers, not the people measuring risk rigorously based on scientific principles. One of the greatest pieces of applied wisdom, which became apparent after the 2008 crash to nearly everyone, is the following:

A fool with a tool is still a fool.[261]
—*Saying*

The funny thing is the following: if you explain to a tool-using fool that using the tool is foolish, you, from the perspective of the fool, are the fool:

Talk sense to a fool and he calls you foolish.[262]
—EURIPIDES *(ca. 480–406 BC), Greek tragedian*

Bottom Line

The human factor makes it difficult to predict, plan, and control things.

Risk can be defined as "exposure to change." Mr. Spock thinks it would be illogical to assume that all conditions remain stable. There is no safety. Only varying states of risk. And failure.

Risk is not the same as uncertainty. Risk is not a number. "Exposure to change" means a lot of bad things could happen that are not predictable, plannable, controllable, and quantifiable. Markets are not determined by fundamental laws; the human factor is to blame.

Boring is good; good investing is boring.

Wealth preservation is difficult, and risk management is not a science. If this were untrue, Nobel laureates would be good at it.

A fool with a tool is still a fool. Some tools are like a chainsaw: a highly efficient tool for those who are well trained in the tool; a potential source of self-mutilation for everyone else.

———

Risk management is difficult. Montaigne's axiom applies.

MONTAIGNE'S AXIOM

Believe those who are seeking the truth; doubt those who find it.
—André Gide

Montaigne's axiom states that nothing is so firmly believed as that what we least know. Everyone believes in something. Markets change when beliefs change. When managing risk, dogma is dangerous. Have a laugh. There is no proof of the universe not being a joke.

Nothing is so passionately believed as what we least know. The prevailing ideology is difficult to escape. The mind is like a parachute; it ought to open.

Political correctness is the opposite of truth-seeking and is generally for little people. Truth is what works. Talk is cheap, except when Congress does it. Those who say don't know, and those who know don't say.

Believe those who seek truth, rather than those who claim to have found it. Certainty is unwisdom, the mother of fools. The wise err and doubt. Wisdom might or might not come with age. Prevention is the daughter of intelligence as experience is expensive.

If you're Apple and the lights suddenly go off at Samsung, you had better be able to make a lot of money.

Gill's Law and the Musical Chairs Effect

Dogma and Truth

In the years after the dot-com bubble burst, many investors experienced risk according to one of the aforementioned definitions of risk (for example, risk being equal to exposure to change, etc.) as market environment and return expectations changed. The same was true after the equities bull market of 2003–7 and probably after all other bull markets. Things change.

One of the problems of long episodes or trends is that one tends to think that things cannot change. Terms like "new economy" or "this time is different" or TINA ("there is no alternative" to equities) pop up and imply continuation for just a bit longer. Up until 2007, it was nearly inconceivable that US real estate could fall in value. But things changed. House prices did indeed fall with great fanfare, and despite governmental assurance that implied they would not. As George Bernard Shaw, who won a Nobel Prize in 1925 and an Oscar in 1938, put it, entirely unrelated to finance, but applicable to wealth preservation nevertheless:

> [I]t is not disbelief that is dangerous to our society: it is belief.[263]
> —GEORGE BERNARD SHAW (1856–1950), Irish dramatist,
>   critic, and political activist

Fighting strong-held beliefs with analysis and reason can be an uphill battle:

> It is usually futile to try to talk facts and analysis to people who're enjoying a sense of moral superiority in their ignorance.[264]
> —THOMAS SOWELL (b. 1930), American economist

Everyone believes in something. However, holding false beliefs is generally referred to as being delusional. Being delusional is a human fallibility and is dangerous in relation to wealth preservation. (Being delusional is, of course, dangerous to many other activities as well; river rafting, skydiving, glue sniffing, base-jumping off antennas, etc.) David Rosenberg, a strategist repeatedly ranked in Institutional Investors' All-Star rankings when at Merrill Lynch, put it unerringly:

> *In the arena of wealth management, there is no room for dogma.*[265]
> —DAVID ROSENBERG *(b. 1960), Canadian economist*

This idea can be traced to the most famous stock operator, who put it when reminiscing:

> *A man does not swear eternal allegiance to either the bull or the bear side. His concern lies with being right.*[266]
> —EDWIN LEFÈVRE *(1871–1943), American journalist and writer*

The idea of being right will be central to the idea of nowcasting discussed in chapter ten. *The Economist*, a weekly magazine, was not holding back punches when it wrote in 2008:

> *[H]uman beings are fallible: lazy, stupid, greedy and weak; loss-averse, stubborn, and prone to inertia and conformism. All that makes them poor decision-makers, often incapable of their own happiness.*[267]
> —*The Economist*

At one level, dogma, beliefs, faith, and uncertainty are related. On another level, a discussion of dogma, beliefs, faith, and uncertainty could become emotionally charged, as someone's strongly held beliefs are complete and utter nonsense to someone else. To some historians, dogma is the number one cause for Homo sapiens killing one another. George W. Bush, who seems to be on a first-name-basis with God, claimed God told him:

> *George, go and end the tyranny in Iraq.*[268]
> —*God*

(Since I am a financial analyst and not a psychoanalyst, I will not inquire what modern psychiatry says about people who hear voices and act upon them.[269]) Imagine Mr. Bush had said: "A creature on Alpha Centauri has told me through my hair blower to invade Iraq." Everyone would have thought him mad. However, by adapting a common belief system, only parts of the world population thought he was mad. For some people, Mr. Bush's remarks made perfect sense. For others, the line of communication between Bush and divinity does not matter, and the whole situation was a bit awkward. It is a matter of belief. Furthermore, perhaps God was pulling George's leg:

> Even the gods love jokes.[270]
> —PLATO (428/427 or 424/423 to 348/347 BC), Greek
> philosopher

In any case, the George-go-and-end-tyranny episode potentially caused the trend of thousands of years from polytheism to monotheism to reverse. As one "flaneur, with focus on probability (philosophy), probability (mathematics), probability (logic), probability (real-life), deadlifts, Lebanese wine, dead languages" put it:

> My God isn't the God of George Bush.[271]
> —NASSIM NICHOLAS TALEB (b. 1960), Lebanese American
> risk analyst and author

Galileo Galilei, the college dropout autodidact who had *eppur Si muove* written on his tombstone and whose "home office" period was unrelated to a pandemic, also thought that there could not just be one:

> I do not feel obliged to believe that the same God who has
> endowed us with sense, reason, and intellect has intended us to
> forgo their use.[272]
> —GALILEO GALILEI (1564–1642), Italian polymath and
> science revolutionist

Political Correctness and Dishonesty

Caveat lector: the topics of belief and dogma are tricky, especially when combined with ridicule. However, the topics of belief and dogma are central to this book. What investors believe is driving nearly everything. This is how the author of *The Art of Asset Allocation* put it:

> Markets usually change when beliefs change, not fundamentals.[273]
> —DAVID DARST *(b. 1947), American investment strategist*

The distinctions between truth and untruth, reality and fiction, science and superstition, fact and opinion are elementary building blocks when dealing with uncertainty. Ridicule and cynicism are part of the analyst's toolkit and are all different forms of honesty, the search for the truth, essentially the opposite of political correctness. Not even dogma survives ridicule:

> *The final test of truth is ridicule. Very few dogmas have ever faced it and survived.*[274]
> —H. L. MENCKEN *(1880–1956), American journalist and literary critic*

Political correctness is dishonest as it bends truth and skews facts to avoid offense. Offense can destroy political capital, hence the incentive for political correctness. Research is defined as seeking or investigating truth and ought to be honest and therefore must be politically *incorrect* by definition. Reason, logic, and thoughtfulness apply. Occasional and potential offensiveness, therefore, is not the purpose of this book but an unfortunate side effect. Not I, but an arrogant genius might word it as follows:

> *Words ought to be a little wild for they are the assault of thoughts on the unthinking.*[275]
> —JOHN MAYNARD KEYNES *(1883–1946), British economist*

Salman Rushdie, ranked by the *Times* in 2008 as thirteenth on a list of the fifty greatest British writers since 1945, also thinks that offense is important:

> *What is freedom of expression? Without the freedom to offend, it ceases to exist.*[276]
> —SALMAN RUSHDIE *(b. 1947), Indian-born British essayist and author*

The link between wisdom and freedom and freedom of speech and tyranny was made hundreds of years ago in Cato's *Letters*:

> *Without Freedom of Thought, there can be no such Thing as*
> *Wisdom; and no such Thing as publick Liberty . . .*[277]
> —JOHN TRENCHARD *(1662–1723), English writer, and*
>   *Thomas Gordon (1691–1750), Scottish writer*

The recent reverse-enlightenment and limitation of free speech in the United States, the woke movement, is quite a serious affair. The limitation of free speech is somewhat an early indicator for stronger forms of tyranny to come.

There is a pragmatic remedy to books that offend. Some books come with a disclaimer. One such book warns from offense early on:

> *To prevent angering the little people community, we suggest that*
> *this book be placed on the very highest shelf possible.*[278]
> —BOBBY HENDERSON *(b. 1980), American satirist and*
>   *founder of Pastafarianism*

Talk and Persuasion

Oratory is a skill that is applicable to many situations, mainly where diplomacy is required:

> *A diplomat . . . was a person who can tell you to go to hell in such*
> *a way that you actually look forward to the trip.*[279]
> —CASKIE STINNETT *(1911–98), American travel writer and*
>   *magazine editor*

There is a saying that talk is cheap. Genius, it is not:

> *Mediocrity can talk;*
> *but it is for genius to observe.*[280]
> —ISAAC D'ISRAELI *(1866–1948), British writer and scholar*

There are exceptions to nearly all rules. If talk is cheap, there is at last one exception:

Talk is cheap—except when Congress does it.[281]
—CULLEN HIGHTOWER *(1923–2008), American salesman*
   and sales trainer

In finance, and presumably elsewhere, too, oratory skill is required in the sales department, not in R&D (research and development):

Those who say, don't know;
and those who know, don't say.[282]
—*Anonymous old trader with a Brooklyn accent in the 1980s*

Whether this one quotation above can describe Wall Street all in one sentence, I will leave aside for now. In any case, the distinction between babbling and thoughtfulness is old. The anonymous old trader with a Brooklyn accent in Michael Lewis's *Liar's Poker* might have been a Taoist:

Those who know don't talk.
Those who talk don't know.[283]
—LAO TZU *(ca. 6 BC), Chinese philosopher*

The divider that separates talk and wisdom was well articulated by Thomas Macaulay, Secretary of War under Queen Victoria:

The object of oratory alone is not truth, but persuasion.[284]
—CHARLES KNIGHT *(1791–1873), English publisher, editor*
   and author

Baltasar Gracián, the Spanish Jesuit whose writings were lauded by the likes of Schopenhauer and Nietzsche, recommended discriminating. He thought one could not dine off words, which are wind, or off politeness, which is but polite deceit. One of his aphorisms from 1647 related to worldly wisdom states:

Distinguish the Man of Words from the Man of Deeds.[285]
—BALTASAR GRACIÁN *(1601–58), Spanish philosopher*

Idealism and Cynicism

My first line of defense for using ridicule as an analytical tool in the search for truth and wisdom is Gill's law, named after Brendan Gill, an American who wrote for the *New Yorker* for six decades:

> *Not a shred of evidence exists in favor of the idea that life is serious.*[286]
> —BRENDAN GILL *(1914–97), American writer*

Seriousness, therefore, is a constraint to the open-minded, the seeker of truth, i.e., the analyst. Truth is pragmatism made simple:

> *Truth is what works.*[287]
> —WILLIAM JAMES *(1842–1910), American philosopher and psychologist*

Cynicism is potentially an analytical tool too:

> *The power of accurate observation is commonly called cynicism by those who have not got it.*[288]
> —GEORGE BERNARD SHAW *(1856–1950), Nobel laureate (Literature)*

This means, if you are called a cynic by someone, it is he who has the reality deficit, not you. Cynicism might be a function of age, a character trait of those who have been around the block on multiple occasions:

> *Idealism is what precedes experience;*
> *cynicism is what follows.*
> —DAVID T. WOLF *(b. 1943), American author*

As an analyst for whom accurate observation, bias-awareness, and pragmatic interpretation are key, one, therefore, ought to be an occasional cynic and not (always) serious:

> *Seriousness is the only refuge of the shallow.*[289]
> —OSCAR WILDE *(1854–1900), Irish author*

I do respect serious people, though, despite my kids wearing a T-shirt with the above quotation printed in front when they were in nursery school. Patrick Jake "P. J." O'Rourke, über-libertarian, and author of *Parliament of Whores*, modernized Oscar Wilde's quote:

> Earnestness is stupidity sent to college.[290]
> —P. J. O'ROURKE *(b. 1947), American political satirist and journalist*

Ridicule and cynicism sometimes apply to a certain situation, are appropriate even, and sometimes are not. Not making fun of Nicolás Maduro, Francois Hollande, Jeremy Corbin, North Korea's "crazy fat kid" (a John McCain term), or the 2016 and 2020 presidential candidates in the United States makes no sense when trying to understand reality. Even silliness can add perspective and applies every now and then:

> Silly things do cease to be silly if they are done by sensible people in an impudent way.[291]
> —JANE AUSTEN *(1775–1817), English novelist*

Whether this last quotation applies to a Silicon Valley billionaire sending an electric roadster into space and selling flamethrowers via Twitter, I'm not sure. (The latter certainly had some appeal to the arsonists among us.) But then, progress depends on silliness, at least in part:

> The reasonable man adapts himself to the world, the unreasonable man persists in trying to adapt the world to himself. Therefore all progress depends on the unreasonable man.[292]
> —GEORGE BERNARD SHAW

Folly and Belief

A couple of years ago at a party at the leading superconductivity research center in Japan, the researchers, presumably having a good time, poured different types of alcohol on their superconductor. It turned out that the superconductors become more efficient when red wine was poured on them; an example of sensible people being silly. There are times when the greatest wisdom lies in seeming not to be wise. This idea can be traced further back than to Jane Austen. In a book titled *The Art of Worldly*

Wisdom, a book almost entirely composed of three hundred maxims with commentary, Baltasar Gracián wrote:

> *Make use of Folly.*[293]
> —BALTASAR GRACIÁN *(1601–58), Spanish philosopher*

I believe the following pieces of wit and wisdom have merit and, in one form or another, apply to the topic of dogma in finance. If some of these remarks are offensive, it is not the messenger's fault. Personally, I find the way in which they apply to finance and the current political environment shocking. It goes without saying that these quotations were taken out of context; Bertrand Russell and H. L. Mencken were presumably not thinking of MMT (Mugabe Maduro Theory, sometimes referred to as Modern Monetary Theory to make it sound more intelligent) when they penned the lines below. I must assume, therefore, that, at least to some extent, the applicability of these references lies in the eye of the beholder.

> *The fact that an opinion has been widely held is no evidence whatever that it is not utterly absurd.*[294]
> —BERTRAND RUSSELL *(1872–1970), British philosopher*

> *The most common of all follies is to believe passionately in the palpably not true. It is the chief occupation of mankind.*[295]
> —H. L. MENCKEN *(1880–1956), German American journalist*

Furthermore, appearance can inform as well as delude the observer:

> *People think that I must be a strange person. This is not correct. I have the heart of a small boy. It is in a glass jar on my desk.*[296]
> —STEPHEN KING *(b. 1947), American horror author*

Montaigne's axiom is related to holding false beliefs. It is typically stated as follows, although there are many variants of this wording:

> *[N]othing is so firmly believed, as that what we least know . . .*[297]
> —MICHEL DE MONTAIGNE *(1533–1592), French philosopher*

Montaigne, a Renaissance celebrity, most famously known for his skeptical remark, "Que sçay-je?" ("What do I know?"), goes on warning us from astrologers, fortune-tellers, or, to use the Wall Street variant, fortune-sellers, etc. which is still good advice four hundred years later and is most applicable to the realm of finance. Montaigne's advice is sound. However, escaping from delusions, false beliefs, inapplicable ideologies and ideas, babblers, etc. is exceedingly difficult:

> No one can escape the influence of a prevailing ideology.[298]
> —LUDWIG VON MISES *(1881–1973), Austrian School*
> *economist*

Believe it or not, Frank Zappa, who thought communism does not work because people like to shop, said more or less the same thing as von Mises:

> *A mind is like a parachute. It doesn't work if it is not open.*[299]
> —FRANK ZAPPA *(1940–93), American musician*

Many people having a biased view on reality was not lost on Earl Russell:

> *Man is a credulous animal, and must believe something; in the*
> *absence of good grounds for belief, he will be satisfied with bad*
> *ones.*[300]
> —BERTRAND ARTHUR WILLIAM RUSSELL, *3rd Earl Russell*
> *(1872–1970), Nobel laureate*

The idea is old. Caesar said more or less the same thing:

> *People readily believe what they want to believe.*[301]
> —JULIUS CAESAR *(100–44 BC), Roman general and politician*

This means the idea that people can hold on to false beliefs is ancient, traceable at least back to Demosthenes (384–322 BC).

Doubt and the Beginning of Wisdom

I have been supplementing my research with quotations since the early 1990s. When writing this book, I was surprised by how many quotations I had been attributing incorrectly. For this book, I tried to find the original source of every quotation I use, as outlined in the preface. Here is my favorite fake Buddha quote:

Do not believe in anything simply because you have heard it. Do not believe in anything simply because it is spoken and rumoured by many. Do not believe in anything simply because it is found written in your religious books. Do not believe in anything merely on the authority of your teachers and elders. Do not believe in traditions because they have been handed down for many generations. But after observation and analysis, when you find that anything agrees with reason and is conducive to the good and benefit of one and all, then accept it and live up to it.[302]
—*Anonymous, but probably not Buddha*

This is rather good advice; very applicable to the field of finance, irrespective of where it originated and who did the exact wording. There is a huge debate about the origin of this quotation and variants thereof, all of which I will skip for now. Below is a handier version of the potentially fake Buddha quotation from above, one of my top ten. André Gide was the winner of the Nobel Prize in Literature in 1947.

Believe those who are seeking the truth;
  doubt those who find it.[303]
—ANDRÉ GIDE *(1869–1951), French author*

Voltaire saw this very well:

Doubt is not a pleasant condition,
but certainty is an absurd one.[304]
—VOLTAIRE *(1694–1778), French philosopher*

The doubt bit even made it into a German proverb:

Gewissheit ist die Mutter der Narren. (Certainty is the mother of fools.)[305]
—*German proverb*

Letting go of certainties is not easy, but it is a prerequisite for clear and creative thinking:

Creativity requires the courage to let go of certainties.[306]
—ERICH FROMM *(1900–80), German philosopher*

Voltaire was a doubter. Being a doubter in eighteenth-century France was risky. Voltaire's solution? Same as Gordon Gekko's: Switzerland. There he was free to write what he thought instead of what the authorities thought he should write. We should rate him highly:

> When we forget to honor Voltaire we shall be unworthy of freedom.[307]
> —WILL DURANT (1885–1981), American historian

The French Enlightenment, which includes Voltaire, was influential for the second-most-important freedom-related one-pager in history; the United States Declaration of Independence from July 4, 1776. (Fun fact: George III, king of England, kept a diary. His entry for July 4, 1776: "Nothing of importance happened today.")[308]

George Iles, similarly to André Gide and anonymous-but-not-Buddha, links doubt to wisdom:

> Doubt is the beginning, not the end, of wisdom.[309]
> —GEORGE ILES (1852–1942), Canadian author

Stability and Error

Mahatma Gandhi, who was nominated for the Nobel Peace Prize five times, recommended modesty. It is the leave-your-ego-outside-when-entering-the-meeting-room idea mentioned in the previous chapter.

> It is unwise to be too sure of one's own wisdom. It is healthy to be reminded that the strongest might weaken, and the wisest might err.[310]
> —MAHATMA GANDHI (1869–1948), Indian leader and nonviolent civil rights activist

This last quotation disfavors central planning, the belief in central planning being one of the main tenants of socialism. It is not obvious then that India, once the world's byword for great riches, chose socialism after independence. After World War II, India was in a much better position to prosper than was China. It didn't. India was free and had escaped the ravages of the war. China wasn't and hadn't. China was torn apart by civil war and a brutal Japanese invasion. However, by 2017, China was more than four times richer than India based on GDP per capita. India erred. (Well, China erred too. It just corrected its error more speedily as it freed up markets quicker.)

Risk management (as opposed to risk measurement) deals with changing one's portfolio according to an ever-changing environment or changing rules that happened to have worked fine in the past. The future is uncertain. The only thing we really know for sure is that the status quo is going to change. As economist Hyman Minsky put it:

> Stability is unstable.[311]
> —HYMAN MINSKY (1919–96), American economist

Every mariner knows that a calm sea is a storm in the making. Risk management is the thought process that balances the investment opportunities with the probability of capital depreciation. This means that it is subjective. It also means that someone with investment experience will most likely have a competitive advantage over someone who has none. To some extent, investing and managing risk are like musical chairs—if you are slow, you lose early.

Bottoms and Skin in the Game

Prevention and Experience

There are two types of risk management: prevention and cure. The two tasks are entirely different. Preventing disaster is forward-looking and creative, while responding to a disaster, the cure, is reactive and stressful. Both are important tasks in the tool kit of any investor. Prevention is nobler though.

> Prevention is the daughter of intelligence.[312]
> —WALTER RALEIGH (ca. 1554–1618), English writer, soldier, and explorer

While preventing disaster is laudable, accidents—or worse, disasters— happen. When the accident or disaster is exogenous, the investor will naturally find himself in the position of "getting out of trouble" mode. Exogenous shocks also happen to prudent and foresighted investors (while endogenous accidents and disasters do not—or do to a lesser extent.) Given that exogenous shocks happen, skill (or the lack thereof) and leverage (or the lack thereof) matter most. In other words: (1) experience matters, and (2), a shock can be disastrous for the slow and over-leveraged investor but a great opportunity for the alert and well-funded investor.

Experience matters for obvious reasons. Investors who lived through and survived 1998 and 2008 have more experience than those who have not. As poet Heinrich Heine, born Harry Heine, put it:

> *Experience is a good school. But the fees are high.*[313]
> —HEINRICH HEINE *(1797–1856), German poet*

Note that experience is not the same as age:

> *With age comes wisdom, but sometimes age comes alone.*
> —*Anonymous, sometimes attributed to Oscar Wilde (1854–1900), Irish author*

When exposed to risk, the maxim of "learning by doing" applies, as already outlined in relation to the iron law of failure. Someone who has dug himself out of a hole once in the past might have an edge next time around, certainly relative to someone who thought this could never happen to him, that is, never imagined finding himself in a hole. However, there is the argument to the contrary. Value investor, business founder, and *Forbes* columnist David Dreman argued in 1996 that investors in fact do *not* learn from experience:

> *There is an impressive and growing body of evidence demonstrating that investors and speculators don't necessarily learn from experience. Emotion overrides logic time after time.*[314]
> —DAVID DREMAN *(b. 1936), American investor and author*

Wisdom and Plagiarism

Of course, there are investors who learn, and those who do not and continue repeating their mistakes. This indicates that those who learn have an edge over those who make the same mistakes repeatedly. If this is true, we then could argue that experience is existent in the financial world but is scarce. This could serve as an explanation as to why some investment managers can charge horrendous fees and why others cannot.

A cynic might turn this notion around and argue that some investment managers can charge horrendous fees because those who pay the horrendous fees have no experience. Connecticut-based John Webster gave some good advice in relation to hedge funds in 2003, as the boom of investors flocking to hedge funds was already well underway:

> *Investors will want to make sure that they don't start out with the money and the hedge funds start out with the experience, and then when all is said and done, the hedge funds have the money, and the investors have the experience.*[315]
> —JOHN WEBSTER *(b. 1957), Greenwich Associates*

Replace "hedge funds" with "smart beta providers," "risk parity funds," or "ESG funds," and you pretty much have the situation at the time of writing, seventeen years later. John Webster's advice is robust; the items on offer change. Personally, I am a great believer in the learning-by-doing dictum, as already outlined earlier. This is all terribly embarrassing, at least from one perspective, as it means I belong to Will Roger's third category:

> *There are three kinds of men. The one that learns by reading. The few who learn by observation. The rest of them have to pee on the electric fence for themselves.*[316]
> —WILL ROGERS *(1879–1935), American humorist*

Rogers's three-stage learning model is old, i.e., it has withstood the test of time well:

Man has three ways of acting wisely. First, on meditation; that is the noblest. Secondly, on imitation; that is the easiest. Thirdly, on experience; that is the bitterest.[317]
—CONFUCIUS *(551–479 BC), Chinese philosopher*

Although being in Will Rogers's third category is a bit embarrassing, there is a pro-pee-on-the-fence-yourself argument; it is the learning-by-doing argument discussed two chapters ago. You cannot plagiarize wisdom:

We can be knowledgeable with other men's knowledge, but we cannot be wise with other men's wisdom.[318]
—MICHEL DE MONTAIGNE *(1533–1592), French philosopher*

One observation I made is that some investors demand risk management expertise pre-disaster and others post-disaster, the second group being much larger than the first. Investment banks were selling mortgage-backed collateralized debt obligations (CDOs) *prior* to the 2008 crash and tail-risk insurance *after* the crash.

They could not have done it the other way around. Most firms sell what people want. This might or might not be a good product or service. It is exceedingly difficult to actively create demand for something out of thin air. Selling tail-risk insurance prior to the event would have been an uphill battle, as per the following adage:

We never know the worth of water till the well is dry.[319]
—THOMAS FULLER *(1654–1734), English physician, writer, and adage collector*

Controlling risk means being aware that the well will indeed dry out eventually, i.e., risk is exposure to change. The iron law of failure applies.

Experience and Delusion

Experience matters. I believe Oliver Wendell Holmes Sr., a popular teacher at Dartmouth College, because, allegedly, he was the only one who could keep the class awake, put it well:

The young man knows the rules,
but the old man knows the exceptions.[320]
—OLIVER WENDELL HOLMES SR. *(1809–94), American*
   polymath

There are some caveats though; after all, there is no fool like an old fool. Or, as two-time US Open winner Lee Trevino put it:

The older you get,
the better you used to be.
—LEE TREVINO *(b. 1939), American golfer*

Timing in relation to experience being applicable can also be tricky:

Experience—a comb life gives you after you lose your hair.[321]
—JUDITH STERN *(b. 1942), American writer*

Gerald Ashley, author of a book called *Uncertainty and Expectation*, presented an intuitive way of classifying different kinds of information that we can use as a proxy for skill and experience and for its pricing:

"Data	*Facts that can be used for reasoning, discussion, or calculation.*
Information	*Data with context, obtained from investigation, study, or instruction.*
Knowledge	*Information with meaning and understanding.*
Wisdom	*This term can be ridiculed, but let's say it is knowledge with insight.*"[322]

The careful reader will immediately recognize the knowledge pyramid discussed in the previous chapter, albeit in a four-layered and reversed form. The market price is related to the preceding list; the further down we go on the list, the more value is added and the higher the price in the marketplace.

Data and information, we get through a download from a data provider or by watching investment shows on TV. It is free or cheap for a reason. Knowledge, we pick up at school or by reading cleverly written books.

It is not entirely free and requires effort. Knowledge is often described as "properly justified true belief."[323]

Having the right beliefs is thus not just a matter of intellectual importance, but it is of the utmost practical importance, too, as already discussed elsewhere. Holding false beliefs is the same as being delusional.

The forming of beliefs was an evolutionary push toward efficiency, rather than accuracy. In simpler times, beliefs were formed by our sensory experiences. Seeing was believing, as the saying goes. Doubt might have gotten our early ancestors eaten. It was better to be safe than sorry. Almost by definition, our early ancestors did not become philosophical about the rustling in the grass ahead of them when coming out of the cave.

Wisdom and insight, we acquire through experience. Wisdom—easily ridiculed, as Gerald Ashley put it earlier—cuts to the core. Wisdom is never all ornament and no substance; any veneer is backed by a strong reality. There are multiple definitions of what wisdom entails. Most definitions entail a component of sound judgment and decision-making in real world situations. Wisdom is practical.

Applying wisdom is a goal potentially never achieved by most investors, including—stating the obvious—this one. However, avoiding folly is both wise and doable. No one holds a monopoly in folly. Many witty one-liners in this book are applicable to avoiding investment folly. However, there is no wisdom—or "folly-avoidance"—without experience. It is very unlikely that investment and risk management experience will trade cheaply any time soon:

> Experience is one thing you can't get for nothing.[324]
> —Saying

Accidents and Funding

Accidents happen despite Master Oogway suggesting otherwise.

> There are no accidents.[325]
> —MASTER OOGWAY in Kung Fu Panda

"Accidents happen" is a catchy slogan for promoting insurance. However, accidents do not just happen. In certain kinds of systems, large accidents, though rare, are both inevitable and normal, as already alluded to when discussing the iron law of failure. These accidents are a characteristic of the system itself. The coffee maker or entertainment system of a commercial aircraft is not supposed to bring down the aircraft, but both have done so in the past.

An airliner is a good example of a complex system: a large mass containing explosive fuel, flying at high speeds, and operating along a fine boundary between stability and instability. As chaos theory suggests, small forces can upset the system, causing a chain of events that result in the destructive release of the large amount of energy stored in the system. Interestingly, sometimes efforts to make those systems safer, especially by technological means, can make the systems more complex and therefore more prone to accidents.[326] As Albert Einstein most likely never put it:

> *Any intelligent fool can invent further complications,*
> *but it takes a genius to retain, or recapture, simplicity.*[327]
> —Ernst F. Schumacher *(1911–77), German-born English*
>   *economist*

It does not take too much imagination to adapt the airliner analogy to the world of finance.

The investor's capital should be stable and secured. Investors who use leverage face the risk of the foreign capital, the financing, i.e., the debt, being torn from under their feet at the worst possible time. Many of LTCM's trades would have been profitable if it had been able to hold on to its assets for some months longer (and some brokers/dealers had not traded against them). Since LTCM in 1998, there have been other investors that found themselves in dire straits as funding was impaired, hedge funds, banks, endowment funds, etc.

Assuming sound funding, an exogenous shock can be a great investment opportunity instead of a disaster. Typically, markets overreact to good, and especially to bad news; that is, market prices overshoot on the downside. The extraordinary sharp fall in equity markets in March 2020 caused by the response to the pandemic is a recent example. In a sharp downturn, weak hands and poorly funded entities become forced sellers.

Citadel founder and CEO Ken Griffin, who, when in London, lives down the road from the queen, made the point well in 2001:

> *If you're Avis and the lights suddenly go off at Hertz,*
> *you had better be in a position to make a lot of money.*[328]
> —KEN GRIFFIN *(b. 1968), American hedge fund manager*

There is an element of irony in this quotation as the lights nearly went off at Citadel, Ken Griffin's firm, in 2008.[329]

In a stressful market environment, the wheat is separated from the chaff. While the majority panic and run for the exit, some investors—the ones who have no need to worry about their funding—could be facing a great investment opportunity. This is the reason why, for example, hedge fund managers introduce lockups or seek "permanent capital" in the secondary markets. It is also the reason why Warren Buffett bailed out Salomon Brothers after the Treasury bond scandal in 1990–1991 and offered to bail out LTCM when it was in distress after the Russian default in 1998. Trying to catch the proverbial falling knife obviously has its quirks as one does not know whether one is lunging for a falling, recently sharpened, battle-ready *tsurugi* (a double-edged samurai sword) or a butter knife.

Most investors are not Ken Griffin or Warren Buffett. Ms. Becky Quick of CNBC's *Squawk Box* fame gave some advice "for the rest of us." She argued during the September 2008 turmoil:

> *Bottoms are better to watch than to try and catch.*[330]
> —REBECCA "BECKY" QUICK *(b. 1972), American television*
>   *journalist*

Bottom Line

Beliefs are important. Markets change when beliefs change.

One's own beliefs could be wrong. There is no room for dogma. Seriousness can be shallow. Beware of babblers. Make use of folly.

Montaigne's axiom implies one can have great conviction in things unknown as well as unknowable. Certainty is the mother of fools, doubt the beginning of wisdom. We know that things will change though.

Experience is expensive but matters. Experience cannot be faked, and wisdom cannot be plagiarized. A fox has an edge over a lamb. Accidents do not just happen. Being well funded is sound risk management advice. Market panic can present opportunities to the well-funded.

———

Not everything in life is uncertain. There are things that work repeatedly. The law of capital is one of these things.

THE IRON LAW OF CAPITAL

*Those who do not learn from history
are doomed to repeat its mistakes.*

—George Santayana

The iron law of capital states that capital goes where it is welcome and well treated. The "law" was coined by Citibank chairman Walter Wriston in my lifetime, but the idea has been around far longer, and I trace it back many centuries. The key is that "capital" is not just money; it is people and ideas too. Think of it as the five Bs: bucks, businesses, brains, bodies, and blueprints.

The most prominent contemporary example for welcoming capital is the United States of America. At the other end of the spectrum is Venezuela. The US is to Venezuela what capitalism is to socialism and what Milton Friedman is to Karl Marx.

Good risk management requires a sense of humor. You need to view the world from many angles to manage risk, and humor forces multiple perspectives.

The list of "cannots" is a libertarian's delight. These are ten axioms embraced by President Ronald Reagan and Margaret Thatcher. With so much talk of inequality, here is a timely "cannot": "You cannot lift the wage earner by tearing down the wage payer."

My purpose is to help you make more wise decisions and fewer foolish ones. Besides humor, the best way I know to avoid losses? Learn the lessons of history, and do not confuse brains with a bull market, i.e., stay humble. As the Klingons say on *Star Trek*, a fool and his head are soon parted. Simply put, there is no applied wisdom without applied history. Fools are condemned to repeat mistakes from the past, as Santayana knew they would.

An example of ignoring history? Not understanding the iron law of capital could result in "going Venezuela." That is not a compliment. It describes a society that "does the wrong thing repeatedly and with great conviction."

Chávez and the Lessons of History

Humor and Condensed Wisdom

Not Winston, but Charles Churchill once said:[331]

> *A jest is a very serious thing.*[332]
> —CHARLES CHURCHILL *(1732–64), English poet and satirist*

Humor is the root of all truth.

> *The love of truth lies at the root of much humor.*[333]
> —ROBERTSON DAVIES *(1913–95), Canadian novelist*

The following story needs to be seen in exactly that context:

> *"What do you want to be when you grow up?" I asked my friend's little girl.*
>
> *"I want to be Prime Minister of Canada someday," she replied.*

"If you were Prime Minister, what would be the first thing you would do?" her parents asked her. Both were NDP [social-democratic party in Canada] supporters.

"I'd give food and houses to all the homeless people," the little girl replied.

"Welcome to the NDP Party!" her parents said, beaming with pride.

"Wow . . . what a worthy goal!" I told her. I continued, "But you don't have to wait until you're Prime Minister to do that. You can come over to my house, mow the lawn, pull weeds, and sweep my yard, and I'll pay you $50. Then I'll take you over to the grocery store where the homeless guy hangs out. You can give him the $50 to use toward food and a new house," I said to the little girl.

She thought that over for a few seconds, then she looked me straight in the eye and asked,

"Why doesn't the homeless guy come over and do the work, and you can just pay him the $50?"

"Welcome to the Conservative Party," I said, with a smile.

Her parents still aren't speaking to me.[334]

—Anonymous

While this jovial entry into this chapter is supposed to entertain, there is more to it:

When a thing is funny, search it carefully for a hidden truth.[335]
—GEORGE BERNARD SHAW *(1856–1950), Irish dramatist and political activist*

The following is neither literally true, nor is it politically correct. But there is a hidden truth. It would not be funny for some of us otherwise.

Trump loves Kim Kardashian. You know, one more "K" and she would have his favorite initials.[336]
—GRAHAM NORTON *(b. 1963), Irish talk-show host*

Not only is there truth in humor, jokes, and satire; there is wisdom too:

A joke is like condensed wisdom.[337]
—CHARLES LEWINSKY *(b. 1946), Swiss screenplay writer and
author*

Humor, like beauty, is supposedly in the eye of the beholder. However, understanding how things work is not. Sometimes humor helps us to understand things; adds perspective.

A sense of humor is a sense of proportion.[338]
—KHALIL GIBRAN *(1883–1931), Lebanese American artist,
poet, and writer*

Wit and Science
Understanding complex issues requires different perspectives. In general, perspective matters, and it particularly matters in risk management. A sense of humor, therefore, is a risk management tool:

*A sense of humor judges one's actions and the actions of others
from a wider reference and finds them incongruous. It dampens
enthusiasm; it mocks hope; it pardons shortcomings; it consoles
failure. It recommends moderation.*[339]
—THORNTON WILDER *(1897–1975), American playwright
and novelist*

Lord Keynes is famed for saying that in the long run, we're dead. Charlie Chaplin said the same thing:

In the end, everything is a gag.[340]
—CHARLIE CHAPLIN *(1889–1977), English comic actor*

One need not be a practitioner of *laughter yoga* to appreciate the benefits of humor. Without it, all is lost:

*If you lose the power to laugh,
you lose the power to think.*
—CLARENCE DARROW *(1857–1938), American lawyer*

Losing the power to think can be dangerous:

The distrust of wit is the beginning of tyranny.[341]
—EDWARD ABBEY *(1927–89), American essayist and novelist*

Wit and wisecracking are not the same though; the former is more serious:

Wit has truth in it;
wisecracking is simply calisthenics with words.[342]
—DOROTHY PARKER *(1893–1967), American satirist and*
  writer

Skepticism and science are elementary for progress. Starting a sentence with "the funny thing is" is not entirely unscientific. The following piece of wisdom is often attributed to Russian-born scientist and science fiction writer Isaac Asimov:

The most exciting phrase to hear in science, the one that heralds
new discoveries, is not "Eureka!" but "That's funny . . ."[343]
—*Anonymous, potentially Isaac Asimov (1920–92), American*
  author

This was not lost on Vienna-born, Trinity College–teaching Ludwig Wittgenstein:

If people did not sometimes do silly things,
nothing intelligent would ever get done.[344]
—LUDWIG WITTGENSTEIN *(1889–1951), Austrian-British*
  philosopher

Klingons and Baboons
I herein claim that ridicule, too, is an analytical tool. Ridicule, too, adds perspective. One just needs to look hard enough:

Look for the ridiculous in everything and you will find it.[345]
—JULES RENARD *(1864–1910), French author*

If we do not understand the joke, the ridicule, or the irony, we might be missing a certain perspective. Perspective and open-mindedness are key sensory instruments when dealing with uncertainty. The opposite is the opposite:

> *Single-mindedness is all very well in cows or baboons; in an*
> *animal claiming to belong to the same species as Shakespeare it*
> *is simply disgraceful.*[346]
> —ALDOUS HUXLEY *(1894–1963), English writer*

Open-mindedness is to single-mindedness and mindlessness what wisdom is to ignorance and foolishness:

> *Some folks are wise*
> *and some are otherwise.*[347]
> —TOBIAS SMOLLETT *(1721–71), Scottish author*

This idea is, as so many others that are presented in this book, ancient:

> *The smaller the mind*
> *the greater the conceit.*[348]
> —AESOP *(ca. 620–564 BC), Greek fabulist*

Given that one aim of this book is to avoid foolishness, one ought to be open-minded. The practical relevance of avoiding foolishness being a good idea is related to survival and best described by the following proverb:

> *A fool and his head are soon parted.*[349]
> —*Klingon proverb*

Speaking of *Star Trek*:

> *Dad, why does* Star Trek *have a successful socialist society?*
> *Because it's fiction, son.*
> —*Old joke*

We cannot deal with serious issues, such as dealing with uncertainty and adapting to change, without covering all known perspectives, as Winston Churchill suggests:

It is my belief, you cannot deal with the most serious things in the world unless you understand the most amusing.[350]
—WINSTON CHURCHILL *(1874–1965), British statesman*

So, *Charles* Churchill was right; a joke is indeed a serious thing. *Winston* Churchill, whose political tenure in the British Parliament spanned almost fifty-five years and the reigns of six monarchs, was on to something too: missing a certain perspective means we do not really understand what is going on. Understanding what is "going on" is important:

The proper operation of man is to understand.[351]
—THOMAS AQUINAS *(1225–1274), Italian priest, theologian, and philosopher*

Understanding the joke is part of understanding what is going on. More importantly, if we do not understand the joke, the joke might be on us; as the poker proverb (from 1979) states:

If after ten minutes at the poker table, you do not know who the patsy is—you are the patsy.
—*Poker wisdom*

While humor helps us understand, it is wise decisions that add value. However, "wise decisions" are an ideal. I treat "wise decisions" as an impossibility by nearly all investors, certainly in a continuous and robust fashion. More importantly, it is the avoidance of the opposite of wisdom, foolishness, which adds the value. Foolishness is not the same as stupidity; foolishness is the lack of wisdom. Stupidity is a given; foolishness is avoidable. It is losses, especially large ones, which kill the rate at which capital compounds. Avoiding foolishness helps mitigate losses. The purpose of this book, therefore, is to help you not be the patsy. The book should help save your ass(ets).

Karl Marx and the History Challenged

History and Rhymes

The best book I own is *The Lessons of History* by Will and Ariel Durant, first published in 1968. It is only one hundred and two pages long, with reasonably large letters. I also own *The Story of Civilization,* which is comprised of eleven tomes, each several hundred pages of small print. The latter is, of course, a much tougher read. The one hundred and two pages of the first book are a summary of the lessons from the eleven tomes. One of my favorite fake Mark Twain quotations in relation to the lessons of history, of which there are numerous variants, is the following:

> *History does not repeat itself—at best it sometimes rhymes.*[352]
> *—Anonymous, nearly always attributed to Mark Twain*

This means one not only needs to see the joke, as Winston Churchill suggested, but spot the rhyme too.

One point of this book is that there is no *applied wisdom* without *applied history.* The lessons derived from examining five thousand years of history should not be ignored. However, some people in public service (and in other professions) do exactly that. They believe they know better and delude themselves into thinking that they have captured the moral and intellectual high ground.

However, when the elite political and academic intelligentsia are out of sync with the lessons of history, they almost always eventually fail. The reality is that Stein's law, as well as the iron law of failure, apply:

> *Those who do not learn from history are doomed to repeat its mistakes.*[353]
> —GEORGE SANTAYANA *(1863–1952), Spanish American philosopher*

I believe this to be one of the top ten pieces of wisdom in this book. If a successful investor feels the urge to write a list of his cardinal rules, Santayana's one-liner is almost always included in one form or another.

Jorge Agustín Nicolás Ruiz de Santayana y Borrás, born in Madrid, who taught philosophy at Harvard and was an influence on Bertrand Russell, among others, is often used in relation to some foolish behavior of some sort. The complete economic and social breakdown of Venezuela is a contemporary example of Santayana's one-liner. Venezuela has ignored the lessons of history, using Cuba as a blueprint to reform, rather than Singapore or South Korea.

So, while history is a tutor to some of us, it is also a comedian for most of us:

> *There is no humorist like history.*[354]
> —WILL DURANT *(1885–1981), American historian and*
>   *history popularizer*

As much fun as it is to ridicule Nicolás Maduro, the former bus driver who currently runs Venezuela, it is a bit unfair as he might not get the joke. He might not spot history:

> *History never looks like history when you are living through it.*[355]
> —JOHN W. GARDNER *(1912–2002), American politician*

Santayana's don't-learn-from-history wisdom has some practical implications for many investors:

> *Those who don't study history are doomed to repeat it. Yet those*
> *who do study history are doomed to stand by helplessly while*
> *everyone else repeats it.*[356]
> —TOM TORO *(b. 1982), American cartoonist for the New*
>   *Yorker*

While Santayana's quotation means we should learn from history, Rafiki sees learning from history as an option:

> *Oh yes, the past can hurt. But from the way I see it, you can*
> *either run from it, or . . . learn from it.*[357]
> —RAFIKI, *shaman from The Lion King*

Georg Wilhelm Friedrich Hegel, a German philosopher who influenced Karl Marx profoundly, begs to differ. Hegel had his reservations regarding Rafiki's "learning-by-doing" dictum stated above.

> *The only thing we learn from history is that we learn nothing from history.*[358]
> —FRIEDRICH HEGEL *(1770–1831), German philosopher*

The cartoon that goes with the Hegel quotation shows AOC dozing off in history class when the tutor talks about the millions of lives lost to socioeconomic experiments that went wrong, socialism in her case.[359]

Property Rights and Parking Spaces
When in doubt as to whether to side with Rafiki or Hegel, I recommend Rafiki. Rafiki seems more serious; more real. Unlike Hegel, Rafiki understands options. Life must be lived forward, not backward, paraphrasing Søren Kierkegaard, a critic of Hegel. The learning-by-doing dictum does not work for everyone though:

> *Experience teaches only the teachable.*[360]
> —ALDOUS HUXLEY *(1894–1963), English writer*

Learning from history is clearly not for everyone. The mayor of New York City, confirming Hegel from earlier and advocating centralized urban planning, suggests the Big Apple ought to "go Venezuela":

> *The biggest obstacle to progress is the idea of private property.*[361]
> —BILL DE BLASIO *(b. 1961), American politician and mayor of New York City*

The funny thing is it's the other way around:

> *Where there is no property,*
> *there is no justice.*[362]
> —JOHN LOCKE *(1632–1704), English philosopher*

To John Locke, the above is as clear as a demonstration in Euclid. To Bill de Blasio, it is not. Property rights are one of six of Niall Ferguson's "killer apps" that can explain the rise of the West relative to the rest of the world over the past four to five hundred years or up until quite recently.[363] Mr. de Blasio's thinking can be summed up in a single sentence:

> *The theory of Communism may be summed up in the single sentence: Abolition of private property.*[364]
> —KARL MARX AND FRIEDRICH ENGELS, *in the* Communist Manifesto *of 1848*

As a disclaimer I should note here that I never really understood Marx. Karl, that is. I believe it was his mum who applied wisdom:

> *I wish Karl would accumulate some capital, instead of just writing about it.*[365]
> —*Mother of Karl Marx, allegedly*

According to at least one founding father of the United States, protecting property rights is the one thing Mr. Blasio should be doing wholeheartedly:

> *Government is instituted to protect property of every sort, as well that which lies in the various rights of individuals, as that which the term particularly expresses. This being the end of government, that alone is a just government which impartially secures to every man whatever is his own.*[366]
> —JAMES MADISON (1751–1836), *Founding Father and fourth president of United States*

My ridicule of Mr. de Blasio's comment could be too harsh; the abolition of private property and a planned economy does indeed offer at least some benefits that might be applicable to New York City:

> *Under capitalism, people have more cars.*
> *Under communism, they have more parking spaces.*[367]
> —WINSTON CHURCHILL (1874–1965), *British statesman and prime minister*

Robin Hood and Innovation
Personally, I prefer to debunk private-property naivete with history. Using economics works too though:

> *Nobody spends somebody else's money as carefully as he spends his own. Nobody uses somebody else's resources as carefully as he uses his own. So if you want efficiency and effectiveness, if you want knowledge to be properly utilized, you have to do it through the means of private property.*[368]
> —MILTON FRIEDMAN *(1912–2006), American economist*

The idea to equalize incomes; to redistribute wealth from those who work to those who do not want to; to increase the role of government in the name of equality; the idea to increase living standards for everybody is arguably very laudable and should be applauded. (And, at the polls, most often is.) However, these ideas, while morally sound when examined superficially and without any sense for history, eventually fail. In a game of competition, it makes no sense to limit one's survival probability; it is unwise to do so. Baroness Thatcher, the milk snatcher, knew this from the socialist misery that was the UK prior to her bringing it back to the first world:

> *Socialist governments traditionally do make a financial mess. They always run out of other people's money. It's quite a characteristic of them.*[369]
> —MARGARET THATCHER *(1925–2013), the Iron Lady*

(Fun fact: GDP per capita in pre-Thatcher Britain grew by 48 percent from 1960 to 1978, while Germany grew by 75 percent and France by 92 percent in the same period. GDP per capita in Britain from 1979, the year Thatcher became prime minister, to 2010 grew by 81 percent, compared to 48 percent in Germany and 47 percent in France.[370])

Modern-day Robin Hoods eventually run out of financing. Whether we call it socialist or social-democracy or the third way or the Green New Deal does not really matter. A society that gives incentives for trade, ingenuity, and innovation, and is generally business-friendly prospers. A society that gives disincentives for trade, ingenuity, and innovation, and is generally business-unfriendly does not. One need not be an optimist; rationality suffices:

> *Without trade, innovation just does not happen. Exchange is to technology as sex is to evolution. It stimulates novelty.*[371]
> —MATT RIDLEY *(b. 1958), British banker, journalist, politician, and author*

Capital and Applied History

Safety and Profits

The idea of *applied history* is to understand the present against the backdrop of the past. Applied history allows us to determine whether all things economic are getting better or getting worse. If history does indeed rhyme, then the sequential falling of dominos might not be entirely random or unpredictable. If history does rhyme, then there are trends and feedback loops; trends and feedback loops being possible departures from randomness.

My favorite definition for the iron law of capital, sometimes referred to as Wriston's law of capital, is named after Walter Bigelow Wriston. Walter Wriston was a banker and former chairman and CEO of Citicorp. As chief executive of Citibank/Citicorp (later Citigroup) from 1967 to 1984, Wriston, according to economist Henry Kaufman, was "the most influential banker of his day, and probably since."[372] The term "Wriston's law of capital" was coined by publisher Rich Karlgaard from *Forbes* magazine in an article on his blog, *Digital Rules*, in 2006:

> *Capital will always go where it's welcome and stay where it's well treated . . . Capital is not just money. It's also talent and ideas. They, too, will go where they're welcome and stay where they are well treated.*[373]
> —WALTER BIGELOW WRISTON *(1919–2005), American banker*

The key is that "capital" is not just money; it's people and ideas too. When discussing the Santa Claus principle in the next chapter, I will be referring to "capital" as the five Bs, as in businesses, brains, bodies, blueprints, and bucks. Without the five Bs, there are no five Cs (cash, car, credit card, condominium, and country club membership). Bs come before Cs.

I believe that the iron law of capital has some predictive power. It allows us to identify trends in real time. It allows identification of economic policy folly. Rational analysts were making fun of Chávez long before Venezuela went Cuba. However, learning from past economic folly is not for everyone.

> *I suppose some people would judge that, on balance, Mao did more good than harm.*[374]
> —DIANE ABBOTT *(b. 1953), British Labour Party politician*

The *Communist Manifesto* was written in 1848. History has taught some of us a lot since then. If you replace the word "chains" with "brains," the quotation below is reasonably consistent with the iron law of capital and capital flight today.

> *Workers of the world unite, you have nothing to lose but your chains.*[375]
> —KARL MARX *(1818–83), German revolutionary socialist*

Chains and Brains

The most prominent contemporary example for welcoming capital is the United States of America. For most of its short history, the US has been a magnet for capital, i.e., risk capital, people who want to work hard, people who want to study hard, people who are unwelcome elsewhere, patents, ideas, talent, blueprints for big bombs, etc. It is no coincidence that Silicon Valley is in the United States. (Neither is it a coincidence that Crypto Valley is in Zug, Switzerland.)

One of the most positive, history-changing events I can think of, apart from the Battle of Salamis in 480 BC, where the Greeks stopped the Persians' expansion, is the Manhattan Project. The Manhattan Project did not just occur randomly in the US. The people behind the Manhattan Project left Europe, Germany mainly, for the US. They brought along their capital, relationships, brains, blueprints, and ideas.

Imagine for a moment how the twentieth century could have evolved if Germany had not been a Semitic anti-magnet but, like the US, a magnet. The brains would have stayed. The bomb would have gone off elsewhere, and London's architecture would be, how shall I put this, newer. (The assimilation of various ethnic and religious groups in the US obviously did not go as smoothly as these lines might imply. But that is beside the point made here.) Jim Rogers, who once told a female interviewer that if she knew how bullish he is on commodities, he would be asked to leave the room, articulated the iron law of capital well:

> *Capital never cares whether you're black, white, Communist, socialist, Christian, or Muslim. All it cares about is its safety and its profit. It goes where the opportunities are.*[376]
> —JIM ROGERS *(b. 1942), American investor*

Here is a 2012 quotation that implies that the then-finance minister of France sort of gets the iron law of capital, but then sort of does not:

> *France remains an attractive country for investment. We have no intention to make France inhospitable, but we are in a period of crisis. It is logical that the wealthiest should make a contribution.*[377]
> —PIERRE MOSCOVICI *(b. 1957), French politician*

To many, what I herein call "the iron law of capital" is simply common sense. Mr. Moscovici understood the hospitality bit. However, he still wants to rip off those with the capital; capital here is broadly defined as money, brains, ideas, etc. The emigration of French people into freer nations is going from one all-time high to the next. (There is also inbound immigration to France, for example, from the Maghreb region or Eastern Europe. The same logic applies, i.e., economic opportunities being a magnet for the by-comparison-oppressed. A French engineer sees opportunities in London while an Algerian vegetable farmer spots them in Marseilles.)

One result of the French leaving France is that London, the UK's capital, is the fourth-largest French city when measured by the number of French citizens. And it is typically not the lazy ones who emigrate and seek better opportunities than at home.

Savvy, or shall I say industrious, people tend to leave a sinking ship early, taking their capital with them. The prime minister of New Zealand, Robert Muldoon (1921–92), was almost certainly wrong when he said that it would lift the IQ of both countries, when commenting on the exodus of New Zealanders to Australia. Brains and blueprints are mobile.

Here is perhaps my all-time favorite quotation:

> *Chávez is the best president Colombia has ever had.*[378]
> —*Colombian homeowner*

If you just laughed out loud, I can assure you the rest of this chapter will contain absolutely nothing you don't already know. Brain drain is a big part of the iron law of capital.

The ideas behind the iron law of capital are incredibly old. The following text is from the 1520s; an early defense of the nonpaternalistic approach:

> *Christendom (or shall we say the whole world?) is rich because of business. The more business a country does, the more prosperous are its people. . . . Where there are many merchants, there is plenty of work. . . . It is impossible to limit the size of the companies. . . . The bigger and more numerous they are, the better for everybody. If a merchant is not perfectly free to do business in Germany, he will go elsewhere, to Germany's loss. . . . If he cannot do business above a certain amount, what is he to do with his surplus money? . . . It would be well to let the merchant alone, and put no restrictions on his ability or capital. Some people talk of limiting the earning capacity of investments. This would . . . work great injustice and harm by taking away the livelihood of widows, orphans, and other sufferers . . . who derive their income from investments in these companies.*[379]
> —AUGSBURG, *1520s.*

Chávez never understood this, and Venezuela is suffering as Santayana predicted it would. From the perspective of an optimist, Venezuela is currently learning by doing. Although, W. Edwards Deming—an authority on quality management, who had to implement statistics into manufacturing in Japan first, before he became recognized at home—might suggest otherwise:

> Learning is not compulsory . . . neither is survival.[380]
> —W. EDWARDS DEMING (1900–93), American statistician,
>   author, lecturer, and consultant

Venezuela was the fourth-richest country by GDP per capita in 1950 and the richest major economy in Latin America as recently as 1982. If you believe that blaming Chávez for the downfall of Venezuela is far too simplistic, you might be right. But a saint, he is not. Mr. Gartman on Maduro's idea of declaring Chávez a saint in 2016:

> We remain "fans" of Mr. Maduro, the President of Venezuela because he sets the bar high for lunacy, which only he is able to leap above and re-set.[381]
> —DENNIS GARTMAN (b. 1950), American investment
>   newsletter writer

Equality and Misery

Wriston's law of capital suggests that capital just moves on when it is not welcome and well treated. Therefore, the Chávez-is-the-best-president quotation from earlier is not just comical; it is also full of applied historical wisdom. Socialist animosities (and governmental malpractice) toward the private sector resulted in benefits for its neighbors. It is the reason why it is not just Venezuela that is "going Venezuela." (In the past, I have used the term "going Venezuela" to describe a society or its administration that "does the wrong thing repeatedly and with great conviction."[382])

Argentina and Egypt are two examples of socioeconomic systems that were doing reasonably well a hundred years ago. However, their societies and economies and well-being have been deteriorating continuously ever since. South Korea and Singapore are two examples of the exact opposite. All five countries, Venezuela, Egypt, Argentina, South Korea, and Singapore, can continue their current socioeconomic trajectory for a long time longer. To paraphrase Tobias Smollett from earlier: some are wise, and some are otherwise.

The fascination with Venezuela is the speed of deterioration. (The clownish demeanors of Chávez and Maduro help with the ridicule.) It took only fifteen to twenty years to go from "reasonably well" to the sorry state the country is in today. And it can get progressively worse for an awfully long time too. Winston Churchill knew what the road to hell is paved with, as he articulates here:

> *Socialism is a philosophy of failure, the creed of ignorance, and the gospel of envy, its inherent virtue is the equal sharing of misery.*[383]
> —WINSTON CHURCHILL *(1874–1965), winner of the 1953 Nobel Prize in Literature*

The iron law of capital allows making educated guesses about the movement of capital, and therefore, about ongoing failure or future prosperity. Certain patterns are repeatable. The "going Venezuela" idea is based on historical patterns and implies repeatability, i.e., capital flight when the authorities intervene, for example, in the name of equality; hence the term "the road to hell is paved with good intentions."

This is called the Samaritan's dilemma: an attempt to do good may actually cause harm. Venezuela has not learned from history; it is quite "insane." As Albert Einstein most likely never put it, but is often misquoted as saying nevertheless:

> *Insanity: doing the same thing over and over again and expecting different results.*[384]
> —*Narcotics Anonymous*

Today the above quotation, and variants thereof, is an investment proverb. One can use this fake Einstein quotation for nearly any rant on anything that differs from one's own view. Quoting Einstein obviously sounds smarter than quoting Narcotics Anonymous. As someone put it in relation to the quotation being misattributed to Einstein repeatedly:

The definition of insanity is quoting Einstein over and over and expecting to be thought to be clever each time.[385]
—*Anonymous*

What this last quotation means for your author and his psychoanalytic personality profile is beyond the scope of this book, fortunately. Allow me to move on then, with Wriston, rather than with Freud.

The Ten Cannots and the Spirit of Capitalism

Max Weber (1864–1920), the German political economist and sociologist, who dissented with Karl Marx and believed that human values affect how people act throughout history, coined the term "spirit of capitalism" about the massive influx of (Protestant) merchants, skilled workers, and industrialists. History does indeed rhyme, and those who do not remember the past are most likely condemned to repeat it. Venezuela did not remember the past. Many socialist governments in Europe do not remember the past. They think there is a new way or a third way. In relation to contemporary political Europe, one is tempted to ask: where are the grownups?

Any man who is not a socialist at age 20 has no heart.
Any man who is still a socialist at age 40 has no head.[386]
—Georges Benjamin Clemenceau *(1841–1929), French journalist and statesman*

To Clemenceau's point:

Amen and awoman.[387]
—Emanuel Cleaver *(b. 1944), Democrat, end of congressional prayer*

Another case in point: a survey conducted by the Royal Statistical Society asked some UK members of Parliament a simple question: "A coin is tossed twice. What is the probability of getting two heads?" Fifty-three percent of Conservatives got the answer right, but only 23 percent of members of the Labour party did. (But over 70 percent of each party expressed confidence when dealing with numbers.)[388]

Robert Anton Wilson, too, like Clemenceau, thinks it takes about twenty years, which some just call growing up.

> *It only takes 20 years for a liberal to become a conservative without changing a single idea.*[389]
> —ROBERT ANTON WILSON *(1932–2007), American author*

Vladimir Putin concurs with Clemenceau:

> *Whoever does not miss the Soviet Union has no heart.*
> *Whoever wants it back has no brain.*[390]
> —VLADIMIR PUTIN *(b. 1952), president of Russia*

There is even a proverb along those lines:

> *Be wise with speed;*
> *A fool at forty is a fool indeed.*[391]
> —EDWARD YOUNG *(1683–1765), English poet*

Clemenceau, who had a French aircraft carrier named after him, might have gotten his one-liner from Cicero:

> *To be ignorant of the past is to be forever a child.*[392]
> —CICERO *(106–43 BC), Roman politician, orator, and philosopher*

Grownups and Immaturity

Clemenceau's idea of not transforming from being juvenile-romantic into something more serious, therefore, is quite old. Presidential contender Bernie Sanders and Britain's leader of the opposition, Jeremy Corbyn, according to English historian Peter Hennessy "a man of herbivorous ways and carnivorous views," knew this very well; after all, the juvenile-romantic were a large part of their constituencies. It is therefore quite understandable that the left in the UK want the voting age reduced to sixteen, and in California, the fifth-largest economy on the planet if it were a country, there is the idea to reduce it to fourteen:

Some California legislators have proposed lowering the voting age to 14—as if California politics are not immature enough already.[393]

—THOMAS SOWELL *(b. 1930), American economist and Marxist in his twenties*

Rejecting unfreedom (and Santa Claus), one would have thought, is part of growing up, as Karl Popper experienced:

I remained a socialist for several years, even after my rejection of Marxism; and if there could be such a thing as socialism combined with individual liberty, I would be a socialist still. For nothing could be better than living a modest, simple, and free life in an egalitarian society. It took some time before I recognized this as no more than a beautiful dream; that freedom is more important than equality; that the attempt to realize equality endangers freedom; and that, if freedom is lost, there will not even be equality among the unfree.[394]

—KARL POPPER *(1902–94), Austrian-British philosopher*

Singapore's Founding Father, Lee Kuan Yew, took Clemenceau's wisdom to improve democracy. He thought grownups should have more votes.

[I] am convinced, personally, that we would have a better system if we gave every person over the age of 40 who has a family two votes, because he or she is likely to be more careful, voting also for his or her children. He or she is more likely to vote in a serious way than a capricious young person under 30.[395]

—LEE KUAN YEW *(1923–2015), Founding Father and prime minister of Singapore*

Another idea to modify democracy is to only allow grownups with a stake in governance to vote, i.e., those who pay taxes and own property and shares of domestic companies. They have skin in the game. People with skin in the game, one could assume, are less prone to fall for infantile fluke ideas. People with skin in the game see many shades of gray of the game that bystanders, spectators, and free riders do not:

> *You don't realize how easy this game is until you get up in that broadcasting booth.*[396]
> —MICKEY MANTLE *(1931–95), American baseball player*

As much as I enjoyed Clemenceau's wit, mentioned earlier, when picking it up when I was around forty, there is a counter-quip that is not entirely without merit:

> *The duty of youth is to challenge corruption.*[397]
> —KURT COBAIN *(1967–94), American musician and Nirvana front man*

Cobain might have been quoting Edward Abbey, an inspirational leader for environmentalists and ecowarriors. The quote is often erroneously attributed to Thomas Paine (ca. 1737–1809), the English-born American political activist, philosopher, political theorist, and revolutionary.

> *A patriot must always be ready to defend his country against his government.*[398]
> —EDWARD ABBEY *(1927–89), American author and essayist*

The Cannots and Campus Liberalism

The following bullet points are "cannots" based on historical precedence. To some extent these cannots capture the spirit of the Founding Fathers of the US. I believe they stem from Rev. William J. H. Boetcker (1873–1962), an American religious leader who lectured around the United States about industrial relations at the turn of the twentieth century. He authored the following pamphlet, titled *The Ten Cannots,* in 1916. At one time President Ronald Reagan used them in a speech, wrongly attributing them to Abraham Lincoln. Margaret Thatcher also picked from this list, the list being a libertarian's delight:

> *You cannot bring prosperity by discouraging thrift.*
> *You cannot help small men by tearing down big men.*

You cannot strengthen the weak by weakening the strong.

You cannot lift the wage earner by pulling down the wage payer.

You cannot help the poor man by destroying the rich.

You cannot keep out of trouble by spending more than your income.

You cannot further brotherhood of men by inciting class hatred.

You cannot establish security on borrowed money.

You cannot build character and courage by taking away man's initiative and independence.

You cannot help men permanently by doing for them what they could and should do for themselves.

These cannots have aged well. Suffice to say that they are not widely distributed on US college campuses.

Trends and Mean Reversion

Two immensely powerful concepts in finance are trends and mean reversion. (In finance, mean reversion is the assumption that prices oscillate around an average and that this average functions like a magnet when prices deviate too far from it.) A trend is often feeding on itself, sometimes referred to as a positive or negative feedback loop, and can go on for an exceptionally long time; much longer than is generally and often expected. One of my favorite fake Keynes quotations is along those lines.

> *Financial markets can remain irrational far longer than you can remain solvent.*[399]
> —A. GARY SHILLING *(b. 1937), American financial analyst and beekeeper*

Trends can last hundreds of years, one example being the decline of China—for most of human history, the largest economy. As one Shanghai resident put it, commenting on the long decline and the ensuing mean reversion:

> *We've had a couple hundred bad years, but now we're back.*[400]
> —Shanghai resident

I believe this last quotation summarizes the last couple of hundred years of Chinese history very well in just one sentence. China was great once, prior to the man-made disasters, from the Taiping Civil War of the nineteenth century to the "misnomered" Great Leap Forward and cultural revolution in the twentieth century. The idea of mean reversion, i.e., the good times making way for rough patches, is as old as civilization:

> We are now suffering the evils of a long peace. Luxury, more deadly than war, broods over the city, and avenges a conquered world.[401]
>
> —JUVENAL (ca. 55–140), Roman poet

Applying Stein's law ("If something cannot go on forever, it will stop.") to finance, as discussed in chapter one, implies that trends end eventually. The end of the trend could be viewed, colloquially, as the reversion to the mean of some sort. In the case of China, it was Deng Xiaoping opening markets in 1978 that resulted in the turning point from misery to riches. Deng Xiaoping understood what herein is called the iron law of capital and elsewhere is generally referred to as good economic sense and mental health. Mao didn't. Capital left, or, as sadly was the case under Mao, died. Venezuela also mean reverted under Chávez, like China under Deng Xiaoping, just in the opposite direction.

Many market observers have noted that the iron law of capital might be on sabbatical. The well-intended interventions by the various authorities could mean that nothing has been learned from history and that it is not just Venezuela that is going Venezuela, but many industrialized economies too. William White, the chairman of the Economic Development and Review Committee at the Organization for Economic Cooperation and Development (OECD) in Paris and former chief at the Bank of International Settlements, put it well:

> Rate manipulation below the free market level distorts the investment calculation, systematically misallocating capital towards low yielding business ventures. The longer ZIRP [zero interest rate policy] lasts, the more the yield-starved investors desperately take reckless risks and the more capital flows into

doubtful investments yielding ever lower returns. ZIRP thereby has the counterproductive consequence of eroding the productivity of capital as well as to slow down capital accumulation, with a prolonged and deepened recession as the final result.[402]
—WILLIAM R. WHITE *(b. 1943), Canadian economist*

The West and parts of Asia, supported intellectually by scholarly Keynesians, just keep on spending. There are many ways to reduce debt and take from those with wealth, inflation being probably the most politically palatable and elegant. However, history teaches us that there are other ways to get to the money. Ludwig von Mises pointed this out a long time ago:

> *The unprecedented success of Keynesianism is due to the fact that it provides an apparent justification for the deficit spending policies of contemporary governments. It is the pseudo-philosophy of those who can think of nothing else than to dissipate the capital accumulated by previous generations.*[403]
> —LUDWIG VON MISES *(1881–1973), Austrian School economist*

Warren Buffett has found a way to reduce deficit spending and improve democracy:

> *I could end the deficit in 5 minutes. You just pass a law that says that anytime there is a deficit of more than 3% of GDP all sitting members of congress are ineligible for re-election.*[404]
> —WARREN BUFFETT *(b. 1930), American investor and businessman*

Expropriation and Options
One of my favorite fake Thomas Jefferson quotations is the following:

> *The democracy will cease to exist when you take away from those who are willing to work and give to those who would not.*[405]
> —*Anonymous, but most likely not Thomas Jefferson*

It's still applied wisdom, perhaps just not Jefferson's. Real assets should do well in times of debt monetization. However, if the real assets get nationalized, the investor loses everything, or whatever the authorities think is the "fair share."

Expropriation is an option, an option for the government. The bearer of wealth, the investor, is short that option. As China-born, London-based, Australia-raised Sir Michael Hintze, founder of CQS, a hedge fund, put it in 2013 in relation to Europe becoming a bit more aggressive in going after its citizens' money:

> One of the things that concerns me in the context of the Euro-zone is expropriation. Cyprus was a bail-in, with depositors' savings taken away to make up for the shortfall and it was done at the direction of government. This now seems to be the new template.[406]
> —MICHAEL HINTZE (b. 1953), British-Australian hedge fund manager

Michael Hintze's grandparents fled Russia after the 1917 Bolshevik revolution; hence, speculating a bit, Mr. Hintze's sensitivity to expropriation. Vladimir Putin, formerly with the KGB, did not appreciate the Cyprus bail-in of 2013 and expropriation of Russian "investors" either. Before the bail-in, he said:

> Such a decision, if it's adopted, will be unfair, unprofessional and dangerous.[407]
> —VLADIMIR PUTIN (b. 1952), Russian politician

Many Russian oligarchs have "invested" in Cyprus; hence Putin's unease of the Eurozone's sticky fingers. Tensions with Russia, Russia being classified by George Soros in Davos in January 2018 as a "dictatorship and Mafia state," can escalate. The First World War was not started because Bosnia's Che Guevara, Gavrilo Princip, finished his sandwich, left the café, and shot Franz Ferdinand and his wife. This might have been the trivial trigger, the butterfly's wing flap that caused the first domino to fall. Big events can have trivial beginnings, as Cicero mused in chapter two. Whether Mr. Putin had a Klingon proverb in mind when he said the above, I do not know. He might have.

> *Fool me once, shame on you.*
> *Fool me twice, prepare to die.*
> —*Klingon proverb*

Bottom Line

There is an iron law of capital. It states that capital goes where it is welcome and well treated. Capital is not just bucks, but businesses, brains, bodies, and blueprints; the five Bs. They, too, go where they are welcome and well treated.

Some folks are wise, and some are otherwise. Fools are condemned to repeat mistakes from the past. Investors can use this in the sense that failure is somewhat predictable *before* the fools have unleashed their full potential.

Trends and mean reversion are powerful concepts in history and universally applicable to the field of finance. An extended period of economic bliss can be followed by a period of despair. Stein's law and the law of failure dictate that the bliss ends eventually.

Expropriation is an option for a government that is finished kicking the can further down the road. The investor is short that option.

———

Life is full of options. Learning from history is an option. For some of us, expecting presents from Santa is an option too.

THE SANTA CLAUS PRINCIPLE

Eloquence may exist without
a proportional degree of wisdom.
—Edmund Burke

Santa brings the presents. Presents are for free. The Santa Claus principle states that there is something for free. If you believe only kids believe in Santa, you are mistaken.

Freedom is an option. An option allows choice. Central planning eliminates options. A prisoner has fewer options. No one risks his life to get to Cuba. There once was a saying, "rich as an Argentinian." No more. Freedom also means the right to make a complete fool out of yourself and seek unwisdom.

Central planning works in theory though. It is therefore taught on campus. However, campus liberalism is like Neil Diamond music. It's not good and belongs in the past, yet there is a group of people who think that it will eventually catch on if only they keep playing it. Neil deGrasse Tyson suggests one ought to make America smart again, prior to making it great again.

Applied Economics and Ripple Effects

Santa and the Government

In 1961, during the Soviets' nuclear testing at the North Pole, a little girl wrote a letter to JFK, asking if Santa Claus was okay. Kennedy wrote back to her, saying that he spoke with Santa and that he was okay. Santa is a matter of belief. Some grownups believe in him too. Santa Claus was issued a pilot's license from the United States government in 1927. Finland reserves the postal code 99999 for Santa Claus. Not everyone believes in Santa Claus though:

> I never believed in Santa Claus because I knew no white dude
> would come into my neighborhood after dark.
> —DICK GREGORY (1932–2017), African American comedian
>   and civil rights activist

"Santa Claus" stands for receiving presents without putting up an effort. Some economies are currently thinking of paying a fixed salary, a basic income of say $3000 per month, to every single working-age citizen from the government coffers, no strings attached. It is a potential vote-winner. Presents without work? Sounds great. The intentions are good, and the first-order effect is just wonderful.

Thomas Sowell, an economist currently in his early nineties, did a lot of writing. He is famous for, among many things, his down-to-earthness and pulling no punches:

> Too often what are called "educated" people are simply peo-
> ple who have been sheltered from reality for years in ivy-cov-
> ered buildings. Those whose whole careers have been spent in
> ivy-covered buildings, insulated by tenure, can remain adoles-
> cents on into their golden retirement years.[408]
> —THOMAS SOWELL (b. 1930), American economist, social
>   theorist, and political philosopher

One of his books was cleverly titled *Applied Economics*. The term has its roots in the nineteenth century. Mr. Sowell takes a common-sense approach to economics. The subtitle of the book is "Thinking Beyond Stage One." One of the key aspects of the book is to demonstrate the ripple effects of all sorts of political, socioeconomic, and economic policy decisions.

The first stage of a new policy, for example, according to Sowell, is what makes the policy initiator look good. The problem is, though, that the policy initiator is not responsible for the ripple effects, the later stages. A contemporary example is generous immigration in, say, Sweden. The first-order effect is giving refuge to human beings in need. A higher-order effect, one that was not foreseen, or one that was consciously ignored, is pregnant native-born mothers being turned away from maternity wards due to a lack of capacity. The costs of failure, i.e., the higher-order effects, are not carried by the initiator. Harry Browne found one way of putting it:

> The free market punishes irresponsibility. Government rewards it.[409]
> —HARRY BROWNE (1933–2006), American libertarian writer and politician

Since around 2016, Nassim Taleb has called those who cannot see beyond stage one and who are unaware of their blindness "Intellectuals Yet Idiots" (IYI).

> Typically, the IYI get the first order logic right, but not second-order (or higher) effects making him totally incompetent in complex domains.[410]
> —NASSIM NICHOLAS TALEB (b. 1960), Lebanese American risk analyst and author

The idea of a cause having multiple effects is not new, of course:

> Every cause produces more than one effect.[411]
> —HERBERT SPENCER (1820–1903), English philosopher

Wishful Thinking and Good Intentions

Everyone has an ax to grind. However, some have a strong incentive to focus only on the first stage, as in "lying." It is not just, or not always, economic ignorance. Take the minimum wage as an example. The first stage is unskilled labor getting a minimum wage for executing simple tasks, sometimes referred to as menial work. That is the first stage, the romantic bit. It's wonderful.

The romantic bit is popular with voters for whom minimum wage is an increase in income. As Dennis Gartman, not the biggest fan of retributive taxes and income redistribution, put it in 2011:

> *Of course the average American wants the minimum wage raised. They want puppies that are house trained too, they want to believe that a new driver really will lengthen their drives by 25 yards, they really do believe that by taking one pill or another one can lose 25 lbs. in two weeks while still eating desserts and French fries galore, they believe that Big Time college football is clean and that the bike riders in the Tour de France are also, they believe in Santa Claus, in Mr. Putin's benevolence, in Berlusconi's contrition et al.*[412]
> —DENNIS GARTMAN *(b. 1950), American investment newsletter writer*

The wishful thinking of voters who cannot or will not think beyond stage one is called the Santa Claus principle. The term Santa Claus principle was coined by Ludwig von Mises in relation to the interventionalist argument of Keynes, and the redistributive idea is kept alive by all those who expect personal or political advantage from government spending.

> *An essential point in the social philosophy of interventionism is the existence of the inexhaustible fund which can be squeezed forever. The whole system of interventionism collapses when this fountain is drained off. The Santa Claus principle liquidates itself.*[413]
> —LUDWIG VON MISES *(1881–1973), Austrian School economist*

What Mr. Sowell calls the first stage is the one that politicians point out when running for office or when accumulating political capital. It's the *good intentions* in "the road to hell is paved with good intentions."

> *Little evil would be done in the world if evil never could be done in the name of good.*[414]
> —MARIE VON EBNER-ESCHENBACH *(1830–1916), Austrian writer*

Saving typewriter manufacturing jobs is the "good intention." The ensuing structural deficits and high unemployment is "the road to hell" bit. The "hell" bit (in the "road to hell") is stages two, three, and four; the ripple effects. In the case of minimum wage, stages two to four are less supply at the artificial higher price, i.e., fewer job opportunities. A drop in the quality of work, as in "why bother?" A black market, i.e., employers as well as employees driven into illegality. (In Italy and Spain, for example, it is estimated that about a third of GDP is produced in the underground [black] market, as interventionism resulted in the costs of doing business legally becoming prohibitively expensive.)

The funny thing about minimum wage is that it is the political left that introduces it and goes on to blame the entrepreneurs for responding to the higher costs. This is how one writer put it when a minimum wage raise in Ontario, Canada, did not work as planned:

> *It was the socialists, union activists, and politicians who cut the bottom rungs off the economic ladder. Now they're blaming gravity for the damage done to the unskilled workers who fell off the ladder as a result.*[415]
> —MATTHEW LAU *(b. 1994), Canadian writer*

Minimum Wage and Upside Mobility
The reference to gravity is particularly well chosen as entrepreneurs' response to higher costs is so obvious to anyone with only the slightest modicum of business-savvy. The negative consequence of minimum wage that I think is most fascinating, and perhaps the one that is least appreciated, is that minimum wage robs the least skilled of learning experience; it destroys upside optionality. There is less "learning by doing." In

this regard, Mr. Sowell tells the story of Mr. Frank Winfield Woolworth (1852–1919), later destined to become head of a store chain that bore his name.[416]

> *Welfare can give you money but it cannot give you job experi-*
> *ence that will move you ahead economically.*[417]
> —THOMAS SOWELL *(b. 1930), American economist*

In 1873, Woolworth was a country bumpkin with no work experi-ence, i.e., a very unpromising-looking prospect. He got a menial job at a shop and asked the owner what he would get paid, to which the owner exclaimed: "Pay you!? You don't expect me to pay you, do you? Why you should pay me for teaching you the business." Woolworth did menial work, without pay, for the first three months, which allowed him to move up the learning curve and gain experience.

The owner gave Woolworth an option; hence the question of who is paying who is not trivial. Woolworth learned the business and moved on to do very well in life. Minimum wage eliminates that option. With minimum wage, Woolworth would have stayed at his family's farm, milk-ing cows at 5:30 a.m. The story ends with Woolworth, much later in life, making his former employer a partner in the F. W. Woolworth retail chain, ending up paying him for the option, i.e., for teaching him the business. Sowell claims, rightly, in my opinion, that these ripple effects, i.e., what he calls the later stages, are often (deliberately) ignored. Minimum wage is only clever from a very superficial perspective, i.e., the first stage. Sowell recommends looking beyond this first stage.

> *When you set minimum wage levels higher than many inexpe-*
> *rienced young people are worth, they don't get hired. It is not*
> *rocket science.*[418]
> —THOMAS SOWELL, *a Marxist in his twenties*

The reason why so many trained economists currently promote min-imum wage is because there is empirical evidence that minimum wage does *not* kill jobs. However, killing jobs is a first-order effect. The lost optionality is not accounted for in the empirical findings, i.e., is ignored. Calling anyone an IYI might seem a bit harsh, but then, what else do you call someone who ignores higher-order effects and isn't aware of their presence? Here is an attempt to phrase it a bit more nicely:

> *Socialism in general has a record of failure so blatant that only an intellectual could ignore or evade it.*[419]
> —THOMAS SOWELL

This last quotation is consistent with Taleb's IYI moniker as well as dysrationalia and the Nobel disease, both mentioned in chapter one.

Freedom and the Five Bs

Servitude and Options

There are multiple definitions for freedom; below I list just one:

> *I'm single because I was born that way.*
> —MAE WEST *(1893–1980), American actress*

Almost all definitions of freedom involve the absence of imprisonment in one form or another. *Braveheart* got it right despite William Wallace having a wrong-way-round Argentinian flag painted on his face:

> *It's all for nothing if you don't have freedom.*[420]
> —MEL GIBSON *(b. 1956), American actor and filmmaker, as William Wallace*

The Swiss's fourteenth-century equivalent to William Wallace was called Arnold von Winkelried. According to legend, not history, at the Battle of Sempach on July 9, 1386, when the Confederates (the good guys)[421] were not able to break through the Austrian lines, it is reputed that Winkelried threw himself onto the enemy spears, shouting, "Take care of my wife and ahhhhhh!"[422]

In one cartoon I came across, one guy says related to this period: "Back then, the Swiss were farsighted, had grandiose ideas, and didn't allow themselves to be pushed around!" to which the other guy says: "How times have changed!" This is a reference, among other things, to many Swiss politicians and intellectuals thinking it to be a good idea to bow and buckle to the might of the European Union, giving up what Winkelried fought for. Margaret Thatcher, who MP Clement Freud (1924–2009) called Attila the Hen, knew all this:

> *The Swiss have flourished mightily outside the European Union. They have enjoyed prosperity, stability and liberty, and one might be forgiven for thinking that no one would be foolish enough to want to upset that happy state of affairs. But the Europeans and the pro-European Swiss federal government do not see it that way.*[423]
> —MARGARET THATCHER *(1925–2013), British stateswoman and prime minister of the United Kingdom*

(Fun fact: after the Swiss decided against joining the European Economic Area [EEA] in 1992 [the referendum was "sold" as a stepping stone to joining the EU], the Europhiles said Switzerland was economically toast. It was not, prospered, and lived happily ever after.

After the British decided to leave the EU in June of 2016, the Europhiles immediately went on arguing that it was now Britain that was toast. It most likely is not.)

Horoscopes and Planning

I once claimed that from the perspective of the Swiss, the European Union ("EU") appears socialist, i.e., unfree. (One meme on the Internet shows a picture of the USS Enterprise from Star Trek and below the cube spaceship from The Borg. On top of the picture showing the USS Enterprise it says: "What socialists think they are getting." Below the Borg picture it says: "What they are actually getting.")[424] The last time this became apparent to everyone was during the campaigns for the French elections in April and May of 2017; France not being a hotbed for entrepreneurialism, despite the word coming from there.[425] (As George W. Bush never said but is often quoted as saying nevertheless: "The problem with the French is that they don't have a word for entrepreneur.") To be fair to French socialists, they do use clever tools as one socialist contender for the presidency revealed ahead of the 2017 elections:

The horoscopes are favorable.[426]
—Jean-Luc Mélenchon *(b. 1951), French politician and*
   Chávez admirer

Well, they weren't. He lost.

Peter Thiel, once described as an outspoken libertarian provocateur, and most likely a student of demographics, has an alternative take on Europe:

Europe, def.: museum of old people doing nothing.[427]
—Peter Thiel *(b. 1967), American entrepreneur and*
   cofounder of PayPal

People from the new side of the Atlantic often have a different perspective on Europe than the people who actually live there. This is how *The Economist*, a British magazine, phrased it in 2003:

EUROPE, viewed from across the Atlantic, is often looked on
as a depressing place—not so much the old continent as the
dark continent: economically stuck, politically and morally con-
fused, militarily feeble and populated most visibly by pensioners,
trade-unionists, anti-Semites and terrorists.[428]
—*The Economist*

Economist Ludwig von Mises made the interesting point that there is no big difference between socialism and interventionism.[429] He argues that advocates of middle-of-the-road policies, i.e., social market economies, capitalism with a heart, the third way, socialism with a this-or-that face, etc., allow markets to allocate capital based on market factors but intervene when the outcome is not socially desirable. This, of course, means that the market is allowed to do only what the authorities want it to do. The authorities regulate the outcome. This is closer to outright socialism than it is to free markets. In Ludwig von Mises's words:

[T]he market is free as long as it does precisely what the gov-
ernment wants it to do. It is "free" to do what the authorities
consider to be the "right" things, but not to do what they consider
the "wrong" things; the decision concerning what is right and

*what is wrong rests with the government. Thus the doctrine and
the practice of interventionism ultimately tend to abandon what
originally distinguished them from outright socialism and to
adopt entirely the principles of totalitarian all-round planning.*[430]
—LUDWIG VON MISES *(1881–1973), Austrian School
economist*

Planning is a good idea in theory though:

*Theoretically, planning may be good. But nobody has ever fig-
ured out the cause of government stupidity—and until they do
(and find the cure), all ideal plans will fall into quicksand.*[431]
—RICHARD FEYNMAN *(1918–88), American physicist*

Interventionism can be compared to certain male spiders who are
gobbled up by their cannibalistic female spouse after mating. The first-
round effect involves an element of fun; the selfish genes acting unselfishly
and having a good time. Incentives are straightforward, and intentions
are good. However, one of the follow-on effects is death. It's a reversal of
the "short-term pain for long-term gain" idea.

Take Cuba for example. The first-round effect was getting rid of the
gambling business and cigar-smoking fat people in pinstripes. (Capitalists
are often caricatured as such.) However, it went downhill from there; as
the revolution triggered the socioeconomic negative feedback loop, that
then did its predictable thing, i.e., brought misery to almost everyone
(who did not leave).

In the twenty years prior to Castro's revolution, from 1939 to 1958, GDP
per capita grew by 67 percent. In the twenty years that followed, it grew by
28 percent. (This compares to 67 percent and 55 percent in El Salvador over
the same time spans.)[432] Cuba is a case of short-term gain for long-term pain.

The function of socialism is to raise suffering to a higher level.[433]
—NORMAN MAILER *(1923–2007), American author and
political activist*

Cuba is now run by thin cigar-smoking people. In Venezuela, a country "going Cuba" over the past decade or two, 74 percent of the population

lost an average of 8.7 kilograms per person over one year alone.[434] The comical-if-it-weren't-so-sad aspect of all this is that some Westerners—who might or might not have lost touch with reality—turn the weight loss into a positive; after all, who does not want to shed some pounds for good health reasons, they say. (Nicolás Maduro looks well-fed though.)

The practical relevance for the investor is that the negative consequence of seeking equality of outcome is hundreds of years old, and George Santayana's idea of history punishing the history-challenged is applicable. Choosing unfreedom is unwise.

Freedom and Options

I herein claim that freedom is an option. Or, more precisely, freedom is a series of options. Most definitions of freedom involve the concept of choice in one form or another. The enslaved, the unfree, have fewer choices.

Choice is quite human:

> *It is the ability to choose which makes us human.*[435]
> —MADELEINE L'ENGLE *(1918–2007), American writer*

A free person or business has options, i.e., more precisely, holds long positions in a series of options. An option is often referred to as the freedom to choose. Pizza or sushi tonight is an option for free people. A prison sentence is punishment by limiting optionality. There is, simplifying a bit, no sushi in prison. (I am quite sure that there are numerous exceptions to this "rule," Pablo Escobar's incarceration being a prominent one.)

Socialism, therefore, is a form of punishment as it limits the upside optionality of its people and businesses. It's a special form of punishment as the ensuing pain is often self-inflicted, a bit like self-mutilation. (Whether tattooed and pierced people have a leaning toward the political left, I have not checked.) Putting it much more eloquently:

> *Only free men can negotiate; prisoners cannot enter into contracts.*[436]
> —NELSON MANDELA *(1918–2013), South African politician and freedom fighter*

At one level, the lack of optionality, i.e., the lack of freedom, is one of the reasons the Soviet Union, Egypt, Argentina, Venezuela, etc., have failed, whereas the United States, Britain, Singapore, Botswana, South Korea, Switzerland, etc. have not. The latter-mentioned countries are where the options are. Cubans risk their lives to get to the United States. No American ever risked his life to get to Cuba. The United States, from the perspective of a Cuban, is where the options are. The same is, of course, true for people risking their lives leaving the Soviet-controlled area during the cold war or leaving North Korea today. The movement of people is from an area with fewer options, i.e., less freedom, toward areas with more options. Free movement and migration of the five Bs (businesses, brains, bodies, blueprints, and bucks) is toward "more optionality" and away from "fewer options." As Warren Buffett put it in early 2017, enthusing about the United States:

> One word sums up our country's achievements: miraculous ... Above all, it's our market system—an economic traffic cop ably directing capital, brains, and labor—that has created America's abundance.[437]
>
> —WARREN BUFFETT (b. 1930), American investor and businessman

The free-market system that allocates capital efficiently can be described as follows:

> What modern capital markets do very well is raise large amounts of capital from a broad base of investors who are persuaded to give their money to perfect strangers with precious little idea of what these fortunate recipients are going to do with it.[438]
>
> —ANDREW REDLEAF and RICHARD VIGILANTE, American hedge fund managers

Campus Liberalism and Neil Diamond Music
Warren Buffett, presumably with the help of Carol Loomis (b. 1929), the American journalist who writes/edits for Mr. Buffett and wrote about him as

early as 1966,* has the gift of bringing complexity to the narrowest of points. Ayn Rand, too, made a similar remark, but not as efficiently articulated.

> *America's abundance was created not by public sacrifices to the common good, but by the productive genius of free men who pursued their own personal interests and the making of their own private fortunes.*[439]
> —AYN RAND *(1905–82), Russian American novelist and philosopher*

Sometimes I ask stupid questions, entirely unaware of my ignorance, of course.

> *Philosophers are adults who persist in asking childish questions.*[440]
> —ISAIAH BERLIN *(1909–97), Russian-British social and political theorist*

A couple of years ago, I was talking to a Yellow Cab driver in New York on the way from JFK to Manhattan. He told me how tough his life was as a Yellow Cab driver, given the competition that was Uber. I was his first passenger that day, and it was noon. I asked where he was from originally. (That was not an infantile question as he wasn't a native American.) He was originally from Soviet-controlled Romania, and, as an eighteen-year-old, together with his brothers in the early 1980s, risked his life to swim over the Danube and cross Soviet-controlled territory toward freedom. I then asked whether there were any regrets.

---

* In April 1966, Carol Loomis wrote an article called "The Jones Nobody Keeps Up With." Published in *Fortune,* Loomis' article shocked the investment community by describing something called a "hedge fund" run by an unknown sociologist named Alfred Jones. (She coined the term *hedge fund* in that article, as Jones referred to his fund as a "hedged fund.") Jones' fund was outperforming the best mutual funds even after a 20 percent incentive fee. A successful but then largely unknown hedge fund, focusing on long-term investments in Omaha, "Buffet Partnership" [sic], also got a mention in that article. Carol Loomis started to edit Warren Buffett's annual investor letters in 1977, and they became close friends. Misspelling "Buffett" in 1966 was not held against her. All the typos in this book should be treated accordingly.

That, from his perspective, was a stupid question. He had no regrets at all. Even not living the often-cinematically-glorified American dream, essentially an option, and being forced to compete with Uber, is better than having no options at all. As far as I can tell, no Westerner ever swam over the Danube to get to Romania. He felt sorry for his buddies left behind. He probably thought I was a disillusioned Sanders voter or a Neil Diamond fan.

> *Socialism is like Neil Diamond music. It's not good and belongs*
> *in the past, yet there's a group of people who think that it will*
> *eventually catch on if only they keep playing it.*[441]
> —JEFFREY EVAN BROOKS *(b. 1976), American author*

Some American authors avoid the term *socialism* and call it *campus liberalism* instead. This is in relation to how education in the US is organized and a reference to what is thought and taught there. Campus liberalism is also like Neil Diamond music, of course. A case in point:

> *My daughter's immigrant friend, asked during her dissertation*
> *defense why she had not dealt with the Marxist interpretation*
> *of her topic: "I grew up in Eastern Europe during the Cold War.*
> *I do not indulge in recreational Marxism."*[442]
> —CHARLES MURRAY *(b. 1943), American political scientist*

Tyranny and Unwisdom

Money and Success

I claim here that freedom is the most important thing. Take Argentina as an example. In Latin America, the saying goes "rich as an Argentinian." It refers to some hundred years ago when the country was one of the richest on the planet. No more. In 1913, Argentina's GDP per capita was 82 percent of that of the United States. By 2016, it was 36 percent. Argentina has grown 2.8-fold over this period, the US 6.5-fold. South Korea, one of the winners over the past hundred years, grew fifty-four-fold over the same period. Cuba, one of the losers over the past hundred years, grew 2.6-fold, nearly the same as Argentina. Brazil, a country not entirely immune to socioeconomic folly, grew around tenfold, the same as Greece.[443]

Freedom is one of the main difference makers. Evita's husband, Juan Perón, most likely having good intentions, curtailed optionality for citizens and businesses. And that is putting it very amicably. Quite in contrast to Lee Kuan Yew, who modeled Singapore after Western standards and embraced, with some limitations, free speech and freedom principles. (If a Western hippie or surfer dude imports drugs into Singapore and gets caught, he is governmentally whipped, causing a media outcry in the West; the whipping being a bit "unwestern" does not change the line of argument made here.) This is how the founder of Singapore referenced both optionality and the lack thereof:

> *Wealth springs from entrepreneurship, which means risk taking. . . . The only way to raise the living conditions of the poor is to increase the size of the pie. Equality of incomes gives no incentive to the resourceful and the industrious to outperform and be competitive.*[444]
> —LEE KUAN YEW *(1923–2015), Founding Father and former prime minister of Singapore*

John Ciardi phrased the risk-taking bit, the optionality, as follows:

> *The Constitution gives every American the inalienable right to make a damn fool of himself.*
> —JOHN CIARDI *(1916–86), American poet*

Many Americans follow Ciardi to the letter. And that is a good thing. Not all options end up in the money. (An option that is in the money has intrinsic value, whereas an option that is out of the money does not.) Investment life can be unfair though:

> *Wise men profit more from fools than fools from wise men;*
> *for the wise men shun the mistakes of fools, but fools do not imitate the successes of the wise.*[445]
> —CATO THE ELDER *(234–149 BC), Roman statesman*

Fooling around a bit at times, and briefly, is not the same as unwisdom:

> *Everyone is a damn fool for at least five minutes every day.*
> *Wisdom consists in not exceeding that limit.*[446]
> —ELBERT HUBBARD *(1856–1915), American polymath*

Freedom fighters see the optionality in "freedom" almost by definition:

> *Freedom is not worth having if it does not connote freedom to*
> *err and even to sin.*[447]
> —MAHATMA GANDHI *(1869–1948), Indian lawyer and*
> *leader of independence*

(The "even to sin" bit is often left out when this quotation is used.) Regarding optionality, another freedom fighter said more or less the same thing:

> *Money won't create success;*
> *the freedom to make it will.*[448]
> —NELSON MANDELA *(1918–2013), South African politician*
> *and anti-apartheid revolutionary*

In other words, freedom is an option—an option to err (an option to sin), an option to make money, an option to speak freely and fool around, an option to multiply consentingly, an option to talk complete nonsense on subjects one has no knowledge about during a pandemic for example, etc.

Freedom has its limitations though:

> *Tyranny is always better organised than freedom.*[449]
> —CHARLES PÉGUY *(1873–1914), French poet*

Tyranny and Free-world Bashing

I am quite certain that Putin, Erdogan, et al. agree wholeheartedly with this last notion. Tyranny and corruption are not all bad; they can pay well. It really depends on which side of the brown paper bag you are on, the giving or the receiving end. The miscreant increases his own optionality by taking it away from his underlings. As a matter of fact, tyranny and corruption can work for both parties, with the cost being an economic externality that will only boomerang in the future. For Karl Popper there are just two types of government:

> *You can choose whatever name you like for the two types of government. I personally call the type of government which can be removed without violence "democracy", and the other "tyranny."*[450]
> —KARL POPPER (1902–94), Austrian-British philosopher

Vladimir Putin's net worth is estimated to be between $70–200 billion, on an annual salary of $125,000. The family of Wen Jiabao has controlled assets worth at least $2.7 billion. The net worth of Xi Jinping's extended family was once estimated to be around $376 million, on Xi Jinping's official salary of around $22,000 per year. (He is fighting corruption, though, thereby skewing his own optionality asymmetrically to the upside by getting rid of the competition.) The net worth of Hosni Mubarak, Egypt's former military leader, is officially estimated to be around $1.2 billion, with some estimates being multiples of that. These are just some randomly picked examples from a list that is rather long.

One comical aspect of inequality zealots and free-world bashers, sometimes referred to as "Piketty et al.," is that they hardly ever point toward the extreme tyranny, corruption, injustice, and inequality in the nonfree world. A socialist is essentially a hippie who refuses to grow up.[451]

> *Son: Dad; when I grow up, I want to be a socialist.*
> *Dad: You can't do both, Son.*
> —Old joke

Tyranny, stating the obvious, is not the same as leadership:

> *The supreme quality for leadership is unquestionably integrity. Without it, no real success is possible, no matter whether it is on a section gang, a football field, in an army, or in an office.*
> —DWIGHT EISENHOWER (1890–1969), thirty-fourth US president and five-star general in WWII

Tyranny and corruption might be a function of the lack of leadership. I assume many tyrants enjoyed *Dallas* in the 1980s too:

> *Once you get rid of integrity, the rest is a piece of cake.*[452]
> —J. R. EWING, *president of Ewing Oil (1977–80)*

However, the trade-off between *government redistribution* and concentration of wealth is no trivial matter for those with responsibility:

> *The fiscal policy of a government may make or break a society, excessive taxation, or the entry of a government into production and distribution, can stifle incentive, enterprise, and competition, and kill the goose that lays the revenues. On the other hand, an excessive concentration of wealth may tear a society to pieces by promoting revolution.*[453]
> —IBN KHALDUN *(1332-1406), Maghrebian Muslim historian and occasionally referred to as one of the fathers of the social sciences*

Pigs and Brains

Corruption and autocracy can be "justified" though. If we assume Vladimir Putin's net wealth is indeed $200 billion and assume further that the sum of wealth attributed to his reign, i.e., the value he "added" to society, is, say, $1 trillion, we can look at this as Putin just taking a generous cut, i.e., akin to having a 20 percent operating margin. If we assume further that the alternative to prosperity and happiness is Boris Yeltsin, then a 20 percent cut for Putin makes perfect sense. This is how one minister of propaganda put it, justifying the authorities taking a generous cut:

> *We pigs are brainworkers. The whole management and organisation of this farm depend on us. Day and night we are watching over your welfare. It is for your sake that we drink that milk and eat those apples.*
> —SQUEALER, *fictional character, a pig, in George Orwell's* Animal Farm

Putin, a Swiss luxury watch aficionado, among other things, is at times quite popular in Russia though. A couple of years ago there was a commonality between Putin and Obama as both leaders were acting in the best interest of Russia.

Golden Geese and Degeneration

Trial-and-error-style risk-taking increases the number of options and therefore also the number of options that end up having intrinsic value, i.e., increase wealth of society. Nassim Taleb summarized it well:

> *Trial and error is freedom.*[454]
> —NASSIM NICHOLAS TALEB *(b. 1960), Lebanese American risk analyst and author*

Soaking the rich is a bit like shooting the messenger of bad news in medieval times:

> *Soaking the rich would not only be profoundly immoral, it would drastically penalize the very virtues of thrift, business foresight and investment, that have brought about our remarkable standard of living. It would truly be killing the goose that lays the golden eggs.*[455]
> —MURRAY ROTHBARD *(1926–95), American economist*

Killing golden-egg-laying geese is quite dangerous. Many historians think societies and empires fall from suicide, not murder. As Abraham Lincoln thought:

> *America will never be destroyed from the outside. If we falter and lose our freedoms, it will be because we destroyed ourselves.*[456]
> —ABRAHAM LINCOLN *(1809–65), American politician and sixteenth president of the United States*

Societies do not fail overnight. Degeneration from prosperity to misery can take decades. If we can spot degeneration, we can assess the slow disappearance of optionality. Abraham Lincoln called the degeneration and loss of options: "falter and lose our freedoms." Degeneration was not lost on Thomas Sowell. In 2002, he wrote:

There was a time when we honored those who created the pros-
perity and the freedom that we enjoy. Today we honor the com-
plainers and sue the creators. Perhaps that is inevitable in an era
when we no longer count our blessings, but instead count all our
unfulfilled wishes.[457]
—THOMAS SOWELL *(b. 1930), American economist*

Lee Iacocca, the father of the Mustang, probably felt the same way.
The following is a response to a question asked by a congressman seeking
to hear a defense for Lee's $20.6 million in compensation for basically
saving Chrysler:

That's the American way. If little kids don't aspire to make money
as I did, what the hell good is this country?
—LEE IACOCCA *(1924–2019), American automobile*
    executive

There is a limit even to freedom:

Too much of a good thing is just that.
—*Saying*

This is the reason why some radio stations introduced Bee Gees–free
days in the 1980s; it was just too much of a good thing. Too much of
something might even be risky, potentially having adverse effects:

Too much of a good thing is bad. Too much of a bad thing is bad
too. So, "too much" must be bad.
—MOKOKOMA MOKHONOANA, *South African social critic*
    and satirist

Brains and Education
President Trump wanted to make America great again. (At the time of
this writing, his disciples took the Capitol building on January 6, 2021.)
Neil deGrasse Tyson, the Carl Sagan of the twenty-first century, suggested
a detour at the time:

We all want to Make America Great Again. But that won't hap-
pen until we first Make America Smart Again.[458]
—NEIL DEGRASSE TYSON *(b. 1958), American astrophysicist*

Whether Neil deGrasse Tyson had Hank Johnson, member of the
US House of Representatives from Georgia's 4th district, in mind, who,
during a House Armed Services Committee hearing in March 2010, asked
an admiral whether Guam would "tip over and capsize" when US troops
are sent there, I do not know.[459]

Perhaps deGrasse Tyson was thinking about the person who was
amazed about the enormous coincidence that the wind was able to carve
a large piece of rock in South Dakota in a manner that resembles four
dead presidents. Or about the American couple who wondered why the
Brits built Windsor Castle so close to a major airport. The US education
system has room for improvement. Teachers' incompetence is one of
Thomas Sowell's evergreen issues:

> *Letters from teachers continue to confirm the incompetence*
> *which they deny. A teacher in Montana says that my criticisms*
> *of teachers are "nieve." No, it was not a typographical error. He*
> *spelled it that way twice.*[460]
> —THOMAS SOWELL *(b. 1930), American economist and author*

Nearly every parent wants his offspring to have a good education. Education is important. Lack of education is a handicap. However, handicaps
can be compensated for:

> *Me having no education, I had to use my brains.*[461]
> —BILL SHANKLY *(1913–81), Scottish footballer and manager*

Sowell and deGrasse are not alone in pointing out deficiencies in the
US education system. George W. Bush was also worried about education:

> *[R]arely is the question asked: Are . . . is our children learning?*[462]
> —GEORGE W. BUSH *(b. 1946), American politician and forty-*
> *third president of the United States*

Mr. Bush—who, as the governor of Texas in the 1990s, successfully
increased education funding, set higher standards for schools, deregulated

the economy, and reformed the criminal justice system—was more into economics than linguistics and grammar:

> *More and more of our imports come from overseas.*[463]
> —GEORGE W. BUSH, *only US president that has run a marathon*

In many places, young people go to the streets for education. Below are some anonymous pro-education placards from the March for Science, Washington, DC, April 22, 2017:

- *You know things are serious when the introverts arrive.*
- *My homoeopath thinks this [march for science] is a bad idea.*
- *Atoms are like Sean Spicer. They make up everything.*
- *Bacteria is the only culture Trump has!*

It's not all bad though. Professors in the US get paid well, demonstrating society's high appreciation for education:

> *America believes in education: the average professor earns more money in a year than a professional athlete earns in a whole week.*
> —EVAN ESAR *(1899–1995), American humorist*

Bottom Line

Applied economics means debunking Santa. What looks socioeconomically good at first sight, often isn't. The reason for this is that a market intervention, even if it's just a nudge, has multiple effects. The part of the intervention that looks good to voters is often a first-order effect. The ripple effect is often ignored. No one person is responsible for the ripple effect; the negative consequences are socialized. By investing some time in thinking about these higher-order effects, the investor will gain a clearer picture of reality. Faux sophistication, unwisdom, and Santa should only deceive the youngest of voters.

Freedom, prosperity, and the five Bs (businesses, brains, bodies, blueprints, and bucks) are interlinked. It's all for nothing if you don't have freedom. The freest are best off. If the government allows the market to do the "right" things, but not what it deems the "wrong" things, it is the government who makes the allocation decisions. When this happens, Santayana's those-who-do-not-learn-from-history-are-doomed truism applies.

Freedom is an option. Imprisonment is the removal of options. If this is true, then interventionism is punishment, or, in its most aggressive form, suicide. As investors we need to spot the removal of options. We need to know whether Cubans are risking their lives to get to Florida, or Floridians are risking their lives to get to Cuba. Choosing unfreedom is unwise.

Freedom is the most important thing. Killing golden geese is borderline suicidal. Money won't create success; the freedom to make it will. Prosperity won't create happiness; the free pursuit of it will. Repression won't create misery; the lack of options will.

––––––––

You ought to know what you don't know, as life is like a box of chocolates.

GUMP'S LAW

*One of the greatest pieces of economic wisdom
is to know what you do not know.*
—John Kenneth Galbraith

Gump's law states that life is like a box of chocolates in the sense that you do not know what you are going to get.

While easier said than done, one of the greatest pieces of economic wisdom is to know what you do not know. At poker and in life, there is always a patsy. You need to make sure it is not you. Ignorance, per se, is not nearly as dangerous as ignorance of ignorance.

There is indeed a basic law of stupidity. Stupidity is the deliberate cultivation of ignorance. Doris Day got it right: *que sera, sera*. Wizards err. Bear Stearns was fine, they said. It wasn't. True wisdom is less presuming than folly.

Doubt is good. (Another pun on Gordon Gekko's most famous one-liner.) After all, skepticism is the first step toward truth. However, beware of scaremongers. When it bleeds, it leads. We will not all die within ~~twelve~~ ten years if we do not tackle climate change.

Those who have knowledge do not predict. Those who predict do not have knowledge. Yoda was right: "Difficult to see. Always in motion is the future."

Life and a Box of Chocolates

Wizards and Errors

At the beginning of 2014, seventy-two out of seventy-two financial strategists surveyed by *Bloomberg*, "financial strategist" being a less derogatory term than "guru," predicted that interest rates would rise throughout the year. Rising interest rates was the consensus at the time. Interest rates fell in 2014. At the beginning of 2019, fifty out of fifty economists surveyed by the *Wall Street Journal* thought that ten-year Treasury yields would not fall below 2 percent during the year. They did. Remember:

> *The herd instinct among forecasters makes sheep look like independent thinkers.*[464]
> —EDGAR FIEDLER *(1929–2003), American economist*

It is not only financial strategists and economists who should refrain from forecasting; historians should avoid it too:

> *It is always a mistake for the historian to try to predict the future. Life, unlike science, is simply too full of surprises.*[465]
> —RICHARD J. EVANS *(b. 1947), British historian*

Forrest Gump's mother said pretty much the same thing:

> *My momma always said, "Life is like a box of chocolates. You never know what you're gonna get."*[466]
> —FORREST GUMP, *fictional soldier, runner, entrepreneur, and investor*

Forrest Gump was an early investor in a "fruit company" that did rather well.[467] In honor of Gump's momma, I herein call acknowledging uncertainty "Gump's law."

One ought to know what one does not know. Wizards err. In 1993, the Organization for Economic Cooperation and Development (OECD) analyzed forecasts made between 1987 and 1992 by various governments, as well as by the International Monetary Fund (IMF) and the OECD itself. The governments and the IMF should have guessed or flipped a coin, rather than forecast: not only were the forecasts abysmally wrong, but they would have been better forecasts had they binned their models and simply assumed that the numbers would be the same as the year before.[468]

Knowledge and Ignorance
John Kenneth Galbraith, a leading scholar of the American Institutionalist school who also collaborated on and narrated a PBS TV series, *The Age of Uncertainty*, put it most eloquently.

> *One of the greatest pieces of economic wisdom is to know what you do not know.*[469]
> —JOHN KENNETH GALBRAITH *(1908–2006), Canadian American economist*

Leave out the word "economic" and the quote works just as well, better even. The applicability of Galbraith's wisdom to risk management was well put by Mrs. Thatcher:

> *It is always important in matters of high politics to know what you do not know. Those who think they know, but are mistaken, and act upon their mistakes, are the most dangerous people to have in charge.*[470]
> —MARGARET THATCHER *(1925–2013), British stateswoman and prime minister of the United Kingdom*

The last thing you want in high office, therefore, are people with personality disorders, egotistical traits that are borderline narcissistic, who are delusional and have an easily inflammable temper. I believe this applies to the corporate and financial world too.

I believe in learning by doing, as pointed in chapter three. In some instances, the path from ignorance to applied wisdom can be swift:

When I was a boy of 14, my father was so ignorant I could hardly stand to have the old man around. But when I got to be 21, I was astonished at how much the old man had learned in seven years.[471]
—MARK TWAIN *(1835–1910), American author*

Knowing what you do not know is easier said than done:

It takes considerable knowledge just to realize the extent of your own ignorance.[472]
—THOMAS SOWELL *(b. 1930), American economist*

The idea of knowing one's limitations, including one's own ignorance, is incredibly old. Old is good. Old means battle-tested. Concepts and ideas that are not applicable disappear over time. Concepts and ideas that are applicable survive over time. This one has survived:

Real knowledge is to know the extent of one's ignorance.[473]
—CONFUCIUS *(551–479 BC), Chinese philosopher*

The idea of distinguishing between what one knows and what one does not was not lost on the writers of *Game of Thrones*:

A wise king knows what he knows and what he doesn't.[474]
—TYWIN LANNISTER, *lord of House Lannister*

Tywin Lannister must have gotten his leadership skills from *Poor Richard's Almanack*:

The first Degree of Folly, is to conceit one's self wise;
the second to profess it; the third to despise Counsel.[475]
—BENJAMIN FRANKLIN *(1706–90), American polymath*

Yoda and the Invisible Gorilla
The practical relevance is that ignorance of one's ignorance is risky:

Ignorance per se is not nearly as dangerous as ignorance of ignorance.[476]
—SYDNEY J. HARRIS *(1917–86), American journalist*

To Sydney Harris's point:

> *Bear Stearns is fine! Keep your money where it is.*[477]
> —JIM CRAMER *(b. 1955), American television personality*

To Jim Cramer's point:

> *Difficult to see. Always in motion is the future.*[478]
> —YODA

This means, with regards to the future, we are blind, and it is especially important that we know about the degree of our blindness. Daniel Kahneman, cocreator of prospect theory and coauthor of the most important scientific paper I have ever come across, points out two important facts about our minds in relation to the fascinating invisible gorilla:

> *We can be blind to the obvious, and we are also blind to our blindness.*[479]
> —DANIEL KAHNEMAN *(b. 1934), Israeli-born American psychologist*

The invisible gorilla is a selective attention test in video format. The video shows two groups of people passing basketballs. One team is wearing white shirts, the other black. The viewer is instructed to count how many times the players wearing white shirts pass the basketball. Twenty-four seconds into the video an actor in a gorilla suit walks into the frame center, pounds his chest, and moves on. The fascinating bit is that only around 50 percent of viewers see the gorilla when watching for the first time. They are too busy counting passes. They are blind to reality and quite surprised about their blindness once it has been revealed to them.

Knowing what one does not know helps thinking and helps separate between dogma and reason:

> *It [the encounter with Marxism] taught me a number of lessons which I have never forgotten. It taught me the wisdom of the Socratic saying, I know that I do not know. It made me a fallibilist, and impressed on me the value of intellectual modesty.*

And it made me most conscious of the differences between dog-
matic and critical thinking.[480]
—KARL POPPER *(1902–94), Austrian-British philosopher*

The idea that one ought to know what one does not could well be more than three thousand years old:

True wisdom is less presuming than folly. The wise man doubts
often, and changes his mind; the fool is obstinate, and doubts
not; he knows all things but his own ignorance.[481]
—AKHENATON *(ca. 1385–ca. 1350 BC), Egyptian pharaoh, or*
   Kemetic saying, or ancient Egyptian proverb

This made it into a Chinese proverb:

Deep doubts, deep wisdom;
small doubts, little wisdom.
—*Chinese proverb*

Plato, to Nietzsche "a bore," said Socrates took it a step further:

The only true knowledge is knowing that you know nothing.[482]
—SOCRATES *(470–399 BC), Greek philosopher*

Shakespeare, who only left his wife a bed in his will and whose children were presumed illiterate, was quoting Socrates then:

The fool doth think himself wise,
but the wise man knows himself to be a fool[483]
—WILLIAM SHAKESPEARE *(1564–1616) English dramatist,*
   playwright, and poet

Crystal Ball and the One-eyed Kings

The idea of knowing one's ignorance is loosely related to the Socratic paradox: if the only thing you know is that you know nothing, then how do you actually "know" that you know nothing? According to Socrates, to some a parasitic, antisocial pederast, the route to wisdom begins with wondering. To achieve any level of wisdom, one must first acknowledge one's own ignorance. The quotation is a starting point to gaining knowledge and, ideally, wisdom. Although it is generally attributed to Plato's Socrates, it cannot be found phrased like this in any of Plato's works. For this argument, however, the origin does not matter that much in this instance. What matters is that some semi-blind investors have an edge over others trotting erroneously and ignorantly in the dark:

> *In the country of the blind, the one-eyed man is king.*[484]
> —*Proverb*

In an article titled "Cracks in the Crystal Ball," John Kay, a visiting professor of economics at the London School of Economics and op-ed writer, who often hits the proverbial nail squarely on its head by ridiculing the more comical parts of the financial profession, wrote the following:

> *Economic forecasters . . . all say more or less the same thing at the same time; the degree of agreement is astounding. [But] what they say is almost always wrong.*[485]
> —JOHN KAY *(b. 1948), British economist*

Mr. Kay's remarks are arguably consistent with economists predicting yields to rise at the beginning of 2014. Speaking of crystal balls, Robert N. Veres has expressed a pragmatic approach as to how forecasters should be perceived:

> *Personally, I think everybody who predicts the future with a straight face should be required (by federal law) to change out of the business suit, wrap him/herself in a gypsy shawl, wear one of those pointed wizard's hats with a picture of a crescent moon on it, and make conjuring sounds over a crystal ball. That way, everybody would know exactly what's going on and how much credibility to give the answer.*[486]
> —ROBERT N. VERES *(b. 1951), Author*

Paying attention to forecasts is not just folly; it can also be dangerous:

Anyone who causes harm by forecasting should be treated as either a fool or a liar. Some forecasters cause more damage to society than criminals. Please, don't drive a school bus blindfolded.[487]
—NASSIM NICHOLAS TALEB *(b. 1960), Lebanese American risk analyst and author*

Christina, queen of Sweden, described as being intelligent as well as one of the most educated women of the seventeenth century, knew this, too, and brought it to the point:

Fools are to be more feared than knaves.[488]
—CHRISTINA *(1626–89), queen of Sweden*

There are "laws" to all this, the basic laws of human stupidity.

Human Stupidity and Forecasting

Stupidity and Ignorance

The damage caused by fools and liars needs to be overcompensated for by nonfools and honest people. This is true according to an authority on the subject, the author of *The Basic Laws of Human Stupidity*:

The only way a society can avoid being crushed by the burden of its idiots is if the non-stupid work even harder to offset the losses of their stupid brethren.[489]
—CARLO M. CIPOLLA *(1922–2000), Italian economic historian*

There are many different definitions regarding what constitutes stupidity; below are just two.

Stupid person, def.: A stupid person is a person who causes losses to another person or to a group of persons while himself deriving no gain and even possibly incurring losses.[490]
—CARLO M. CIPOLLA, *author of* The Basic Laws of Human Stupidity

Stupidity is the deliberate cultivation of ignorance.[491]
—WILLIAM GADDIS *(1922–98), American novelist*

Stupidity is not limited to individuals:

One man alone can be pretty dumb sometimes, but for real bona fide stupidity, there ain't nothin' can beat teamwork.[492]
—EDWARD ABBEY *(1927–89), American essayist and novelist*

What Abbey, a self-proclaimed anarchist who, when serving in the military, got promoted twice and then demoted twice, is referring to is called "the too-much-talent effect" that states that "too much of the good thing is just that, too much." This means team performance is increased by adding talent but at one point starts to decrease when more talent is added.

Science writer David Robson, in a very commendable book titled *The Intelligence Trap*, discusses a legendary football match between England and Iceland as an example of this effect. England has the best players in the world, a group of arrogant, overpaid prima donnas to some, whereas Iceland, a country with 364,134 inhabitants, is comprised of a group of, by comparison, nobodies. Iceland kicked England out of the 2016 European men's football tournament 3:2.[493]

One historian argues that human stupidity is something we can count on:

Human stupidity is one of the most important forces in history, yet we often discount it.[494]
—YUVAL NOAH HARARI *(b. 1976), Israeli historian and author*

The following is a definition of *fatuity*. This definition is helpful in spotting folly.

Fatuity, n.: Self-conceited foolishness; weakness of mind with high self-esteem; unconscious stupidity.[495]
—WILLIAM DWIGHT WHITNEY *(1827–94), American linguist and lexicographer*

If you just thought of a tweet-happy, well-coiffed American real estate tycoon-turned-politician Simpsons celebrity, it's not my fault.

Politics and Zappa's Law
One of the problems with stupidity is that it is contagious. If one economy starts introducing economic folly, others must follow suit:

> *We can also do stupid. We also have to be this stupid.*[496]
> —JEAN-CLAUDE JUNCKER *(b. 1954), Luxembourgish politician*

This was the response of the president of the European Commission in relation to the president of the United States announcing the introduction of trade tariffs.

There have been several attempts to quantify stupidity. According to one disputed Albert Einstein quotation, stupidity is infinite. Here I mention an alternative attempt:

> *There is more stupidity than hydrogen in the universe, and it has a longer shelf life.*[497]
> —FRANK ZAPPA *(1940–93), American musician and 1991 presidential candidate*

A variant of this quotation is referred to as Zappa's law: "There are two things on earth that are universal: hydrogen and stupidity." Stupidity need not be just negative though. Napoleon, who was of average height but was made "short" by British propaganda, famously argued that:

> *In politics, stupidity is not a handicap.*[498]
> —NAPOLEON BONAPARTE *(1769–1821), French military and political leader*

Outside of politics, stupidity is indeed a handicap though. John Wayne, an American Western hero, knew this:

> *Life is tough, but it's tougher when you're stupid.*[499]
> —MARION ROBERT MORRISON *(1907–79), American actor known as John Wayne*

Whether John Wayne was referring to dying from climbing to high altitudes or from the Running of the Bulls in Spain is unknown to this author.

A forecast might or might not turn out to be correct. It might be of no value; harmful even, as it might deprive the believer of independent thought. It is more intelligent to know what one does not know: the future. However, there are exceptions for everything. For time travelers, for example, foresight is hindsight:

> I believe that I've made good judgments in the past, and I think
> I've made good judgments in the future.[500]
> —DAN QUAYLE (b. 1947), American politician and former
>   vice president

For the rest of us, i.e., people who do not travel through time and practice some skepticism toward parallel universes and wormholes, it is more conservative to treat uncertainty as uncertainty and act accordingly. This means treating forecasts as a form of entertainment or infotainment or "investainment." At one level, Wall Street research is about being entertained:

> Traders rarely hire economists for their own consumption, but
> rather to provide stories for their less sophisticated clients.[501]
> —NASSIM NICHOLAS TALEB (b. 1960), Lebanese American
>   risk analyst and former trader

Although, if an infinite number of parallel universes do indeed exist, then there must be at least one in which stock market forecasts are taken seriously:

> JOHN OLIVER: You stated that you believe there could be an
> infinite number of parallel universes. Does that mean that there
> is a universe out there where I am smarter than you?
>
> STEPHEN HAWKING: Yes. And also a universe where you're
> funny.[502]

Fads and Butterflies

Hindsight is a wonderful thing. It allows us to ridicule forecasts that went horribly wrong. Some one hundred years ago, it was the automobile that changed everything. One of the all-time greatest forecasts was:

> *The horse is here to stay, but the automobile is only a novelty—a fad.*
> —*A banker*

The car turned out to be the most important product of industrialization, changing not only industry and business practice but also society by revolutionizing mobility. And the advent of self-driving cars is just the next phase. The quotation is attributed to the president of the Michigan Savings Bank advising Horace Rackham (Henry Ford's lawyer) not to invest in the Ford Motor Company in 1903. Rackham ignored the advice and bought $5,000 worth of stock. He sold it several years later for $12.5 million. Potentially, management consultant Peter Drucker was on to something when he said:

> [F]orecasting is not a respectable human activity, and not worth-
> while beyond the shortest of periods.[503]
> —PETER DRUCKER *(1909–2005), Austrian-born American*
>   *management consultant*

Professor Tetlock of *Superforecasting* fame said pretty much the same thing, referring to the butterfly effect discussed earlier and, in the footnote to the quote, making fun of a strategist who looks foolish only two years into a hundred-year forecast:

> *In a world where a butterfly in Brazil can make the difference*
> *between just another sunny day in Texas and a tornado tearing*
> *through a town, it's misguided to think anyone can see very far*
> *into the future.*[504]
> —PHILIP TETLOCK *and* DAN GARDNER, *authors of*
>   *Superforecasting*

Drucker and Tetlock's statements are consistent with the approach of one of the most respected hedge funds, Renaissance Technologies, founded by James Harris "Jim" Simons in 1982, a prize-winning mathematician and former code breaker. One of Renaissance's attributes is that it only hires natural scientists. Renaissance aims to find small market anomalies and inefficiencies. Using statistical models, Renaissance predicts the future movement of financial instruments within a specific time frame. Their algorithms "just" look for short-term patterns in the data in a way that is entirely agnostic to financial theory taught at business schools or the state of the economy or some forecaster's opinion thereof. The forecasting, therefore, is done in "the shortest of periods." Jim Simons in his own words:

> [W]e look at anomalies that may be small in size and brief in time. We make our forecast. Then, shortly thereafter, we reevaluate the situation and revise our forecast and our portfolio. We do this all day long.[505]
> —JAMES SIMONS *(b. 1938), American mathematician and hedge fund manager*

Renaissance's approach seems to work, judging by the magnitude and consistency of their performance. However, the barriers to entry are high. Jim Simons has been thinking of numbers and shapes since he was three years old.[506] Deep quant is not for everyone.

Forecasting future technology is difficult. But forecasting the use of existing technology is difficult too. An associate of David Sarnoff (RCA) said in the 1920s that "the wireless music box [the radio] has no imaginable commercial value. Who would pay for a message sent to nobody in particular?" In 1940, Theodore van Kármán of the National Academy of Science said jet engines and rockets would be of no future use because there was no material tough enough to stand up under their high combustion temperatures. Kármán changed his mind five years later. In 1955 he said of his 1940 prediction, "What I did wrong was to write it down."

In 1943, IBM president Thomas Watson's view was that "there is a world market for maybe five computers." In the same year, Admiral William Leahy of the Manhattan Project said, "The bomb will never go off. I speak as an expert in explosives." So much for expert opinions.

Witches and Wizards

I could go on, and I shall: "In ten years all important animal life in the sea will be extinct" was Paul Ehrlich's "imagination" in 1970. "We will bury you," said Nikita Khrushchev, who US Army Brigadier General Frank L. Howley (1903–93) called "a pig-eyed bag of wind," to western ambassadors during a diplomatic reception in Moscow in 1956. "Castro will last a year. No longer." Those were quite literally the famous last words by Fulgencio Batista, who was deposed by Fidel Castro in 1959. Paul von Hindenburg, who was central in "allowing" Hitler's ascent, in 1931: "Hitler is a queer fellow who will never become chancellor; the best he can hope for is to head the postal department."[507] (Next to Paul von Hindenburg, Neville Chamberlain comes across as a psychoanalyst.)

I cannot resist: "We don't like their sound, and guitar music is on the way out." Decca, rejecting the Beatles in 1962. "The singer has to go" was the assessment of the Rolling Stones' new manager Eric Easton in 1963. At the time of writing, Mick was still going strong-ish. "Children just aren't interested in witches and wizards anymore" was the assessment of a book publishing executive writing to J. K. Rowling in 1996, rejecting *Harry Potter*. She got lucky with her thirteenth publisher.

Harry Warner of Warner Brothers movie studio, when asked about sound in films around 1927, was confident: "Who the hell wants to hear actors talk?" (That is pretty much what President Trump said after Meryl Streep spoke out in January 2017. What Mr. Trump thought when Oliver Stone referred to Fidel Castro as "one of the world's wisest men" or when Jack Nicholson referred to Castro as a genius, I do not know.)

Charlie Chaplin on the prospects of cinema in 1916: "The cinema is little more than a fad. It's canned drama." Marilyn Monroe was told early in her career to learn secretarial work, or else get married. "Reagan doesn't have that presidential look" was the argument of a United Artists executive rejecting Ronald Reagan as the lead in the film *The Best Man* in 1964. Margaret Thatcher, quoted in 1974, thought that "it will be years—not in my time—before a woman will become Prime Minister." She became prime minister five years later. Sometimes even inside information does not help to make accurate forecasts:

Nothing will ever separate us. We will probably be married
another ten years.[508]
—ELIZABETH TAYLOR, *1974, five days before she and Richard*
  Burton announced their divorce

One somewhat comical aspect of these predictions is that many of
them were not entirely unreasonable at the time. All the ridicule draws
heavily on the concept of hindsight.

FUD and Science Fiction

Forecasts and predictions in technology are a great source of comical
relief: a Western Union internal memo from 1876: "This 'telephone' has
too many shortcomings to be seriously considered as a means of communication. The device is inherently of no value to us." In 1934 Albert
Einstein mused: "There is not the slightest indication that nuclear energy
will ever be obtainable. It would mean that the atom would have to be
shattered at will."[509] In 1977, Ken Olson, president, chairman, and founder
of Digital Equipment Corp., loudly thought that "there is no reason for
any individuals to have a computer in their homes."

In 1981, Bill Gates, founder of Microsoft, thought that "640K ought
to be enough for anybody." Speaking of Microsoft; in 2007 Steve Ballmer,
then CEO of Microsoft, mused about the market potential of Apple's
iPhone in an interview at a conference:

> Q: *People get passionate when Apple comes out with something*
> *new—the iPhone; of course, the iPod. Is that something that*
> *you'd want them to feel about Microsoft?*
>
> BALLMER: *It's sort of a funny question. Would I trade 96% of*
> *the market for 4% of the market? (Laughter.) I want to have*
> *products that appeal to everybody.*
>   *Now we'll get a chance to go through this again in phones*
> *and music players. There's no chance that the iPhone is going*
> *to get any significant market share. No chance. It's a $500*
> *subsidized item.*[510]

By 2013, the iPhone alone generated more revenue than the whole of Microsoft.[511] By 2020, thanks to smartphones, UFO sightings had collapsed, as everyone now, at all times, has a camera to record anything out of the ordinary.

Analysis of the track record of forecasters over the past several decades shows that their long-term technology predictions have been wrong about 80 percent of the time, according to a wonderfully titled book, *Fortune Sellers*, by William Sherden in 1998. Another study quoted by Sherden found that nearly every prediction was wrong.

One bizarre thing about "forecasting" is that nearly all of Captain Kirk's gadgets in the original *Star Trek* series from the 1960s, then science fiction, are in existence today: wireless communication, food replicator, scanners including health scanners, computer tablets, lasers, voice activation, talking computers, drones, autopilot, 3D games, etc. (Teleportation and the warp drive being two exceptions.) As Ralph Waldo Emerson most likely never said:

> *Fiction reveals truth that reality obscures.*[512]
> —JESSAMYN WEST *(1902–84), American writer*

Andy Grove, the man behind Intel and its third employee, born Andraz Graf in Hungary, surviving both Hitler and Stalin before immigrating the United States in the late 1950s, applied some form of reverse-Murphy's Law (what can go wrong, will) to technological advancement:

> *In Technology, whatever can be done will be done.*[513]
> —ANDREW GROVE *(1936–2016), American businessman and*
> *semiconductor pioneer*

Tesla and SpaceX founder Elon Musk, who is famous for many things, including sending a roadster into space, selling flame throwers on the Internet, selling candy to rich people as a kid, and giving his kids funny names, thinks along the same lines:

Science is discovering the essential truths about what exists in
the Universe, engineering is about creating things that never
existed.[514]
—ELON MUSK *(b. 1971), South African–born American*
    entrepreneur and engineer

The foresightedness of science fiction is bizarre because many experts
from that time who predicted how the world would look like in the year
2000 made, by the year 2000, complete fools out of themselves.

[I] would take even money that England will not exist in the
year 2000.[515]
—PAUL EHRLICH *(b. 1932), American biologist in 1969*

Blood and Pessimism
By 2018, scientists and futurists were falling over themselves, warning
vociferously that everyone's job will be replaced by artificial intelligence
and robots by 2030, except, perhaps, the jobs of hairdressers and Elvis
impersonators. This is, of course, nonsense. (Androids will be doing great
Elvis impersonations.) It's Malthus's mistake. But the experts know that
scaremongering gains attention. Media studies show that negative news
outweighs positive news by about seventeen to one.

If it bleeds, it leads.
—*Old saying in newspaper industry*

In the late 2010s, all sorts of people, including scientists and socialists,
were falling over themselves, warning vociferously that we are all going to
die soon if nothing is done regarding climate change. The fearmongering
was briefly interrupted during 2020 by virus-related fearmongering, presumably to resume after the pandemic is over.

The world is going to end in twelve years if we don't address
climate change.[516]
—ALEXANDRIA OCASIO-CORTEZ *(b. 1989), American*
    politician and activist

The solution? Windmills, a technology that is around fifteen hundred years old. Given that science fiction writers seem to make better long-term predictions than the intelligentsia, ask yourself: have you ever seen a science fiction movie where energy is generated by windmills? (That said, let us hope that the writers behind the *Terminator* series got it all wrong, and Orwell and Huxley were delusional when penning *1984* and *Brave New World*.)

Fear sells well. One practical aspect of this book is to be able to spot fearmongering: fearmongering being a potentially dangerous departure from reality. FUD (fear, uncertainty, and doubt) is an important tool in the charlatan's tool kit. It works nearly all the time. Fearmongering is a huge problem in finance. Human nature is so much more attracted to bearish opinions than it is to positive ones.

> *Pessimism sells. For reasons I have never understood, people like to hear that the world is going to hell, and become huffy and scornful when some idiotic optimist intrudes on their pleasure.*[517]
> —DEIRDRE MCCLOSKEY *(b. 1942), American professor of economics, history, English, and communication*

Investors need to adjust for this.

Skepticism and Truth

Reality Deficits and Survival Probability

Authors have an incentive to be negative. Authors who write negatively are perceived as more critical and therefore more intellectual, more serious. Skepticism is a serious thing:

> *Skepticism is the first step towards truth.*[518]
> —DENIS DIDEROT *(1714–84), French philosopher*

Optimists are perceived as a bit bland. In the US stock market, the optimists are much more often right than perma-bears. If you say, at the beginning of every year, the US stock market will be up at year's end, you will be right roughly two-thirds of the time. However, it is the optimists that are much more often ridiculed, called naive, as well as branded "sales-oriented," arguably the worst accusation for an analyst. I agree with Benjamin Disraeli:

> *It is much easier to be critical than to be correct.*[519]
> —BENJAMIN DISRAELI *(1804–81), British politician, two-time prime minister, and novelist*

An investor has an incentive to be correct, while talking heads and salespeople have an incentive to be heard. The reason why scaremongering and generally being negative works is that humans seek out news of dramatic, novel, negative events. The reason for this is that our brains evolved in a hunter-gatherer environment where anything novel or dramatic had to be attended to immediately for survival. We no longer defend ourselves against saber-toothed tigers coming around the corner, but our brains have not caught up.

Sherden on the difference between forecasting and science fiction:

> *The main difference between technology forecasting and science fiction is that the former is sold under the pretense of being factual.*[520]
> —WILLIAM SHERDEN, *consultant and author of* Fortune Sellers

Nassim Taleb, a satirist when it comes to making fun of economists, highlights the difficulty of forecasting well:

> *Prediction requires knowing about technologies that will be discovered in the future. But that very knowledge would almost automatically allow us to start developing those technologies right away. Ergo, we do not know what we will know.*[521]
> —NASSIM NICHOLAS TALEB *(b. 1960), author of the* Black Swan

The ultimate and heavily quoted and re-quoted forecast related to investments is from Irving Fisher, professor of economics at Yale University, who was quoted in 1929: "Stocks have reached what looks like a permanently high plateau." With the benefit of hindsight, we know today that stocks halved in the years after that piece of scholarly "wisdom" and then halved again and then halved once more before all was said and done.

Ego Inflation and Hubris
Speaking of scholarly wisdom: a weekly newsletter from the Harvard Economic Society from November 16, 1929, argued:

> *A severe depression like that of 1920–21 is outside the range of probability.*[522]
> —*Harvard Economic Society*

Predictions that are "outside the range of probability" like the one stated earlier by the Harvard Economic Society are in clear violation of Gump's law; one really needs to know what one does not know. Book-smartness can be a detriment to doing things successfully, say running a big country.

> *I would rather be governed by the first 2000 people in the Manhattan phone book than the entire faculty of Harvard.*[523]
> —WILLIAM F. BUCKLEY JR. *(1924–2008), American author and journalist*

Overintellectualizing things is often a handicap related to human action. Intellectuals can indeed be bozos when tasks need pragmatism for success.

> *A man of special learning may be a fool as to common relations. And that he who passes for an intellectual prince may be a moral pauper there are examples enough to show.*[524]
> —HENRY GEORGE *(1839–97), American political economist and journalist*

But there is something else: educated (as in book-smart) as well as monetarily successful people can experience ego inflation throughout their careers, as the only feedback they get is positive. After continuous success and positive feedback, this often happens:

As I looked into the night sky, across all those infinite stars, it
made me realise how unimportant they are.[525]
—PETER COOK *(1937–95), English satirist, writer, and*
  comedian

Ego inflation can cause, apart from arrogance, a lack of open-mindedness and intellectual integrity, i.e., a propensity to dogma and materially reduced tolerance and imagination toward alternative outcomes, probabilities, views, and perspectives. This is one way of putting it:

[T]ip-of-your-nose delusions can fool anyone, even the best and
the brightest—perhaps <u>especially</u> the best and the brightest.[526]
—PHILIP TETLOCK *and* DAN GARDNER, *authors of*
  Superforecasting

The following is an alternative, shorter way of referring to narrow-mindedness and lack of imagination:

Middle age is when your broad mind and narrow waist begin
to change places.[527]
—E. JOSEPH COSSMAN *(1918–2002), American businessman*
  and author

Belief and Forecasting
Jan Tinbergen, a Dutch economist who was awarded the first Bank of Sweden Prize in Economic Sciences in Memory of Alfred Nobel in 1969, which he shared with Ragnar Frisch, was a keen observer:

Forecasting is not a strong side of economics.[528]
—JAN TINBERGEN *(1903–94), Dutch economist*

One contemporary economist suggested in 1998 that policy makers are delusional, and do not learn from past mistakes:

One of the great mistakes of the past 30 years of economic policy
has been an excessive belief in the ability to forecast.[529]
—MARTIN FELDSTEIN *(1939–2019), American economist*

This was not lost on Nassim Taleb, author of *Fooled by Randomness* and *The Black Swan*, the latter described in a review by the *Sunday Times* in 2009 as one of the twelve most influential books since World War II.

> *As a practitioner of uncertainty I have seen more than my share*
> *of snake-oil salesmen dressed in the garb of scientists, particu-*
> *larly those operating in economics. The greatest fools of random-*
> *ness will be found among those.*[530]
> —NASSIM NICHOLAS TALEB *(b. 1960), Lebanese American*
>   *risk analyst and author*

On a similar notion, John Kenneth Galbraith suggested forecasters suit up:

> *[I]n monetary matters as in diplomacy, a nicely conformist*
> *nature, a good tailor, and the ability to articulate the currently*
> *fashionable financial cliché have usually been better for personal*
> *success than an excessively inquiring mind.*[531]
> —JOHN KENNETH GALBRAITH *(1908–2006), Canadian*
>   *American economist*

Survival and Entertainment

A portfolio manager "who falls in love with his own ideas" (i.e., believes his own BS) is robbed of the ability to cut losses short. This is what happens:

> *The moment a person forms a theory, his imagination sees in*
> *every object only the traits which favor that theory.*[532]
> —THOMAS JEFFERSON *(1743–1826), American Founding*
>   *Father and third president of the United States*

A reality deficit reduces survival probability, i.e., the ability to fight another day. The Harvard Economic Society letter ridiculed earlier ceased publication in 1931, going broke because of the Great Depression. Will Rogers recommends caution when it comes to forecasts by economists:

An economist's guess is liable to be as good as anybody else's.
—WILL ROGERS *(1879–1935), American humorist*

There is arguably great wisdom and wit in this simple one-liner. Gump's mum certainly knew it. This is even though the economists' presentation of the forecasts is often conducted with great fanfare, conviction, and oratorical brilliance. It's a show, a form of entertainment, or "investainment." This is how the authors of *Superforecasting* put it:

> *You might think the goal of forecasting is to foresee the future accurately, but that's often not the goal, or at least not the sole goal. Sometimes forecasts are meant to entertain . . . [S]ome forecasts are meant to comfort—by assuring the audience that their beliefs are correct and the future will unfold as expected. Partisans are fond of these forecasts. They are the cognitive equivalent of slipping into a warm bath.*[533]
> —PHILIP TETLOCK *and* DAN GARDNER

John Kay, an op-ed writer for the *Financial Times*, knows this too:

> *Mostly they [economists] are employed in the financial sector— for their entertainment value rather than their advice.*[534]
> —JOHN KAY *(b. 1948), British economist and columnist*

Case in point:

> *Jan, the bottom line is, before the end of the year, the NASDAQ and Dow will be at new record highs.*[535]
> —MYRON KANDEL *(b. 1930), financial editor and anchor CNNfn/Cofounder, CNN, April 4, 2000*

The NASDAQ halved after April 4, 2000. And then, after halving, it fell another 45 percent. The record highs of 2000 were not reached until April 2015.

Bottom Line

Many an economist could learn something from Forrest Gump's mum: life is like a box of chocolates. Life is simply too full of surprises for forecasting to make sense, it's often chaotic. An abundance of data does not replace thought. One of the greatest pieces of economic wisdom is to know what you do not know. However, in the country of the blind, the one-eyed man has an edge.

Humans respond differently to bad news than to good news. Charlatans know that. Investors need to adjust for the when-it-bleeds-it-leads and FUD phenomena.

Stupidity is plentiful, and overintellectualizing things is dangerous. If a butterfly in the Amazon can cause a tornado in Texas, economic forecasting is a form of entertainment. The horse was here to stay and the automobile a fad; the Great Depression was outside the range of probability; the Titanic was unsinkable; and Pearl Harbor and Fannie Mae were safe.

––––––––

There is overconfidence; *confidence,* the delusional call it.

THE DUNNING-KRUGER EFFECT

The greatest enemy of knowledge is not ignorance;
it is the illusion of knowledge.

—Aphorism popularized by Daniel J. Boorstin

The Dunning-Kruger effect is a cognitive bias in which bozos overestimate their ability. One characteristic of bozos is delusion, i.e., they do not know what they do not know.

While there are those who know that they don't know, there are also those who know that they don't know but nevertheless professionally need to come across as knowledgeable and confident. Feelings and wishful thinking play a part when producing baloney. A healthy dose of doubt is a good baloney detector.

Coin-flipping is underrated when making decisions. Experts err predictably and often. Many of us smile at old-fashioned fortune-tellers. But when the soothsayers use science, we take their predictions seriously. Beware of charlatans using the Barnum effect that suggests they have something for everyone in the forecast. It is how astrology "works."

Only fools, liars, and charlatans predict earthquakes, says the inventor of the Richter scale. Economic forecasting makes astrology look respectable. You do not need forecasts. Fortune cookies suffice.

Unwisdom and the Bozo Explosion

Economic Buffoonery and the Triumph of Stupidity

In a 2005 book, Philip E. Tetlock, a Canadian American scientist specializing in forecasting and decision-making, mentions how experts are often no better at making predictions than most other people, and how, when they are wrong, they are rarely held accountable. Tetlock conducted a set of small-scale forecasting tournaments between 1984 and 2003. The forecasters were two hundred and eighty-four experts from a variety of fields, including government officials, professors, journalists, etc.

The tournaments solicited roughly twenty-eight thousand predictions about the future and found the forecasters were often only slightly more accurate than chance, and usually worse than basic extrapolation algorithms, especially on longer-range forecasts three to five years out. The funny thing is that forecasters with the biggest news media profiles were especially bad at forecasting.[536] Maintaining a media persona takes time and effort, time and effort which are therefore not being put into the core competence anymore.

For a financial professional, resisting the temptation to forecast is not easy. This brings me back to John Kenneth Galbraith, who distinguishes between two types of seers:

> We have two classes of forecasters: Those who don't know—and those who don't know they don't know.[537]
> —JOHN KENNETH GALBRAITH (1908–2006), Canadian American economist

The thing about the second group is that they do not know that they don't know. This is how Dan Lyons of HubSpot fame put it in a chapter he, paraphrasing Steve Jobs, called "The Bozo Explosion":

The thing about bozos is that bozos don't know that they're bozos. Bozos think they're the shit, which makes them really annoying but also incredibly entertaining, depending on your point of view. Shrinks call this the Dunning-Kruger effect, named after two researchers from Cornell University whose studies found that incompetent people fail to recognize their own lack of skill, grossly overestimating their abilities, and are unable to recognize talent in other people who actually are competent.[538]
—DANIEL LYONS *(b. 1960), American journalist and writer*

The bozo explosion is also applicable to investment banking, where people who do well in their field but cannot manage people are promoted to manage people. (The reason for me knowing this is beyond the scope of this book.)

The Dunning-Kruger effect, often applied to Donald Trump during his tenure as president by parts of the media, was well articulated in a 1933 essay titled "The Triumph of Stupidity":

The fundamental cause of the trouble is that in the modern world the stupid are cocksure, while the intelligent are full of doubt.[539]
—BERTRAND RUSSELL *(1872–1970), British philosopher*

The Dunning-Kruger effect is a form of unwisdom; the stupidity a function of overconfidence, single-mindedness, intolerance for opposing views, intellectual nonintegrity, metaforgetfulness (people confusing their current level of understanding with their own peak), a me-bias, and potentially a portion arrogance or the ultimate form of self-delusion: hubris.

As E. Joseph Cossman argued earlier, age does not protect from folly. As the expert ages, his mind can clog; thinking become fuzzier, dogmatic even:

In the beginner's mind there are many possibilities;
in the expert's, there are few.[540]
—SHUNRYU SUZUKI *(1904–71), Zen monk*

Forecasting and the Lack of Doubt
While Galbraith argued earlier that there are two types of forecasters, there are actually three types:

> *There are two types of investors, be they large or small: those who don't know where the market is headed, and those who don't know that they don't know. Then again, there is a third type of investors—the investment professional, who indeed knows that he or she doesn't know, but whose livelihood depends upon appearing to know.*[541]
> —WILLIAM J. BERNSTEIN *(b. 1948), American financial theorist*

Sometimes, some would say often, it is economists with great insight and scholarly accolades that fall into Bernstein's second or third category:

> *[T]he Fed's analytical prowess is top-notch and our forecasting record is second to none.*[542]
> —JANET YELLEN *(b. 1946), American economist and a former chair of the Federal Reserve*

To some, the Fed is always wrong, but never in doubt. However, not all central bankers fall into Galbraith's second class of forecasters:

> *We really can't forecast that well. We pretend we can, but we can't. Markets do very weird things because it reacts to how people behave and sometimes people are a little screwy.*[543]
> —ALAN GREENSPAN (b. 1926), American economist and former chairman of the Federal Reserve

This last quotation came after many years of personal reflection. It is not all bad. Sometimes bureaucrats do indeed make correct forecasts:

> *When I came to the Treasury, they predicted to me that I would become the most unpopular man in Britain. This was the only correct forecast that the Treasury made in the several years that I was chancellor.*[544]
> —NORMAN LAMONT *(b. 1942), British politician and chancellor of the Exchequer (1990–93)*

Forecasts by highly intelligent, knowledgeable, and book-smart people are not always a function of mal-incentive, ignorance, foolishness, or a blown-up ego. At least some forecasts can be attributed to a romantic vein of the forecaster. An idealist can have a bias toward his ideal, a delusion, i.e., a departure from reality. Below are three examples:

> *The Soviet economy is proof that, contrary to what many sceptics had earlier believed, a socialist command economy can function and even thrive.* [545]
> —Paul Samuelson *(1915–2009), American economist in 1961*

> *As the North [of Korea] continues to develop and the South to degenerate, sooner or later the curtain of lies must surely begin to tear.* [546]
> —Joan Robinson *(1903–83), British economist, in 1964 on Korea*

> *By 2005 or so, it will become clear that the Internet's impact on the economy has been no greater than the fax machine's.* [547]
> —Paul Krugman *(b. 1953), American economist, in 1998*

Opinions and Feelings

One of the more comical aspects of studying human behavior is that to this day, there are still supporters of the entente of the four Cs of economic buffoonery (Castro, Chávez, Corbin, and Che). The comical aspect is that these supporters are not found among the least educated but among the most book-smart-educated. Intuitively one would assume the most educated are the least delusional. The romantic vein when forming opinions was spotted well by Herbert Spencer, the Darwin contemporary who coined the term "survival of the fittest":

> *Opinion is ultimately determined by the feelings, and not by the intellect.* [548]
> —Herbert Spencer *(1820–1903), English philosopher*

Some decision-making, of course, is done by the heart. When finding a spouse, in many cases, the heart is involved. When buying a car, the following happens:

> People mistakenly assume that their thinking is done by their head; it is actually done by the heart which first dictates the conclusion, then commands the head to provide the reasoning that will defend it.[549]
> —ANTHONY DE MELLO (1931–87), Indian Jesuit priest

Having a heart is great. Wearing it on your sleeve has its limitations though.

> To wear your heart on your sleeve isn't a very good plan; you should wear it inside, where it functions best.[550]
> —MARGARET THATCHER (1925–2013), British stateswoman

For decision-making in finance, reason and logic are sound alternatives to instinct and feelings.

> [O]ne day your intuition will fail, and you will finally understand that logic is primary above all else. "Instinct" is simply another term for serendipity.[551]
> —TUVOK (b. 2264), Vulcan chief of security, USS Voyager

While logic should be a big part of decision-making under uncertainty, the world is not necessarily a logical place. In a dynamic system in which humans are involved, cause and effect thinking might not be applicable. Centennial James Lovelock, who is best known for his Gaia theory that suggests that living and non-living parts of Earth form a self-regulating system that can be thought of as a single organism , put it well:

> As Newton found long ago, logical thinking does not work with dynamic systems, things that change over the course of time. Quite simply, you cannot explain the working of something alive by cause-and-effect logic. Most of us, especially women, have known this all along.[552]
> —JAMES LOVELOCK (b. 1919), British independent scientist and futurist

Rita Mae Brown said pretty much the same thing:

> *If the world were a logical place,*
> *men would ride side-saddle.*[553]
> —RITA MAE BROWN *(b. 1944), American author*

Risk and Wishful Thinking

In addition, or instead of a romantic vein, wishful thinking—somewhat related to a rosy view of the world of the romantic—is also very human and might override the ability to assess probabilities. Furthermore, the incentive to pump up reality and lie can be quite overpowering. Three examples:

> *No risk.*[554]
> —TIM GEITHNER, *seventy-fifth United States Secretary of*
>   *the Treasury, in response to the question of whether the US*
>   *could lose its AAA credit rating*

> *I have great, great confidence in our capital markets and in*
> *our financial institutions. Our financial institutions, banks and*
> *investment banks, are strong.*[555]
> —HENRY PAULSON, *seventy-fourth Secretary of the Treasury,*
>   *on March 16, 2008*

> *They will make it through the storm.*[556]
> —BEN BERNANKE, *fourteenth chairman of the Federal*
>   *Reserve; "they" being Fannie Mae and Freddie Mac two*
>   *months before they collapsed*

Speaking of storms . . . during a briefing by academics at the London School of Economics on the turmoil on the international markets during 2008, Queen Elizabeth II of England, wonderfully portrayed by a debonair Claire Foy in Netflix's *The Crown*, asked: "Why did nobody notice it?" Professor Luis Garicano, director of research at the London School of Economics's management department, had explained the origins and effects of the credit crisis when she opened a new building. The queen, who is famous for studiously avoiding controversy and never giving away

her opinions, then described the turbulence on the markets as "awful."[557]
As two Nobel laureates put it a year later:

> *If science is defined by its ability to forecast the future, the fail-*
> *ure of much of the economics profession to see the crisis coming*
> *should be a cause of great concern.*[558]
> —GEORGE AKERLOF (b. 1940) and Joseph Stiglitz (b. 1943),
>   American economists

Adair Turner, chairman of the Financial Services Authority in the UK
during the financial crises, summarized the financial crises well in 2018:

> *The excessive risk-taking was allowed by bad regulation justified*
> *by flawed economic theory.*[559]
> —ADAIR TURNER *(b. 1955), British businessman and*
>   *academic*

Economists, one could argue, are around thirty years behind methodologists. Methodologists, some time ago, also did not know what they
didn't know and thought more complexity would improve their forecasts.
The weather, like the economy, is also chaotic, as in the butterfly effect
mentioned earlier.

Oxford University physicist Tim Palmer and other scientists in England
around 1985 started using less-precise simulations to get a range of possible
outcomes. Today, scientists can predict the weather over four days as well
as they used to over just one day. The key insight, Palmer argued in 2018,
was a philosophical shift toward embracing perpetual doubt—seeing it not
as a threat to knowledge, but as the very essence of it. Mark Buchanan, the
author of the highly commendable book *Ubiquity*, sums it up well:

> *Oddly, better knowledge has come about by emphasizing doubt*
> *and uncertainty at every step.*[560]
> —MARK BUCHANAN *(b. 1961), American physicist and*
>   *science writer*

A lie is a lie, and a forecast is a forecast. They are two different things.
However, the original incentive to lie or to forecast can be the same. A
forecast by a government official might not be pure ignorance. The origin

of the forecast, like the origin of a lie, can emanate from the incentive to manipulate markets and investors, i.e., interventionism. When my wife asks me whether we have chocolate in the house, I lie, as I have an incentive to do so. (I would be chocolateless otherwise.) So, as with so many things in life, caveat emptor ("let the buyer beware") applies. Warren Buffett on perma-bears and the incentive to forecast pain:

> *Ever-present naysayers may prosper by marketing their gloomy forecasts. But heaven help them if they act on the nonsense they peddle.*[561]
> —WARREN BUFFETT *(b. 1930), American investor and businessman*

Eisenhower said pretty much the same thing:

> *Pessimism never won any battles.*[562]
> —DWIGHT EISENHOWER *(1890–1969), American general and thirty-fourth president of the United States*

As principals, one ought to beware of agents:

> *Follow Charlie Munger's advice: "Never, ever, think about anything else when you should be thinking about the power of incentives." The world is run by agents. And when agents have the wrong incentives, you get the wrong result.*[563]
> —RUSSELL NAPIER *(b. 1964), British financial market historian*

Prediction and Knowledge

A forecast is biased by definition because it is an opinion. An investment process focusing on facts seems more reasonable than an investment process that focuses on opinions. Leonardo da Vinci might agree with this line of argument were he in finance today. In a section with the subtitle "On Foolishness and Ignorance," Leonardo wrote:

> *The greatest deception men suffer is from their own opinions.*[564]
> —LEONARDO DA VINCI *(1452–1519), Italian polymath*

So not only are forecasts from agents dangerous, but one ought to take care of one's own forecasts too. Another author who wrote on foolishness, Nassim Taleb, was generalizing when he wrote:

> [F]or Mother Nature, opinions and predictions don't count; sur-
> viving is what matters.[565]
> —NASSIM NICHOLAS TALEB (b. 1960), author of Fooled by
>   Randomness

An egomaniac, obviously, would want to beg to differ, most likely unaware of the concept of *qi* (or, to *Star Wars* fans, the Force):

> Those who have knowledge don't predict.
> Those who predict don't have knowledge.[566]
> —LAO TZU (ca. 6 BC), Chinese philosopher

What is quite fascinating is that it is nearly always experts (i.e., often well-educated people who do not suffer from a lack of self-confidence but seldom have skin in the game) who make the silly forecasts. It is as if the silly people knew better.

The funny thing is that with complex problems, laypeople with limited understanding of the subject are often better at forecasting, for it is they who suffer less from overconfidence and are therefore more conservative. The experts' ignorance and ignorance of ignorance is related to the richness of information. The more information there is, the higher the overconfidence of the experts, and therefore, the greater the gap between the experts' opinion and reality.

That said, and to be fair, some people do have a clear picture of the future:

> I have seen the future and it is very much like the present, only
> longer.[567]
> —KEHLOG ALBRAN (pseudonym for authors Martin A.
>   Cohen and Sheldon Shacket)

This last quotation is very much applicable to the concept of "nowcasting," discussed in the last chapter.

Expert Failure and Flipism

Clarke's Law and Permabears

Thomas Malthus, a perma-bear who thought of poverty as humanity's inescapable lot, famously said in 1798:

> *Population, when unchecked, increases in a geometrical ratio.*
> *Subsistence increases only in an arithmetical ratio.*[568]
> —THOMAS MALTHUS *(1766–1834), English demographer*
>   *and political economist*

Modern-day Malthusians are common, often talk about climate change or market crashes, and due to the magnet-like appeal of alarming predictions, easily can find an audience. Paul Ehrlich is special in the sense that not only did he make Malthusian-style apocalyptic, attention-grabbing forecasts; he also stuck with them, even after he was proven wrong.

> *The most intelligent creatures ultimately surviving this period*
> *[the 1990s] are cockroaches.*[569]
> —PAUL EHRLICH (b. 1932), *American biologist in 1968*

Paul Ehrlich will have his way one day, of course, as the law of failure from chapter two implies he will. Everything fails in the end. However, determining the timing of the end is almost impossible. If James Lovelock has his way, the descent of man will be the ascent of machines:

> *They [cyborgs] are as cleverer than people as people are than*
> *plants.*[570]
> —JAMES LOVELOCK *(b. 1919), British independent scientist*
>   *and futurist*

Philosophers do not treat those who do not learn from mistakes lightly. Cicero on catastrophists:

> *Any man can make mistakes, but only a fool persists in his*
> *error.*[571]
> —CICERO *(106–43* BC*), Roman politician, orator, and*
>   *philosopher in 84* BC

Speaking of not learning from mistakes:

Scientists investigated half a century ago the phenomena of experts not learning about their past failings. You can mispredict everything for all your life yet think that you will get it right next time.[572]
—Nassim Nicholas Taleb *(b. 1960), Lebanese American risk analyst*

Imagination and Progress

Malthus's mistake was that he was not able to grasp the idea that human ingenuity can grow exponentially too, i.e., rise "geometrically." Whether it is food production or extracting energy from nature does not matter. "Peak oil" is a laughing matter not just to cynics. Productivity gains during the industrialization of the past two hundred-plus years resulted in parts of the world experiencing exponential wealth increases that exceeded exponential population growth. While this exponential growth did not work for Pacific bluefin tuna, it unmasks Malthus and Ehrlich and their kin, not as fraudsters, but as lacking imagination.

Imagination will often carry us to worlds that never were. But without it we go nowhere.[573]
—Carl Sagan *(1934–96), American astronomer*

Switzerland's most famous patent office employee, too, knew that there are limits to knowledge:

Imagination is more important than knowledge. Knowledge is limited. Imagination encircles the world.[574]
—Albert Einstein *(1879–1955), German-born physicist*

Some politicians do not lack imagination and can indeed assess probabilities:

I have as much chance of becoming prime minister as of being decapitated by a frisbee or of finding Elvis.[575]
—Boris Johnson *(b. 1964), British Brexit campaigner and prime minister, in 2003*

In finance, tricks are often played with exponential growth. The trick is to show something that grows in a chart that does not have a logarithmic scale. This results in the most recent changes being optically larger, i.e., it looks as if the growth went exponential.

So, for example, if you want to scaremonger a bit and show that we all are going to die, you show Homo sapiens' population growth over the last two hundred or two thousand years in a chart that has no log scale. (Essentially the topic of Dan Brown's *Inferno*.) Then you compare it with a chart of Australian rabbits, which went from twenty-four rabbits in 1859 to seventy hundred and fifty million by the 1930s. To cut a long bunny story short, it did not end well for 90 percent of the rabbits.

An expert can give zero probability to a future outcome that he perceives as utterly unlikely. A 2016 example is the election of Donald Trump as president of the United States. The probability was never zero percent. The probability was low, and the whole idea just very unreasonable but not unimaginable. Even the makers of *The Simpsons* thought it was possible as early as the year 2000. They thought of it as a joke, as satire, and were not alone; some still do. Satire is neither difficult nor dead:

> *There's no trick to being a humorist when you have the whole government working for you.*[576]
> —WILL ROGERS *(1879–1935), American humorist*

> *People say satire is dead. It's not dead, it's alive and living in the White House.*
> —ROBIN WILLIAMS *(1951–2014), American actor*

Satire helps us understand reality. Hillary Clinton accusing Donald Trump of lying, or Donald Trump accusing Kim Jong-un of lying is, of course, comical. They all lie, and satire is one way of dealing with that reality. The lack of imagination; the inability to reflect and self-ridicule, and the exclamation that something has zero probability, is called Clarke's (first) law:

If an elderly but distinguished scientist says that something is possible he is almost certainly right, but if he says that it is impossible he is very probably wrong.[577]
—ARTHUR C. CLARKE *(1917–2008), British science fiction author*

Fortuna and Forecasts

The difference between Cassandra, daughter of King Priam and Queen Hecuba of Troy in Greek mythology, and Thomas Malthus was that no one believed Cassandra. (Cassandra was cursed by Apollo to utter prophecies that were true but which no one believed.) To become believable, one ought to use science. It's the trick. Professor Gigerenzer, a well-respected scientist, the author of a highly recommended and pragmatic book titled *Risk Savvy*, and, among other things, director of the (David) Harding Center for Risk Literacy,* put it well:

> *Many of us smile at old-fashioned fortune-tellers. But when the soothsayers work with computer algorithms rather than tarot cards, we take their predictions seriously and are prepared to pay for them.*[578]
> —GERD GIGERENZER *(b. 1947), German psychologist*

Gigerenzer moves on and continues to make fun of forecasters, stressing again that it's just the modern-day forecaster creating the appearance of being a bit more sophisticated than tarot card flippers:

> *[B]lindfolded Fortuna is still at work, calmly spinning her wheel, fooling forecasters and plunging Nobel laureates' hedge funds into ruin.*[579]
> —GERD GIGERENZER, *Risk Savvy risk lecturer*

If you produce a fancy chart that includes the word "debt" on it and forecast the S&P 500 Index will halve, you are almost guaranteed to have

---

* Recommendation to the reader: do the risk quiz on the center's website. It only takes a couple of minutes. See https://www.harding-center.mpg.de/en. If you do poorly on the test, read Gigerenzer's *Risk Savvy*, Bernstein's *Against the Gods*, and Taleb's *Fooled by Randomness*. You will be fine then.

an audience. Many investors are hooked on forecasts, especially bearish ones:

> Permabears create high anxiety—but perhaps that is what some customers secretly want.[580]
> —WILLIAM A. SHERDEN, American consultant and author

The funny thing about perma-bears is that all the ridicule is only in the interim. In the end, they will get it right because the iron law of failure applies to everything: monopolies, economies, hegemonies, the sun, markets, fish, etc. While we tend to pay attention to negative forecasts, we do not necessarily like the messenger of bad news though:

> If you warn 100 men of possible forthcoming bad news, 80 will immediately dislike you. And if you are so unfortunate to be right, the other 20 will as well.[581]
> —ANTHONY GAUBIS (1902–87), American financial analyst

Forecasting is done by experts. One of the issues with forecasting is the inconsistency. A forecaster sometimes gets it right and sometimes wrong. The investment process based on forecasts lacks consistency and therefore is not robust.

> They [market experts] can't predict markets with any useful consistency, any more than the gizzard squeezers could tell the Roman emperors when the Huns would attack.[582]
> —PETER LYNCH (b. 1944), American investment manager

If you apply the quote above to the storming of the Bastille on July 14, 1789, or the storming of the Capitol building on January 6, 2021, it works just as well.

There is good reason for paying attention to experts though. This is how one self-acclaimed radical libertarian put it:

> Always listen to experts. They'll tell you what can't be done and why. Then do it.[583]
> —ROBERT A. HEINLEIN (1907–88), American science fiction author

Gurus and Researchers

Experts err.[584] This does not mean giving advice is a bad business though:

> To err is human,
> but to be paid for it is divine.[585]
> —HOWARD RUFF (1930–2016), American economist and
>   author

As a matter of fact, experts err predictably and often. Nearly 100 percent of studies that find a particular type of food or vitamin that lowers the risk of disease fail to hold up. As much as 90 percent of physicians' medical knowledge has been gauged to be substantially or completely wrong. About two-thirds of the findings published in top medical journals are refuted within a few years. A drug widely prescribed for years to heart-attack victims killed more Americans than did the Vietnam War. These examples are from a book by David H. Freedman (b. 1954), American science and business journalist, of which the book title, subtitle, and cover tagline are quite revealing:

> Wrong: Why Experts* Keep Failing Us—And How to Know
> When Not to Trust Them
> *Scientists, finance wizards, doctors, relationship gurus,
> celebrity CEOs, high-powered consultants, health officials,
> and more.[586]

The German language even has a word for this: Fachidiot, where "Fach" means subject, profession, trade, discipline, and "Idiot" means, well, idiot. (My dictionary translated Fachidiot into "nerd.") The Fachidiot is an expert in one narrow field but is ignorant of his ignorance in other fields, thereby being a fool when dealing with multifaceted and complex problems. The word is somewhat related to Taleb's "IYI" (intellectual yet idiot) and consistent with Robson's intelligence trap.

The problem of expert failure can be traced to man's capabilities as an information processor. Every human organism lives in an environment that generates millions of new bits of information every second, but the bottleneck of the perceptual apparatus does not admit more than one thousand bits per second. We react consciously to only a fraction of the information that is given to us.[587] This is how the 1975 winner of the Turing Award and 1978 holder of the Nobel Prize in Economics put it in 1957:

> *The capacity of the human mind for formulating and solving complex problems is very small compared with the size of the problems whose solution is required.*[588]
> —HERBERT SIMON *(1916–2001), American scientist and economist*

Coin Flipping and Problem Solving

CXO Advisory, an investment-strategy-testing firm, collected six thousand five hundred and eighty-two forecasts for the US stock market offered publicly by sixty-eight experts, bulls and bears employing technical, fundamental, and sentiment indicators during 2005 through 2012.[589] Collected forecasts included those in archives, such that the oldest forecast in the sample was from the end of 1998. For the final report, they graded all these forecasts. The majority failed. The average accuracy by guru was 46.9 percent, while the average accuracy by forecast was 47.4 percent. In other words, flipping a coin is actually the more conservative method to "forecast." Contrarian investor David Dreman analyzed sixty surveys between 1929 and 1993 and found expert failure to be 75 percent, i.e., far worse than coin flipping.[590]

Coin flipping, or flipism, is superior because it results in an accuracy ratio of 50 percent. This means coin flipping is superior to paying attention to forecasters, on average, i.e., statistically speaking. This does not necessarily mean that there are no individuals or firms with superior forecasting skills. Ned Davis, whose well-respected firm Ned Davis Research offers market timing services, suggests coin flipping too:

> *Perhaps the biggest myth in financial markets is that experts have expertise or that forecasters can forecast. The reality is that flipping a coin would produce a better record.*[591]
> —NED DAVIS *(b. 1945), American investment strategist and business founder*

The dispersion of forecasters in the CXO study is very wide. The best forecaster has 68.2 percent accuracy, the worst had an accuracy rate of 20.8 percent. If the accuracy rate is lower than 50 percent, which is the case with the majority, it is more intelligent to flip a coin, rather than pay attention to the forecast. An accuracy rate higher than 50 percent is impressive. However, the observer needs to be able to identify those superior forecasters without much hindsight, thus adding a further element of randomness. On top of that, mean reversion might apply.

The best a forecaster can do in finance for self-promotion is to predict an extraordinary event, for example, a crash. The consumer of the forecast will then have to make sure that the forecaster does not fall into one of the following three categories:

> *Only fools, liars, and charlatans predict earthquakes.*[592]
> —CHARLES RICHTER *(1900–85), American seismologist and active naturist*

This last quotation is the naked truth. (Don't look up the term "active naturist" in the office.)

Charlatans and the 40 Percent Rule

Another trick used by forecasters is the 40 percent rule; a rule that allows the forecaster to be bold without being bold. Just say there is a 40 percent chance of x happening. If x happens, you say, "I told you so," and if it doesn't, you say, "I never said it would happen." It's an art:

> *Pundits and gurus master the art of going out on a limb without going out on a limb.*[593]
> —PHILIP TETLOCK *(b. 1954), Canadian American professor of psychology*

This is how Ned Davis, a Phi Beta Kappa graduate of the University of North Carolina at Chapel Hill, professionally involved in the stock market since 1966, who Louis Rukeyser called "an elf's elf," reflectively summarized it:

*Over the years I have seen scores of very bright investment advi-
sors turn into hugely successful gurus who blaze into the investment business with spectacular forecasts. Yet, I've watched each
and every one of them crash back to earth when a big subsequent
forecast inevitably proved wrong.*[594]
—NED DAVIS *(b. 1945), American investment strategist and
    business founder*

The iron law of failure applies. Note that not all long-term predictions turn out to be false. Pure chance almost eliminates that possibility.
Sometimes there *is* indeed foresight. When two acclaimed economists
were awarded the Nobel Memorial Prize in Economic Sciences in 1990,
Nassim Taleb predicted:

*In a world in which these two get the Nobel, anything can hap-
pen. Anyone can become president.*[595]
—NASSIM NICHOLAS TALEB

In November 2016, Taleb was proven right. He had foresight, as did
James Madison:

Enlightened statesmen will not always be at the helm.[596]
—JAMES MADISON *(1751–1836), Founding Father and fourth
    president of United States*

It's a bit harsh to measure forecasters just by their hits. Personally, I,
like most investment professionals, consume a lot of research, much of
which adds something to the bottom line in one form or another. The
distinction between researcher and guru is important in this regard:

*One important difference between researchers and gurus is that
while gurus often traffic in exotic, dramatic claims, researchers
tend to avoid making extreme claims in much the same way
pilots think twice before reporting UFOs—doing so is a good
way to be branded a flake by colleagues.*[597]
—DAVID H. FREEDMAN *(b. 1954), American science and
    business journalist*

Apologizing up-front for talking my own book; many researchers *are* worth paying attention to for their experience (in watching markets, rather than predicting them), knowledge, analysis, and insight. Robert Shiller and Alan Greenspan, for instance, started talking about the equity market becoming a bit frothy with their "irrational exuberance" remark in December of 1996. The S&P 500 Index was around seven hundred and fifty then and doubled to fifteen hundred after the remark. Howard Marks referred to the following as the greatest investment adage:

> *Being too far ahead of one's time is indistinguishable from being wrong.*[598]
> —*Investment adage*

Shiller and Greenspan's assessments were not without merit. It is just that highly educated people are often too bearish too early *prior* to a major correction and often too bearish for too long *after* a big correction. This means highly educated people are often wrong, precisely as almost everyone else.

Illusory Correlation and the Barnum Effect

Astrology and Fortune Cookies

Whatever the case, following the line of argument of those expert people—in my humble and entirely independent opinion—is worth most investors' while. (Shiller's irrationally exuberant book was published close to the stock market peak of 2000, a marketing bliss, despite his original call being four to five years too early.) However, one of the first things I learned as an analyst was to distinguish between fact and opinion, an idea that I later in life found out we can trace at least back to Plato. My recommendation today is to focus on the former and make fun of the latter. Sherden wrote:

> *Our propensity to believe in predictions consistent with our own beliefs is often exploited by charlatans using what is called the Barnum effect, named in honor of the master showman and*

trickster who advised other tricksters to "have a little something in it for everyone." This tactic is central to the art of astrology, where the believability of predictions or personality analysis is enhanced by including general observations in which customers can see themselves.[599]
—WILLIAM A. SHERDEN, *American consultant and author*

Speaking of astrology, as John Kenneth Galbraith could have put it:

The only function of economic forecasting is to make astrology look respectable.[600]
—EZRA SOLOMON *(1920–2002), American economist*

Even investors with an open mind do not require astrology:

Who needs astrology? The wise man gets by on fortune cookies.[601]
—EDWARD ABBEY *(1927–89), American author and essayist*

Numerous studies discrediting experts have made it clear that expert failure extends far beyond the investment scene. And the problems often reside in man's information-processing capabilities. The expert, like everybody else, is a serial or sequential processor of data who can handle information reliably in a linear manner—that is, he can move from one point to the next in a logical sequence. However, a solution to a complex problem can require configural reasoning. In a configural problem, the expert's interpretation of any single piece of information changes depending on how he evaluates many other inputs.

The configural relationships of a company or the marketplace itself are extremely complex. In addition, research in configural processing has shown that experts can not only analyze information incorrectly; they can also find relationships that are not there—a phenomenon in psychology called illusory correlation.

Illusion and Knowledge
The complexity of the marketplace naturally leads to attempts to simplify and rationalize complex realities. Often investors notice things that are simply coincidental and then come to believe that correlations exist when

none are present. And if they are rewarded by the investment going up, the practice is further amplified. The market thus provides an excellent field for illusory correlation. As Stephen Hawking might have put it:

> The greatest enemy of knowledge is not ignorance;
> it is the illusion of knowledge.[602]
> —Aphorism popularized by Daniel J. Boorstin (1914–2004),
>   American historian and librarian

Much research indicates that subjective models are better than an expert's view, and objective models are better than subjective models. With an intuitive prediction, the expert analyzes the case and, intuitively, weighs the factors. Subjective models use the expert's skill in making judgments but ignore biases. The subjective model uses the expert's analysis of the factors but derives the weights of the factors. This analysis will show how much weight, on average, the experts put on each of the underlying factors.

The idea behind this is as follows: when a person makes a prediction, one gets wisdom mixed with random noise. Intuitive judgments suffer from serious random inconsistencies due to human biases and heuristics. The ideal decision process would eliminate the random noise but retain the real insights that underlie the prediction. A subjective model, therefore, eliminates the noise and retains the core wisdom of the human expert.

The objective model goes one step further. Instead of inferring the weights from the subjective predictions of an expert, the weights are inferred statistically from actual past results.[603]

> Wisdom is what's left after we've run out of personal opinions.
> —CULLEN HIGHTOWER (1923–2008), American salesman
>   and sales trainer

Based on the research of Russo and Schoemaker, from whom I have gotten this, the subjective model is superior to the experts' intuition and inferior to an objective model. For instance, they found that the skill of an oncologist estimating the life expectancy of cancer patients is negative. It is safer to just guess. This makes it like finance, where, as pointed out earlier, it is more intelligent to flip coins than take forecasts seriously. In an appropriately titled best-selling book, *Quiet: The Power of Introverts in a World That Can't Stop Talking*, Susan Cain relates this point to finance and Professor Tetlock's work mentioned earlier:

> *A well-known study out of UC Berkeley by organizational behavior professor Philip Tetlock found that television pundits— that is, people who earn their livings by holding forth confidently on the basis of limited information—make worse predictions about political and economic trends than they would by random chance.*[604]
> —SUSAN CAIN *(b. 1968), American writer and lecturer*

The findings from various guru studies, not just the ones mentioned here, and the applicability to finance can be summarized in one sentence:

> *Our industry is full of people who got famous for being right once in a row.*[605]
> —HOWARD MARKS *(b. 1946), American investor and author*

Humans and the Blame Game

If experts err so badly and are wrong so consistently, will the experts be relieved of their duty to forecast? Probably not. When dealing with uncertainty, an expert's view is likely to be considered in the decision-making process. Consulting an expert is perceived as better than the next best alternative. What is the next best alternative?

One alternative to an expert's view is the view of a nonexpert or a fortune-teller. This might not be considered an alternative at all. Consulting an expert has a further advantage: there is someone to blame if things go wrong. Blaming someone else for one's own mistakes and/or misery is a good starting point, and it is pretty human too.

> *To err is human.*
> *To blame it on someone else is even more human.*[606]
> —BERT BACHARACH *(1898–1983), American columnist and author*

Most financial consultants are not paid for brilliance; they are paid so that someone else (pension fund, insurer, etc.) has a paper trail in place demonstrating that they are not responsible because they paid an expert. This means the blame game is partly about human nature, and partly about managing legal and liability risk.

Nowcasting, discussed in the next chapter, is a further alternative to taking forecasts seriously. Nowcasting is close to the logic behind what Russo and Schoemaker call the "objective model." A strong point could be made that decision-making in finance will become more systematic, disciplined, and oriented toward risk rather than returns. Nowcasting might be an important stepping stone on that path.

Bottom Line

There are all sorts of reasons why forecasters get it wrong: delusion, ignorance of ignorance, overconfidence, incentive to deceive, wishful thinking, unwisdom, idealism, just to name a few. It is not just that there are those who know and those who don't. It is more complicated. The value of the expert lies in the thought process, added perspective, and analysis of content, not in the forecast. In many fields of human endeavor, flipping a coin beats the expert.

Even seers in ancient times knew of the Barnum effect, i.e., make it personal, include something for everyone.

A forecast is an opinion. Our own opinions can be determined by feelings, not intellect and reason. Our own opinions can be deceptive. Wisdom is what is left after we've run out of personal opinions.

———

If investment life is indeed like a box of chocolates, and stupidity is oversupplied, then there is an alternative to forecasting. It goes by the name of nowcasting.

10

THE NOWCASTING APPROACH

It ain't over 'til it's over.
—Yogi Berra

Nowcasting is to forecasting what astronomy is to astrology. Predictions are difficult to make, especially those about the future.

The end of a trend is almost impossible to predict. Waiting 'til the fat lady sings takes patience, and trying to catch a falling knife is risky and unwise. In cases of uncertainty, economic reasoning will be of no value. It's Dornbusch's law.

Bad news can have both a positive or a negative impact on markets. When hooligans storm a government building, markets need not necessarily go down. Predicting news and returns are not the same thing. However, measuring feedback loops in real time takes a bit of randomness out of investment life.

Not fighting the feds, the governmental authorities, is the cardinal rule of investing nowadays. If you need to panic, panic early. Expect the unexpected.

Certain regimes can be determined in real time. The investors' conviction can be much higher on something that is determinable than on something that is just someone's guess. This allows for more robust decision-making. Good decision-making entails robustness of approach and which tool to use at what time.

Dornbusch's Law and Economic Reasoning

Forecasting and Astrology

The term nowcasting is a contraction of "now" and "forecasting." Nowcasting is a reasonably new word, at least in economic finance. It is either the opposite of forecasting or simply a pun on the word "forecasting." The term is used in both economics and meteorology. A forecaster tries to predict the future. (Scientists often show multiple future scenarios based on different assumptions instead of just one forecast.) Empirically, this has proven quite a challenge in many endeavors related to human action as alluded to in the previous chapters and as Mark Twain or Yogi Berra or Niels Bohr might have put it:

> It is difficult to make predictions,
> especially about the future.[607]
> —Adage

In 2015, I claimed that nowcasting is to forecasting what astronomy is to astrology. The term "nowcasting" in an economic context can be defined as follows:

> Nowcasting, def.: Nowcasting is the economic discipline of determining a trend or a trend reversal objectively in real time. Nowcasting is fact-based, focuses on the known and knowable, and therefore avoids forecasting. Nowcasting is the basis of a robust decision-making process.[608]
> —IR&M's definition of nowcasting

Nowcasting and Doubt

Forecasts are an integral part of orthodox asset allocation and are, essentially, guesswork. In other words, guessing is an integral part of how assets are allocated, and risk is taken. However, there are alternatives to guessing. So-called trend followers, for example, do not require a forecast. The same is true for many arbitrageurs.

Trend followers, for example, look at prices, not forecasts. A price is a fact, whereas a forecast is not; it is someone's opinion that might or might have merit. A price is a fact, even if the price is manipulated by central banking or high-frequency trading or seems irrational to seasoned investors because it is driven by young retail investors.

A forecast is biased because it is an opinion. A risk management process focusing on facts seems more reasonable than one that focuses on opinions. A fact is a fact, whereas an opinion isn't. (Forecasting is more entertaining than nowcasting, though, which is why business TV is full of it.) James Picerno, a fellow independent financial analyst, and author of *Nowcasting the Business Cycle*, wrote:

> Given our limited knowledge about the economy (especially when it comes to the economy's _future_ performance), the main goal is less about predicting what's going to happen vs. reducing the doubt about the current state of macro conditions. This seemingly minor bit of intelligence can provide significant value for estimating the current and near-term threat of a new recession.[609]
>
> —James Picerno (b. 1961), American financial analyst and consultant

A trend is a fact and is determinable. Momentum is one approach by which a trend can be determined. A trend is either positive or negative; up or down, essentially. This makes investment life a lot simpler. At the end of 2014, the economic trend in the US was positive, and the economic trend in emerging markets wasn't. The odds favored the former and not the latter. At the end of 2016 both were positive. At the beginning of 2018 both were negative. By mid-2020, both were positive. At one level, it's that simple. Not everything is random. Richard Russell, author of the

Dow Theory Letters, which started in 1958 and was the oldest financial newsletter written by one person, put it succinctly:

> *The primary trend is a law unto itself. It will continue until it dies of exhaustion.*[610]
> —RICHARD RUSSELL *(1924–2015), American newsletter writer*

Richard Russell's quip is of course related to Stein's law, discussed in chapter one. Investors know that the prevailing trend or phase will end eventually, but it makes no sense to try and predict the end. Trying to determine the end of a bear market is like trying to catch the proverbial falling knife in midair. That is too risky. The nowcasting approach discussed here implies one ought to wait until the knife is inert before picking it up. It's safer that way. However, the trend itself is a departure from randomness. It is determinable in real time.

Economic Reasoning and Singing Ladies
Stein's law from chapter one and Russell's remark from before were not lost on Yogi Berra:

> *It ain't over 'til it's over.*[611]
> —YOGI BERRA *(1925–2015), American baseball legend*

The ending not being before the end is even a saying.

> *It ain't over till the fat lady sings.*[612]
> —*Saying*

The saying relates to opera, that, to some, goes on far too long.

> *Opera, def.: Opera is when a guy gets stabbed in the back and, instead of bleeding, he sings.*[613]
> —ED GARDNER *(1901–63), American comic actor, writer, and director*

The two 'til-it's-over-quotes are very much applicable to financial and economic trends. Pattern recognition is as old as humanity itself, that is, depending on one's beliefs on origins, around two hundred thousand years old; or, when judged by the latest findings in Jebel Irhoud, Morocco, around three hundred thousand years old. The distinction between night and day might have been the first pattern to be recognized; it's either/or— there's enough light to hunt, or there isn't. Translate this to today: we are in a liquidity-induced, globally synchronized bull market (at the time of writing), or we aren't (potentially at the time of reading). Trying to predict the beginning of the next bear market is, of course, folly:

> Wall Street's graveyards are filled with men who were right too soon.
> —WILLIAM PETER HAMILTON (1887–1929), editor of the
> Wall Street Journal, first half of the twentieth century

Pattern recognition is an important part of learning. Price trends are just a subcategory of pattern recognition. Some of the patterns used by investors today can be traced back to rice futures trading in Osaka in the seventeenth century. Leaving aside for a moment the idea that investors can indeed be fooled by randomness, i.e., seeing patterns in random data, the "patterns" or trends might not be stable. Economist Hyman Minsky, as already mentioned in chapter five, is famous for the concept of stability not being very stable. Mark Spitznagel, the author of The Dao of Capital, a student of Nassim Taleb, producer of goat's cheese, and investor with a "libertarian bent," phrased the predictability of the first shoe to drop as follows.

> Timing crashes is impossible. If you require a forecast in order for your investment thesis to do well, then I think you're doing it wrong.[614]
> —MARK SPITZNAGEL (b. 1971), American hedge fund
> manager and author

The state of the world is not one that is seeking equilibrium, as it is often assumed in business school economics, but rather the opposite, disequilibrium in the form of instability, chaos, and destruction. Rather than rational agents forcing prices to converge to fair value and equilibrium, there are feedback loops at work that move prices away from equilibrium. If that were not complicated enough, there is often an interventionist government making things even more complicated. Hyman Minsky also reminded us of the iron law of failure from chapter two:

> Each state nurtures forces that lead to its own destruction.[615]
> —HYMAN MINSKY (1919–96), American economist

All of history testifies to the truth of this observation. Greater liquidity leads firms to borrow more than before. But higher levels of debt mean increasing vulnerability to adversity and negative shocks in an ever-changing world. For these reasons, as Minsky put it, stability leads inevitably to instability. It is also for this reason that economists can get things awfully wrong:

> The U.S. economy likely will not see a recession for years to come. We don't want one, we don't need one, and, as we have the tools to keep the current expansion going, we won't have one. This expansion will run forever.[616]
> —RUDIGER DORNBUSCH (1942–2002), German American economist, in 1998

The 1990s expansion did not last forever. Three years after the forecast, the economy was in recession. Robert Lucas, who received the Nobel Prize in Economics for rational expectations theory in 1995, summarized the applicability of economics in relation to investment decisions well:

> In cases of uncertainty, economic reasoning will be of no value.[617]
> —ROBERT LUCAS JR. (b. 1937), American economist

Lucas was referring to Knightian uncertainty, discussed in chapter four, and the market's display of "psychotic behavior." One of the funny things about finance is that bad economic news can be both good and bad for markets: bad, because corporations will earn less in the future; good, because central banks will come to the rescue and inject liquidity. The government coming to the rescue is sometimes referred to as the Greenspan put, that later became the Bernanke put, then the Yellen put, then the Powell put, etc. Investment life would be a lot simpler if bad news were just bad news.

Case in point: when Trump's hooligan mob stormed the Capitol building in January 2021, it was not obvious that the stock market would rise to a new all-time high the next day. A year earlier investors assumed that an unsmooth transition would be a negative. This means understanding what is going on and making predictions about the future are two separate activities. Furthermore, trying to predict tomorrow's news and trying to predict tomorrow's returns are separate endeavors too.

One way to think about the momentum of an economic trend and risk management is with a sailing analogy in combination with Minsky's instability idea.

> Man cannot change the direction of the wind . . . he can only adjust his sails.[618]
> —Sailing wisdom

Exogeneous Risk and Feedback Loops

Every mariner knows that a storm requires a different trim than calmer weather. The key is not to predict the next storm but to respond when circumstances start changing. Rough weather at sea does not change from one minute to the next normally. The same is true for a change of the economic winds normally. There is time to trim the sails normally. "Normally" means, for example, when there is no pandemic. In 2020, the recession came extraordinarily fast, with the economic expansion having peaked around January 2018. A microscopically small virus was the butterfly wing flap that caused the tornado.

There are exceptions to nearly all rules. If the Vogons, an alien race who were considered by Douglas Adams as having the third-worst poetry in the universe, were to attack and vaporize Earth, the nowcaster would look foolish too. This means pattern recognition and nowcasting are helpful when dealing with endogenous risk, that is, risk emanating from the business or credit cycle or any financial market disturbance. However, it is of no value when dealing with exogeneous risk, that is, risk emanating from an external source, say an earthquake that triggers a tsunami that causes a nuclear powerplant catastrophe. (Vogons—a term my spell-checker wanted to change into quite the opposite, i.e., "vegans"—is here used as a proxy for exogeneous risk.)

The practical application of the adjust-his-sails sailing wisdom, and nowcasting in finance, is to become more conservative or hedged when things start to change for the worse. The funny thing is that if everyone "adjusts their sails" at the same time, the whole thing becomes a self-fulfilling prophecy, as the "sail adjusting" has a negative impact on prices, which then leads to more "sail adjusting." A negative feedback loop ensues. This is where the sailing analogy breaks down: the storm at sea is independent of any sail adjusting. The causality only works one way. That is not the case in financial markets.

> *The participants' views influence but do not determine the course of events, and the course of events influences but does not determine the participants' views. The influence is continuous and circular; that is what turns it into a feedback loop.*[619]
> —GEORGE SOROS *(b. 1930), Hungarian-born American hedge fund manager*

Changing circumstances *can* be measured and assessed at all times, though, resulting in decision-making becoming more robust. The practical relevance to Minsky's instability hypothesis is that both at sea and in economics, the current calm is nothing other than the buildup of the next storm. Professor Dornbusch, who held a popular weekly research breakfast and demanded that his students arrive at eight o'clock sharp, put it very well. This is referred to as Dornbusch's law:

> *In economics, things take longer to happen than you think they will, and then they happen faster than you thought they could.*[620]
> —RUDIGER DORNBUSCH *(1942–2002), German American economist*

The Tape and the Feds

One aspect of an economic momentum approach is that it can fail with political intervention. Monetary policy has "gained" as a market force under Greenspan and has become more important ever since. Various central banks are battling a currency war; a "race to the bottom," as some pundits put it.

A central bank is not inherently independent but is a part of the administration; it is a political authority, a governmental institution. (Central banks are independent in the sense that if, for example, they run out of paper clips, they can restock without involving the legislature apparatus.) The applicable wisdom to all this, in a nutshell, is from Martin Zweig:

> Don't fight the Fed.[621]
> —MARTIN ZWEIG (1942–2013), American investor

This, of course, also means you should not go against any other authority. Dennis Gartman likes to point out regularly that "the authorities have bigger margin accounts than you and me." This means, whatever it is they are doing, they can do it for a long while.

Draghi's "whatever it takes" speech in 2012 was a "don't fight the Fed" moment. The trend reversal of falling bond prices of the Club Med states, Italy and Spain mainly, was "measurable" in real time. Furthermore, if there was no other force causing yet another trend reversal, the nowcasting approach allowed the investor to have a high conviction in the direction of the market. (Long risky assets, in the period after Draghi's "whatever it takes" speech.)

Martin Zweig, who at one stage had the most expensive residence in the United States, atop The Pierre on Fifth Avenue in Manhattan, and had the Harley Davidson Hydra-Glide motorcycle ridden by Peter Fonda in *Easy Rider* bolted to the floor in the game room of his home in Connecticut, even goes as far as calling this the cardinal rule of investment decision-making:

> To me, the "tape" is the final arbiter of any investment decision.
> I have a cardinal rule: Never fight the tape![622]
> —MARTIN ZWEIG

(With "tape" he means paying attention to prices. Up until the 1960s, stock prices were transmitted over telegraph lines on ticker tape that included a ticker symbol, price, and volume.) Ned Davis, a financial researcher and business founder who refers to himself as a market historian, referring to Martin Zweig, mentions his first two rules out of nine: rule number one, don't fight the tape, and rule number two, don't fight the Fed.[623]

Luck and Skill

Success and Striking Oil

Next to the cardinal rules of not wanting to fight the Feds or the tapes, there is also a thing called the fundamental law of active management.[624] The fundamental law of active management requires an edge, i.e., some knowledge. It need not be much:

> As an investor, as long as you understand something better than others, you have an edge.[625]
> —GEORGE SOROS (b. 1930), philanthropist and Karl Popper
>   disciple

Once you have an edge and know you have an edge and are not delusional about having an edge, you are set to go. The only thing missing is risk management:

> Make sure you have an edge. Know what your edge is. And have rigid risk control rules.[626]
> —MONROE TROUT (b. 1962), American hedge fund manager

The law of active management suggests that outperformance is a function of two elements: skill and opportunity. If one of the two elements is zero, there is no outperformance; other than the outperformance attributed to luck. Note that luck is a main attribute to many a fortune. As the sixty-seventh richest American who ever lived, based on his wealth as a percentage of the gross national product in 1996, put it:

> Formula for success: rise early, work hard, strike oil.
> —J. PAUL GETTY (1892–1986), American industrialist

Late risers do not strike oil:

> *Inspiration is a guest that does not willingly visit the lazy.*[627]
> —PYOTR ILYICH TCHAIKOVSKY *(1840–93), Russian composer*

> *If you wait for inspiration to write,*
> *you're not a writer, you're a waiter.*[628]
> —DAN POYNTER *(1938–2015), American author and*
> *parachute designer*

That said, there is more than just one formula for success, and the idea of getting up early is disputable:

> *Progress doesn't come from early risers—progress is made by lazy*
> *men looking for easier ways to do things.*[629]
> —ROBERT A. HEINLEIN *(1907–88), American science fiction*
> *author*

Furthermore, rising early bears risks. There is a second mover advantage, as the first mover bears the cost and risk of innovation. Elon Musk did not invent rockets. He just engineers and runs them more efficiently than the government.

> *The early bird may get the worm,*
> *but the second mouse gets the cheese.*[630]
> —*Saying*

Hard Work and Luck

Getty's strike-oil quotation goes well with the law of active management; Heinlein's lazy-man quotation less so. Rising early and working hard comes before getting lucky. This means the striking oil bit, the luck, is not just a function of chance, but effort too. As Thomas Jefferson never said but could have:

> *The harder I work,*
> *the luckier I get.*[631]
> —*Old Amish saying*

A movie star from *Baywatch*, a 1990s swimsuit-advertising TV series, said more or less the same thing:

> *Natural beauty takes at least two hours in front of a mirror.*[632]
> —PAMELA ANDERSON *(b. 1967), Canadian-born American
> actress*

Success almost always requires an effort, even if the success looks random or easily achieved:

> *It takes twenty years to make an overnight success.*[633]
> —EDDIE CANTOR *(1892–1964), American comedian and
> singer*

(The last quotation is what I tell my kids, to which they reply that it didn't take Justin Bieber twenty years.) Eddie Cantor's wit was translated into financial parlance:

> *It is often a long road to quick profits.*[634]
> —HUMPHREY B. NEILL *(1891–1977), author of* The Art of
> Contrary Thinking

The fundamental law of active management is the basis for charging an active fee in asset management:

> *If you're good at something, never do it for free.*[635]
> —THE JOKER, *Batman's nemesis*

Having an edge means having a competitive advantage, i.e., Pamela Anderson's "natural beauty" or Cantor's "twenty years." You still need to put in the effort though. The following is a good summary on the topic, implying that success is a function of both luck as well as action and work:

> *There is indeed an element of luck, and no, there isn't. The pre-
> pared mind sooner or later finds something important and does
> it. So yes, it is luck. The particular thing you do is luck, but that
> you do something is not.*[636]
> —RICHARD HAMMING *(1915–98), American mathematician*

Having a competitive advantage means one can add value by doing something better, faster, or cheaper. Higher enumeration makes sense, as the risk capitalist and his agent share the economics. In finance, Jack Welch's advice might or might not be followed. The following is rule number six from his six rules for successful leadership:

> *If you don't have a competitive advantage, don't compete.*[637]
> —JACK WELCH *(1935–2020), American business executive*

Related to the law of active management, the following might apply:

> *Half the world is composed of idiots,*
> *the other half of people clever enough to take indecent advantage*
> *of them.*[638]
> —WALTER KERR *(1913–96), American writer and theatre critic*

This circles back to Mark Twain's let-us-be-thankful quip in chapter one.

Preparation and Opportunity

A competitive advantage is the economic foundation and logic behind giving a skilled investment manager more flexibility in his area of expertise. The fundamental law of active management in its original form states that the productivity of an active manager is a function of two factors: skill and the opportunity set, i.e., the number of independent decisions a manager can make per, say, year. The "law" was coined by Richard C. Grinold, a physicist-turned-director for risk research who, among other things, helped to wire up the Harvard-MIT Cambridge Electron Accelerator and served as the navigator of the USS *Gainard (*DD-706).

Colloquially, the law of active management means the better you are at striking oil, and the more often you do it, the "luckier" you get. Luck not being random, but a function of opportunity and skill is nothing new, as one actor put it in 1987:

> *I say luck is when an opportunity comes along, and you're prepared for it.*[639]
> —DENZEL WASHINGTON *(b. 1954), American actor*

This is consistent with Louis Pasteur's wisdom from chapter two. The idea of linking success and the opportunity set with getting up early is old:

> Be ready when opportunity comes. Luck is the time when prepa-
> ration and opportunity meet.
> —Roy D. Chaplin Jr. *(1915–2001), American automobile*
> *industry executive*

Well, the idea is very old:

> Luck is what happens when preparation meets opportunity.[640]
> —Seneca the Younger *(ca. 4 bc–ad 65), Roman*
> *philosopher and statesman*

We can trace this idea even further back:

> Chance fights ever on the side of the prudent.[641]
> —Euripides *(ca. 480–406 bc), Greek tragedian*

Skill and Flopping Fish

The search for skill is not enough. Some applied wisdom is required too. This is how Mrs. Savant put it, Mrs. Savant having the highest recorded IQ according to Guinness World Records.

> Skill is successfully walking a tightrope strung between the twin
> towers of the World Trade Center. Intelligence is not trying.[642]
> —Marilyn vos Savant *(b. 1946), American magazine*
> *columnist and author*

It requires intelligence, or in finance parlance, street-smartness to spot the point when either the skill is not applicable anymore or the opportunity set has changed to the risk-takers' disadvantage. One's IQ, fortunately, need not be stratospheric though:

> To invest successfully over a lifetime does not require a strato-
> spheric IQ, unusual business insight, or inside informa-
> tion. What's needed is a sound intellectual framework for

*decisions and the ability to keep emotions from corroding that
framework.*[643]
—WARREN BUFFETT *(b. 1930), American investor and
   businessman*

A stratospheric IQ might even be a negative. This is great news: if you
are not doing well financially, it is because you are too smart:

> *In terms of IQ, probably the best investors fall somewhere above
> the bottom ten percent but also below the top three percent. The
> true geniuses, it seems to me, get too enamored of theoretical
> cogitations and are forever betrayed by the actual behavior of
> stocks, which is more simple minded than they can imagine.*[644]
> —PETER LYNCH *(b. 1944), American investment manager*

Skill is not enough. As circumstances change, the skill that puts the
rubber on the tarmac needs to adapt. It is best to describe to the concept
of life-long learning.

One ought not to forget that adaptability, and therefore change is the
key tool of survival. Maladaptive is the opposite. In a 2004 white paper
called "The Adaptive Market Hypothesis," probably the second most
important scholarly paper I have read over the past thirty-plus years,
Andrew Lo, a professor of finance at MIT, receiver of the Annual CAIA
Leadership Award for Excellence in Alternative Investment Education in
2013, and avid Chinese cook, with scallion pancakes being his signature
dish, put maladaptation as follows:

> *The flopping of a fish on dry land may seem strange and unpro-
> ductive, but underwater, the same motions are capable of pro-
> pelling the fish away from its predators.*[645]
> —ANDREW LO *(b. 1960), American economist and chairman
>   of AlphaSimplex Group*

Things change. In the 1960s, equities were an alternative investment
category for institutional investors. They were perceived as too speculative when compared to bonds. In the 1990s, it was hedge funds that

were perceived as too speculative. Today it is cryptocurrencies that are perceived as too speculative.

Furthermore, markets become more efficient over time as "the market" learns and adapts. In other words, markets become "aware" of how pioneers and first movers exploit market inefficiencies. While skill may remain constant, the reward from applying the skill falls over time. Therefore, one needs to adapt the skill to changing market circumstances, i.e., one needs to evolve to survive. One ought to be a continuous-learning machine:

> *The skill that got Berkshire through one decade would not have*
> *sufficed to get it through the next decade with comparable levels*
> *of achievement. Warren Buffett had to be a continuous-learning*
> *machine.*[646]
> —CHARLES T. MUNGER *(b. 1924), American investor and vice*
>   *chairman of Berkshire Hathaway*

Inertia and Snake Food

Inertia can be bad. The belief and confidence in a purely mechanical, nonadaptive way to generate returns and control risk are potentially disastrous, as circumstances always change (initial opportunity changing due to increased attention, feedback loops, etc.). Potentially, raw intelligence without some form of local or specialist market-savvy is probably as bad as the opposite. In the pursuit of sustainable wealth preservation, as well as survival probability, a balance between the two—intellectual property and adaptability—is best. Both Benjamin Franklin and the founder of *Forbes* magazine knew this:

> *If you don't drive your business,*
> *you will be driven out of business.*[647]
> —B. C. FORBES *(1880–1954), Scottish-born American*
>   *financial journalist and author*

Inertia *can* be bad, but ignorance *is* almost always bad. Imagine you are a frog. Family and friends are skipping about around the pond; all is jolly. Then, with little warning, a clan of snakes enters your familiar and perceived-safe habitat. Doing nothing might be an option. If, for example, the snakes have been Ivy League–educated, they most likely are playful and vegan.

However, if not; if the snakes' kin are more serious, inertia is not a wise option. If you have not been infected by the campus liberal political correctness craze, skepticism toward the snakes expanding territorially might be warranted. One real-world working assumption would be that the snakes need to eat. It is the Gingerbread Man who is jolly, playful, and vegan, but it is the fox who wins the day.

> *For most of human history, it made good adaptive sense to be*
> *fearful and emphasize the negative; any mistake could be fatal.*[648]
> —JOOST SWARTE *(b. 1947), Dutch cartoonist, architect, and*
>   *graphic designer*

Central planners—central planning being one of the main characteristics of campus liberalism—might be able to reduce risk in the frog habitat intermittently, say by keeping interest rates low for a long time. However, the blessings will not last forever, as Bambi's mother knew:

> *It seems long, but it won't last forever.*[649]
> —*Bambi's mother*

Bambi's mother understood Stein's law, discussed in chapter one of this book. What cannot go on forever, won't. Furthermore, financial markets are *carnivorous*, not *vegan*. The penalties for inertia when circumstances change can be high. Responding to change and adapting to regime shifts is a survival measure.

> *I measure what's going on, and I adapt to it. I try to get my ego*
> *out of the way. The market is smarter than I am, so I bend.*[650]
> —MARTIN ZWEIG *(1942–2013), American investor*

The Gingerbread Man thought he had outfoxed the fox. He hadn't. He had a reality deficit and should have gotten his ego out of the way. He did not adapt and therefore became fox food. The irresponsive (and irresponsible) frog from earlier, who is confronted with an imperialist and most likely nonvegan snake entering his habitat, faces becoming snake food:

> *[T]here is no sin punished more implacably by nature than the*
> *sin of resistance to change.*[651]
> —ANNE MORROW LINDBERGH *(1906–2001), American*
>   *author*

Stephen Hawking put it best:

> *Intelligence is the ability to adapt to change.*[652]
> —STEPHEN HAWKING *(1942–2018), English theoretical*
>   *physicist, cosmologist, and author*

Risk and Pax Americana

The weight of the US stock market in the MSCI World Index was 65 percent in June 2020. A lot of thinking in finance is American. The United States of America is the reigning superpower; an economic powerhouse, of which its capital markets are an important part. This creates an American bias in almost anything, including research and culture. (Two thousand years ago, a lot of thinking on anything was Roman. The barbarians in the north had other things to do then.)

One aspect of this bias is related to buying the market or just buying an index fund for the long term and being done with it. In America, it has worked for so long. It was a no-brainer; with the benefit of hindsight, that is. Pax Americana has provided world peace over the past seventy years. The number of violent deaths and the forceful destruction of property has been declining gradually since World War II. (During WWII around twenty-three thousand people were killed in armed conflicts per day. Today around four hundred and sixty people are killed per day. If there had not been a pandemic, that number would have looked quite peaceful by comparison. COVID-19 took an average of six thousand four hundred and fifty lives per day from April to December 2020.[653])

Just buying the stock market is a powerful argument. Companies are the wealth creators of society. They create the wealth that individuals spend on rent and food and that governments spend on almost everything else. So, it is unsurprising that, over the long run, owning bits of the wealth creators is likely to be a good investment.

An American saver who started putting say $10,000 into the stock market at the beginning of every year starting in 1950, i.e., at the beginning of "peace and tranquility," and spent the dividends on yachts, rather than reinvesting in the market, would have compounded at a rate of 5.2 percent per year. This is far superior to compounding nominally at 0.0 percent from putting it under the proverbial mattress. This means an annual savings amount of $10,000 resulted in a pot of $25.3 million at the end of 2020. The mattress strategy would have resulted in the pot being $710,000 after the seventy-one-year period, before inflation is considered. A Japanese investor who did the same thing in his local market would have compounded his capital at a rate of 3.8 percent per year.[654]

Changing the starting point from January 1950 to January 1990 results in the US saver compounding at 4.7 percent and the Japanese saver compounding at 1.1 percent to 2020, thus both beating the mattress. However, the Japanese saver would have been ahead of the mattress only in twelve out of thirty-one years, i.e., at the end of 1999, 2005–7, and 2013–20. A Greek investor doing the same in the local stock market would have compounded capital at -1.0 percent over the thirty-year period.

This means one ought not to generalize US stock market research for the whole world. It is too dangerous. By the end of 2020, the S&P 500 Index had a similar status as the Nikkei 225 Index had by the end of 1989.

Expectations and Surprises
This all means if your local market does not suffer from a total collapse due to, for example, a devastating war, regime-shift induced nationalization, or a monetary policy experiment going wrong, then yes, equities work in the long-term. If not, not.

People from Argentina, Venezuela, Zimbabwe, Egypt, and other people who saw their system fail, or Jewish people who were living in Europe a couple of decades ago, might beg to differ though. They might find the historical returns of the S&P 500 Index mentioned before too simplistic. They know better. A turkey that is still a turkey, rather than a past meal, is lucky. Science writer Mark Buchanan, writing not on January 7, 2021, but in the year 2000, recommends expecting the unexpected:

> *[W]e should learn to expect the unexpected. We live now in a time that is relatively peaceful. This relative calm may endure for another century, or we may see another world war in five years—no one can really say. The United States as a nation may survive for another five hundred years, or crumble in thirty.*[655]
> —MARK BUCHANAN *(b. 1961), American physicist and author*

This last quotation, self-serving as it might be in my case, suggests both nowcasting, i.e., nonguessing the future, as well as active risk management. On Mark Buchanan's point: learning to expect the unexpected is a good attitude and has broader applicability, family planning for example:

> *Expect the unexpected.*[656]
> —BORIS BECKER *(b. 1967), German tennis player*

Sometimes something as trivial as a night out at a Japanese celebrity chef in London can have a life-changing afterplay.

Geeks and Models

Expert Statistics and Risky Speculation

Historical returns are no guarantee of future performance, as nearly any disclaimer in finance states. Even if the math behind a statistical analysis can look complicated, it is still just rearranging the past. This is how one non-quant appealed for skepticism and caution:

> *Investors should be skeptical of history-based models. Constructed by a nerdy-sounding priesthood using esoteric terms such as beta, gamma, sigma and the like, these models tend to look impressive. Too often, though, investors forget to examine the assumptions behind the symbols. Our advice: Beware of geeks bearing formulas.*[657]
> —WARREN BUFFETT *(b. 1930), American businessman and value investor*

The finance literature is quite extensive as to what constitutes speculation and investment or trading versus investing. In this book I do not focus on this distinction because the lines are blurred. Every human action is speculative:

> *Every action refers to an unknown future. It is in this sense always a risky speculation.*[658]
> —LUDWIG VON MISES *(1881–1973), Austrian School economist*

Models and Madness

I strongly believe in the fool-with-a-tool-is-still-a-fool idea mentioned in chapter four on the human uncertainty principle. However, I also believe that the following statement applies well to the field of finance. It may be the bottom line on quantitative analysis and econometric modeling.

> *Essentially, all models are wrong, but some are useful.*[659]
> —GEORGE BOX *(1919–2013), English statistician*

What makes things complicated is that not only does every action alter the future, and therefore the future alters further action; the action causes a reaction too. If I forget to put out the garbage on Friday morning, there are consequences—an opposite reaction, albeit my punishment being beyond the scope of this book. So, not only do actions prompt a response, but inaction, too, prompts a response, making human affairs ultimately more complex than the gravitational pull of heavenly bodies or, for example, a fly "landing" on the ceiling. (The fly approaches the ceiling flying normally, extends its four legs above its head and grabs the ceiling with its front feet, then uses its momentum to swing the rest of the body until the legs are attached to the ceiling. Flies have gooey feet, which keep them there.)

Speaking of heavenly bodies, Sir Isaac Newton—to some, the most influential scientist in history—is said to have lost a lot of money during the South Sea Bubble episode. Newton is often quoted as having said the following regarding the difference between simple natural science and complex human affairs:

*I can calculate the motions of the heavenly bodies, but not the
madness of people.*[660]
—ISAAC NEWTON *(1642–1727), English mathematician,
astronomer, and physicist*

Some of the problems in today's risk management environment are
from relying on historical data and an underappreciation of the reflexive
nature of human affairs. Many models involve forecasting future economic developments based on what has happened in the past. Naturally,
these forecasts consider past trends, volatilities, spikes, and correlations,
but crucially they implicitly assume that the future will resemble the past
in one form or another. History is assumed to rhyme, as mentioned in
chapter six.

The problem with this is that the output of the analysis only tells us
something about risk under "normal" market conditions. The models
often fail when fundamental shifts in the economy occur, such as the out-
break of a financial crisis, a war, or a pandemic. The belief in quantitative
models, and the attitude that can come with it, as well as the hindsight
bias, was well captured by Merton Miller—the prominent Chicago School
economist, who was awarded the Nobel Memorial Prize in Economics
in 1990, a prize he shared with Harry Markowitz and William Sharpe for
their combined efforts on the Modigliani-Miller theorem—in relation to
the demise of Long-Term Capital Management (LTCM), one of the most
spectacular failures in finance.

*In a strict sense, there wasn't any risk—if the world had behaved
as it did in the past.*[661]
—MERTON MILLER *(1923–2000), American economist and
Nobel laureate*

In distressed market conditions, the measured risk under normal market conditions can prove to be useless. Complicating matters are nonlin-
earities. The past might be smooth in the sense that it is nothing else than
the slow approach toward a tipping point, somewhat akin to an inflating
balloon or the slow process of a storm gathering or the patient building
of a house of cards. If the data does not contain the bang, the prick of the

pin, the analysis is pretty much useless, even when Greek letters are used. This was put very well by one risk management practitioner in 1994; i.e., prior to the demise of LTCM and Lehman Brothers:

> When O'Connor [a Chicago-based options trading boutique] set up in London at Big Bang [Thatcher induced deregulation of financial markets in 1986], I built an option risk control system incorporating all the Greek letters—deltas, gammas, vegas, thetas and even some higher order ones as well (the delta of the gamma and the gamma of the vega). And I'll tell you that during the crash it was about as useful as a US theme park on the outskirts of Paris.[662]
> —ROBERT GUMERLOCK (b. 1953), American risk manager

A proverb states that "there is safety in numbers." It's wrong, and there isn't. James Thurber, the writer behind *The Secret Life of Walter Mitty*, which was made into a 2013 film starring Ben Stiller, suggests a pragmatic attitude toward econometric models, and everything else:

> There is no safety in numbers, or in anything else.[663]
> —JAMES THURBER (1894–1961), American cartoonist, author, humorist, journalist, and playwright

Regime Shifts and the Borg

American professor Robert Engle was awarded the 2003 Nobel Memorial Prize in Economic Sciences mainly for his research on ARCH (autoregressive conditional heteroscedasticity). In a nutshell, the key concept is that many financial assets do not move randomly from a regime of low volatility to a regime of high volatility. Rather, a low-volatility environment begets more low volatility, and high volatility begets more high volatility. In other words, once a storm starts to build, it will not just disappear in a puff of thin air. More likely, it will build up, reach its climax, and then revert to the previous state. There is no random flipping from one regime to the next. A former chairman of Merrill Lynch Asset Management put it well:

Most coming events cast their shadows before, and it is on this
that intelligent speculation must be based.[664]
—ARTHUR ZEIKEL *(b. 1932), American businessman and*
   adjunct professor of finance

It is for this reason I occasionally speak about extraterrestrials. An attack by the Borg, an equality-worshipping extraterrestrial life-form, would be quite a surprise. However, below-average equity returns over ten years after the stock market traded at a P/E ratio more than thirty times isn't. The extreme underperformance of Eurozone equities over the past ten to twenty years is not just a random fluke; they have no information technology in their equity indices to speak of and have serious economic troubles there, and these troubles are identifiable in real time. Europe in a nutshell:

> *Now, in Europe 20 years ago, Europe had a simple choice. It was*
> *facing this. And the simple choice was do we cut back our enti-*
> *tlement spending, or do we sacrifice our armies? And Europe, by*
> *and large, made the political choice of let's sacrifice our armies,*
> *cut back on military spending dramatically, keep our entitlement*
> *spending. I'm not putting a value judgment on it. It's a policy*
> *choice.*[665]
> —LOUIS-VINCENT GAVE *(b. 1974), cofounder of Gavekal*
>   *Research*

Certain regimes can be determined in real time. Structural deficits, political buffoonery, an unfolding recession, or a market panic are determinable. This is, of course, quite different from trying to forecast these things. Whether monetary policy is in an easing or tightening mode is also determinable in real time. No guessing is required. The investors' conviction can be much higher on something that is determinable than on something that is just someone's guess. This allows for more robust decision-making.

> *Intelligent decision making entails knowing what tool to use for*
> *what problem. Intelligence is not an abstract number such as*

an IQ, but similar to a carpenter's tacit knowledge about using
appropriate tools.[666]
—GERD GIGERENZER *(b. 1947), German psychologist*

The concepts of business cycles and overvaluation in asset classes are important for investors: it means there are times or states or regimes when financial conservatism is more important or more acute, and there are periods when "all is well" and hedging market risk not a top priority. The nowcaster measures both the continuation of a regime as well as the regime shift; no guessing is required. When the fat lady starts singing, it is time to fasten your seat belts.

The exception to the rule is a sudden exogenous shock like 9/11 or the Tōhoku earthquake and tsunami. Accidents and shocks happen. However, much geopolitical risk is "trending." It starts with tensions and slowly builds up, culminates at one stage, and then levels off. The two world wars are examples of this. The first World War did not just randomly occur when Gavrilo Princip came out of a sandwich shop in Sarajevo and shot Archduke Franz Ferdinand.

There were tensions beforehand. The trivial event, the assassination of Ferdinand and his wife, in this case, was not predictable. The tensions, however, were determinable. The assassination was the butterfly's wing flap, WWI was the tornado, i.e., the falling of dominos initially triggered by one "tiny whiff of air":

> [T]he specific manner by which prices collapsed is not the most important problem: a crash occurs because the market has entered an unstable phase and any small disturbance or process may have triggered the instability. Think of a ruler held up vertically on your finger: this very unstable position will lead eventually to its collapse, as a result of a small (or an absence of adequate) motion of your hand or due to any tiny whiff of air. The collapse is fundamentally due to the unstable position, the instantaneous cause of the collapse is secondary.[667]
> —DIDIER SORNETTE *(b. 1957), French geophysicist and*
>   *author*

Mr. Sornette, a Sinophile who has chopsticks and a knife as perma carry-ons, and thinks the fork is a rigid and barbarian utensil, very inconvenient for the delicate handling of food, makes the important point that it is the long (self-organizing) process and the resultant instability that are the causes of a crash. The causes of a crash or collapse, therefore, are endogenous, the systemic instability being the true cause. The prick of a pin or the butterfly wing flap or that "tiny whiff of air" are often exogenous disturbances that are only triggering factors.

Dirty Harry and Systemic Risk
With interest rates at five-thousand-year lows, government debts, political polarization, threats of cyber warfare, the spread of misinformation rising, and China expanding its power base, it is fair to say that currently there is "tension," partially related to geopolitics and partially related to too much debt and the way the different authorities are handling the situation.

Over the past ten years it has become apparent that it is not only exogenous shocks that matter; a lot of the current uncertainty is endogenous. It is not related to an Austrian amateur painter running amok in Europe but to cracks, friction, and tension within the financial system itself that are the cause for the current uncertainty and difficult investment environment. Some of the uncertainty emanates from within. Warren Buffett suggests not spending too much time trying to forecast panics and quotes Meg McConnell, a senior vice president and head of the Applied Critical Thinking Function in the executive office of the Federal Reserve Bank of New York, in this regard:

> We spend a lot of time looking for systemic risk; in truth, however, it tends to find us.[668]
> —MARGARET M. McCONNELL *(b. 1950), Federal Reserve Bank of New York*

Panics are important to the astute investor. The forecasting track record of nearly everyone being as poor as it is, market stress needs to be identified in real time, i.e., "nowcasted."

During such scary periods, you should never forget two things: First, widespread fear is your friend as an investor, because it serves up bargain purchases. Second, personal fear is your enemy.[669]
—WARREN BUFFETT *(b. 1930), American investor and businessman*

The Warren Buffett quotation is particularly good advice if you're Warren Buffett. Most investors are not Warren Buffett though. Fear being one's friend is true, of course, but applying it in practice is much easier said than done. Not being Warren Buffett is not so bad. Thinking one is Warren Buffett and not knowing that one is not is much worse. Not only does one need to know whether one is lucky, but one ought to know one's limitations too:

A man's got to know his limitations.[670]
—DIRTY HARRY CALLAHAN, *gun-toting, rulebook-ignoring cop immortalized by Clint Eastwood*

Dirty Harry's wisdom, like many quotations in this book, uttered at a time prior to the English language being gender-neutralized, is of course very much related to that of Confucius, and John Kenneth Galbraith discussed in chapter eight, namely that one ought to know what one does not know. People who do not know what they do not know do not need risk management. As Mr. Buffett put it in chapter four, risk is not knowing what you are doing.

Risk management is for investors who do not delude themselves as to knowing the future and instead assess the future in a probabilistic fashion. Applying this to the current situation, it means history might rhyme or might not. Boris Becker and Oscar Wilde are on the same page:

To expect the unexpected shows a thoroughly modern intellect.[671]
⁻OSCAR WILDE *(1854–1900), Irish author*

Callahan's law,* i.e., knowing one's limitations, often comes from experience, as in the "learning-by-doing" adage. Ken Griffin, the founder

---

*   I just made that up.

of Citadel, a hedge fund whose risk intermediation activities at times resembled that of an investment bank, said pretty much the same thing as Mr. Callahan:

> Don't act like a bank, unless you are a bank . . . That was a really
> big lesson learned from 2008.[672]
> —KEN GRIFFIN (b. 1968), American hedge fund manager

In relation to scary periods, Jim Rogers, who predicted in 2012 huge shifts in American society with brokers ending up driving taxis and farmers Lamborghinis, agrees with Buffett:

> Just about every time you go against panic, you will be right if
> you can stick it out.[673]
> —JIM ROGERS (b. 1942), American investor

Intergalactic travelers knew this all along, as was written with large, friendly letters in the *Hitchhiker's Guide to the Galaxy* in relation to a device that looked insanely complicated to operate:

> Don't panic![674]
> —DOUGLAS ADAMS (1952–2001), English author, essayist,
>   humorist, satirist, and dramatist

The risk management angle was put well by André Kostolany, who often distinguished between investors with steady hands or shaky hands. Kostolany, a holder of France's Legion of Honor, the highest French order of merit, both military and civil, recommended having steady hands, rather than shaky ones. The shaky hands panic and sell at the worst possible time; together with nearly everyone else.

> Always be fearful, never panic!
> —ANDRÉ KOSTOLANY (1908–99), Hungarian speculator and
>   author

Not panicking is easier said than done. I believe it is fair to say that nearly all battle-tested investors will agree this last sentence to be true. Looking at a chart from 2008–9 and reflecting as to when it would have been a good idea to buy and when to sell is quite different from having lived through the period while managing risk. Heavily regulated institutional investors had capital requirements and liquidity provisions that "dictated" them to panic. Fortunately, there are indeed alternatives to not panicking:

> *If you're going to panic, panic early.*
> —*Wall Street adage*

Bottom Line

Nowcasting is the economic discipline of determining a trend or a trend reversal objectively in real time. Nowcasting is fact-based, focuses on the known and knowable, and therefore avoids forecasting. Nowcasting is the basis of a robust decision-making process.

The law of active management implies one ought to have an edge and the freedom to exploit it. Hard work and luck play a part. Natural beauty takes an effort. A stratospheric IQ is not required but being prepared helps. There are many surprises. Expect the unexpected.

Not everything is entirely random. Winds cannot be changed, but sails can be adjusted. There is no safety in numbers or anything else. Tensions build, and empires rise and fall. While the whiff of wind that causes a chain reaction cannot be predicted, the stability or instability of a house of cards can be assessed and measured more or less objectively. Wait for the fat lady to sing. Wall Street's graveyards are filled with investors who were right too soon.

CLOSING REMARKS

The art is not in making money;
but in keeping it.
—Proverb

In a chapter titled "Stupidity Spreading Like Wildfire," David Robson in *The Intelligence Trap* almost provides a summary of *Applied Wisdom*:

> *Ultimately, the secrets of wise decision making of the organization are very similar to the secrets of wise decision making for the intelligent individual. Whether you are a forensic scientist, doctor, student, teacher, financier or aeronautical engineer, it pays to humbly recognise your limits and the possibility of failure, take account of ambiguity and uncertainty, remain curious and open to new information, recognize the potential to grow from errors, and actively question everything.*[675]
> —DAVID ROBSON *(b. 1985), British science journalist*

William Somerset Maugham, reputedly the highest-paid author during the 1930s, once said that "there are three rules for writing a novel. Unfortunately, nobody knows what they are." This is most likely applicable to finance and the management of risk. Of course, there is applied wisdom and cardinal rules in finance. But it is much easier to write about it than it is to implement it. It's like parenting. You can read as many books as you want; you're still not prepared for the real thing. It's all learning by doing.

Mishaps and folly are unavoidable. Applying wisdom and avoiding folly is much easier said than done.

This book contains around seven hundred quotations, many of which relate to applied wisdom or applied unwisdom in one form or another. I have been assuming that Sophocles, a contemporary to Euripides from chapter five and chapter ten, who was the most awarded writer in the dramatic competitions of ancient Athens and lived into his nineties, was on to something:

> *A short saying oft contains much wisdom.*[676]
> —SOPHOCLES *(ca. 497–406* BC*), Greek tragedian*

Marie von Ebner-Eschenbach most certainly would have agreed with Sophocles.

> *An aphorism is the last link in a long chain of thought.*[677]
> —MARIE VON EBNER-ESCHENBACH *(1830–1916), Austrian*
> *writer*

This book is not really about wisdom; it's about risk management. Subscribing to the idea of lifelong learning is fun, potentially smart, and most likely rewarding, but it is not wisdom. Investors are not wise. Wisdom is not a state; it is a desirable path at best.

Your author is not wise. There is too much empirical evidence suggesting otherwise. Given that I want this book also to be accessible to a younger audience, I will omit the vocabulary used by my wife after failing in one of my multiple household chores. Suffice to say, the word "wise" does not come up very often. If I wanted to summarize this book in one sentence, it would be: "Avoid folly." But then again, avoiding folly is applying wisdom.

One thing I am quite certain about: my foolish behavior is not unique. I am not the only investor making mistakes. I am not even the only investor with thirty-plus years of experience still making mistakes. It comes with the territory. The learning-by-doing dictum applies. As F. A. Hayek put it in relation to humanity's foolish behavior in the first half of the twentieth century:

We shall not grow wiser before we learn much that we have done
was very foolish.[678]
—F. A. HAYEK *(1899–1992), Austrian economist*

If occasional foolishness is unavoidable, what is one to do? Learn. Learning and surviving failure have upside optionality. Avoid repeated foolishness. Avoid being Chávez. Make fun of him. If you do, at least you have history on your side. The Obama Doctrine applies. Avoiding serial folly is achievable by all investors.

Below I repeat some of my favorite quotations for convenience and in no particular order. (Some of the quotations below might come across as self-serving, I need to admit, as I offer risk management research services to professional investors.)

> ROTHSCHILD: *Buy when the cannons are thundering, and sell when the violins are playing.*

Buy low and sell high is really good advice. The funny thing is that nearly everyone knows this. It is still easier said than done.

> JOHN MAYNARD KEYNES: *When circumstances change, I change my mind—what do you do?*

Circumstances always change. A pragmatic definition of risk is "exposure to change." The Keynes quote captures all the ideas related to adapting to a changing environment, which are essential to survival and prosperity. The difficulty here is that you need to spot the change early.

> WARREN BUFFETT: *Risk comes from not knowing what you're doing.*

Lack of knowledge is only one source of risk. Ignorance, ignorance of ignorance, single-mindedness, delusion, dogma, and hubris also result in a real-world deficit and are just as dangerous.

ANDRÉ GIDE: *Believe those who are seeking the truth; doubt those who find it.*

Fake news, BS, and nonsense are omnipresent. The future is uncertain. Remember the empirical evidence of the intelligence of a forecast being inversely related to the noise of the forecaster. A good baloney-sensing system is quite helpful in finance and elsewhere.

JOHN KENNETH GALBRAITH: *There can be few fields of human endeavor in which history counts for so little as in the world of finance.*

Stein's law, the iron law of capital, the iron law of failure, Clarke's law, etc., are all called laws for a reason. They are often applicable, and therefore serve as a departure from pure randomness. History rhymes. To a certain degree.

PETER THOMAS BAUER: *A safe investment is an investment whose dangers are not at that moment apparent.*

All consumer products are hyped; it is part of selling. As a buyer, if something is too good to be true, it most often is precisely that. There are no safe investments. The way to be safe is to never feel secure.

GEORGE SANTAYANA: *Those who do not learn from history are doomed to repeat its mistakes.*

Spotting folly is, too, a departure from randomness and therefore can be quite helpful. When someone raises minimum wage, you just know what is going to happen to the unemployment rate and the shadow economy. No rocket science is required.

CICERO: *The beginnings of all things are small.*

If a butterfly in the Amazon can create a tornado in Texas, a Pharaoh's nose can alter history, or a failed bank robber can negatively alter the Russian gene pool for generations to come, one ought to exercise intellectual modesty as to how far we can see into the future and our convictions thereof.

HEINLEIN: *Man is not a rational animal; he is a rationalizing animal.*

This quotation puts all debates related to market efficiency at rest. Logical thinking does not work with dynamic systems, things that change over the course of time. You cannot explain the working of social phenomena by cause-and-effect logic very well. All theories where rationality is assumed are wrong. However, man adapts. That we know.

CONFUCIUS: *What you know, you know, what you don't know, you don't know. This is true wisdom.*

When I was seventeen, I thought I knew everything. It turns out I didn't. Separating fact from opinion is helpful. Certainty as to one's opinions is folly. One ought to know at least roughly what one doesn't know: the future, for example.

Throughout this book I also referred to a top twenty-five list of my favorite books related to finance and risk management. (A "top ten" list of books unrelated to finance would include *The Girl with the Dragon Tattoo series, Memoirs of a Geisha,* and *The Gruffalo.*) I list these books not because I believe I know which books are most applicable to financial wisdom and folly but because I am often asked for a list. Some of the books are not financial books, but I believe are very applicable to finance, risk, and uncertainty, nevertheless. I ranked the books by preference, most applicable first.

The Story of Civilization (Will & Ariel Durant), summarized in
     Lessons of History
The Crowd (Gustave Le Bon)
Human Action (Ludwig von Mises)
The Road to Serfdom (F. A. Hayek)
Against the Gods (Peter Bernstein)
Ubiquity (Mark Buchanan)
On the Origin of Species (Charles Darwin)
Risk, Uncertainty, and Profit (Frank Knight)
Fooled by Randomness (Nassim Taleb)

The (Mis)behavior of Markets (Benoit Mandelbrot & Richard L.
   Hudson)
Why Most Things Fail (Paul Ormerod)
Deep Survival (Laurence Gonzales)
Risk Savvy (Gerd Gigerenzer)
Normal Accidents (Charles Perrow)
Extraordinary Popular Delusions and the Madness of Crowds
   (Charles MacKay)
Alchemy of Finance (George Soros)
Statecraft (Margaret Thatcher)
Reminiscences of a Stock Operator (Edwin Lefèvre)
Winning on Wall Street (Martin Zweig)
The Fortune Sellers (William Sherden)
When Genius Failed (Roger Lowenstein)
Liar's Poker (Michael Lewis)
Investment Biker (Jim Rogers)
The World is Flat (Thomas Friedman)
The Mind of Wall Street (Leon Levy)

Ludwig von Mises's *Human Action* is the only book from the list I have
not read cover to cover. *Human Action* was once described as "the most
important book you never heard of." *Human Action* is my go-to reference
book when I need to learn something related to economics. I cannot
remember ever having wasted my time with *Human Action*.

"Human action," what ancient Greek philosophers called *praxeology*,
is like a two-word definition of all things economic. It defines economics
more broadly, much more broadly than the definition of economics of my
formal education, which was largely based off Paul Samuelson's *Economics*. (In the two editions of *Economics* I own, von Mises is not mentioned
once.) As applied wisdom, *phronesis* from chapter one is much more than
just IQ; *praxeology* is much more than just what is taught in economics
class. *Praxeology* is more universal. It is about what people do in the
real world, rather than what they should be doing according to some
mean-variance or IS-LM model, if they were as rational as Mr. Spock.

Speaking of human action: Stephen Hawking, in his last book, *Brief Answers to the Big Questions*, discusses some of the risks related to humanity shooting itself in its collective foot and dying, i.e., go dinosaur and become extinct. He always made fun of the human race not having a particularly good track record when it came to sapiens' intelligent behavior. He recommended, in the end, we should apply wisdom:

> *Our future is a race between growing power of our technology and the wisdom with which we use it. Let's make sure that wisdom wins.*[679]
> —STEPHEN HAWKING *(1942–2018), English theoretical physicist, cosmologist, and author*

To that end, I wish all my readers good health:

> *When you don't have any money, the problem is food.*
> *When you have money, it's sex.*
> *When you have both it's health.*[680]
> —J. P. DONLEAVY *(1926–2017), Irish/American novelist and playwright*

Physical and mental health is much more important than money. Who knew?

I started this book by quoting Voltaire in the preface. I shall end the book with a disclaimer:

> *A witty saying proves nothing.*[681]
> —VOLTAIRE

ACKNOWLEDGMENTS

Like all books, *Applied Wisdom* would not have been possible without the help of countless interactions with family, friends, clients, coworkers, CAIAA and FIF buddies, and critics. Thank you.

In particular, I would like to thank Larry Chen, Andreas Gilgen, Maurice Pedergnana, Cuno Pümpin, and Sanjay Tikku for their involvement, insight, and wisdom when reviewing early parts of the manuscript. A special thanks goes to Peter Douglas for reviewing the whole manuscript. I would also like to thank Leah Spiro for making the project happen and Bill Falloon for his advice and introductions. Particular thanks are also owed to the staff of Radius, namely Mark Fretz and Evan Phail for their patience and hands-on and efficient work.

As cheesy as it may sound, I would also like to thank my wife, not just for putting up with me all these years, but also for being an ego-inflation circuit breaker since 1984.

All remaining errors and follies are my own.

BIBLIOGRAPHY

Abbey, Edward. *A Voice Crying in the Wilderness*. New York: St. Martin's Griffin, 1989.

Abbey, Edward. *The Monkey Wrench Gang*. Philadelphia: Lippincott, 1975.

Ackoff, Russell L. "From Data to Wisdom." *Journal of Applied Systems Analysis* 16 (1989): 3–9.

Adams, Douglas. *Last Chance to See*. London: Heinemann, 1979.

Adams, Douglas. *The Hitchhiker's Guide to the Galaxy*. London: Pan Macmillan, 1979.

Adams, Scott. *God's Debris: A Thought Experiment*. Kansas City: Andrews McMeel Publishing, 2001.

Akerlof, George, and Joseph Stiglitz. "Let a Hundred Theories Bloom." *Project Syndicate*, October 26, 2009.

Allen, Robert S. *Drive to Victory*. New York: Berkley, 1947.

Allison, Graham, and Robert D. Blackwill. *Lee Kuan Yew: The Grand Master's Insights on China, the United States, and the World*. Cambridge, MA: MIT Press, 2013.

Antrim, Minna. *Naked Truth and Veiled Allusions*. Philadelphia: Henry Altemus Company, 1901.

Arkhipov, Ilya and Henry Meyer. "Putin Says Cyprus Bank-Deposit Levy Is Dangerous, Unfair." *Bloomberg*, March 18, 2013.

Ashley, Gerald. *Uncertainty and Expectation: Strategies for the Trading of Risk*. Chichester: John Wiley & Sons, 2003.

Atyeo, Don, and Johnathon Green. *Don't Quote Me*. London: Hamlyn, 1981.

Austen, Jane. *Emma*, vol. 2. London: John Murray, 1816.

Authers, John. "Ed Thorp: the Man who Beat the Casinos, then the Markets, Lunch with the FT." *Financial Times*, February 5, 2017.

Bacharach, Bert. "Now See Here!" *Coshocton Tribune,* August 4, 1968.

Bagehot, Walter. "Dull Government." *Saturday Review,* February 16, 1856.

Bagehot, Walter. *Literary Studies.* London: Longmans, Green, and Company, 1879.

Bańbura, Marta, Domenico Giannone, Michele Modugno, and Lucrezia Reichlin. "Now-casting and Real-time Data Flow." Working Paper Series 1564, European Central Bank, July 2013.

Baran, Paul A. *A Collective Portrait.* New York: Monthly Review Press, 1964.

Barth, James R. *The Rise and Fall of the U.S. Mortgage and Credit Markets.* Hoboken: John Wiley & Sons, 2009.

Beatty, Paul. *Hokum: An Anthology of African-American Humor.* New York: Bloomsbury, 2006.

Beder, Tanya Styblo. "VAR: Seductive but Dangerous." *Financial Analyst Journal* 51, no. 5 (Sept.–Oct. 1995): 12–24.

Bentham, Jeremy. *Panopticon; or, the Inspection House.* Dublin: T. Payne, 1791.

Bernstein, Peter L. *Against the Gods: The Remarkable Story of Risk.* New York: Wiley & Sons, 1996.

Bernstein, William. *The Intelligent Asset Allocator.* New York: McGraw-Hill, 2000.

Berra, Yogi. *The Yogi Book.* New York: Workman Publishing Company, 1998.

Biggs, Barton. *Diary of a Hedgehog: Biggs' Final Words on the Markets.* Hoboken: John Wiley & Sons, 2012.

Biggs, Barton. *Hedgehogging.* Hoboken: John Wiley & Sons, 2006.

Blastland, Michael, and David Spiegelhalter. *The Norm Chronicles: Stories and Numbers about Danger.* London: Profile Books, 2013.

Blumenthal, Steve. "Louis Gave—An Important Paradigm Shift Which Will Define The 21st Century." *Valueweek,* April 8, 2018.

Bookstaber, Richard. *A Demon of Our Own Design: Markets, Hedge Funds, and the Perils of Financial Innovation.* Hoboken: John Wiley & Sons, 2007.

Box, G. E. P. "Science and Statistics." *Journal of the American Statistical Association* 71 (1976): 791–99.

Box, G. E. P., and N. R. Draper. *Empirical Model Building and Response Surfaces.* New York: John Wiley & Sons, 1987.

Boyd, Thomas Alvin. *Prophet of Progress: Selections from the Speeches of Charles F. Kettering.* New York: E. P. Dutton, 1961.

Bradberry, Travis. "8 Signs You're Being Lied To." *HuffPost,* May 28, 2017.

Brown, Rita Mae. *Sudden Death*. New York: Bantam Books, 1983.

Browne, Harry. *Liberty A-Z*. Sacramento, CA: Advocates for Self-Government, 2004.

Buchanan, Mark. "Economists Should Stop Being Quite So Certain." *Bloomberg*, April 11, 2018.

Buchanan, Mark. *Ubiquity: Why Catastrophes Happen*. New York: Three Rivers Press, 2000.

Buchanan, Mark. "The (un)Wisdom of Crowds," *Physics Perspective*, July 10, 2016.

Bühler, Urs. "Charles Lewinsky: 'Im Jüdischen Witz Liefert oft Gott die Pointe.'" *Neue Zürcher Zeitung (NZZ)*, August 23, 2018.

Burton, Jonathan. "Ten Rules to Remember about Investing in the Stock Market." *Marketwatch*, June 11, 2008.

Cain, Susan. *Quiet: The Power of Introverts in a World That Can't Stop Talking*. New York: Random House, 2012.

Capron, Marion. "Dorothy Parker, The Art of Fiction No. 13," *Paris Review* 13, Summer 1956.

Carnegy, Hugh. "France Vows to Maintain Tax Hit on Rich." *Financial Times*, December 30, 2012.

Cerf, Bennet. *Try and Stop Me*. New York: Simon & Schuster, 1944.

Cerf, Christopher, and Victor Navasky. *The Experts Speak: The Definitive Compendium of Authoritative Misinformation*. Expanded and updated edition. New York: Villard, 1998.

Chang, Larry. *Wisdom for the Soul of Black Folk*. Washington, DC: Gnosophia, 2007.

Chew, Lillian. "Shock Treatment." *Risk* 7, no. 9 (Sept. 1994): 63–70.

Chila-Jones, Doreen. *Say What?* Baltimore: Duopress, 2018.

Christie, Agatha. *After the Funeral*. New York: Black Dog & Leventhal, 1953.

Christie, Agatha. *The Mysterious Affair at Styles*. New York: John Lane, 1920.

Christy, Marian. "Winning According to Schwarzenegger." Interview with Arnold Schwarzenegger. *Boston Globe,* May 9, 1982.

Chua, Amy. *Day of Empire: How Hyperpowers Rise to Global Dominance—and Why They Fall*. New York: Anchor Books, 2007.

Churchill, Winston. *The Irrepressible Churchill: Stories, Sayings and Impressions of Sir Winston Churchill*. Edited by Kay Halle. London: Robson, 1987.

Churchill, Winston. *Never Give In!: The Best of Winston Churchill's Speeches*. New York: Hyperion, 2003.

Clarke, Arthur C. *Profiles of the Future*. London: Pan Books, 1962.

Cobain, Kurt. *Journals*. New York: Penguin, 2003.

Cohen, Henry. *Talmudic Sayings: Selected and Arranged Under Appropriate Headings*. New York: Bloch Publishing Company, 1910.

Colman, Nina. *The Friars Club Bible of Jokes, Pokes, Roasts, and Toasts*. New York: Hachette Books, 2001.

Cossman, E. Joseph. *How I Made $1,000,000 in Mail Order*. New York: Prentice Hall, 1963.

Covel, Michael. *Trend Following*. Upper Saddle River, NJ: Prentice Hall, 2004.

Cranston, Maurice William. *Freedom: A New Analysis*. London: Longmans, 1953.

Crisp, Quentin. *Manners from Heaven*. London: Hutchinson, 1984.

Darst, David M. *The Little Book that Still Saves Your Assets*. Hoboken: John Wiley & Sons, 2013.

Davies, Robertson. *A Voice from the Attic: Essays on the Art of Reading*. London: Penguin Books, 1990.

da Vinci, Leonardo. *The Notebooks of Leonardo Da Vinci*. Translated by Jean Paul Richter. New York: Scribner and Welford, 1888.

Davis, Ned. *Being Right or Making Money*. 3rd ed. Hoboken: John Wiley & Sons, 2014. First edition published in 1991 by Ned Davis Research.

de Bono, Edward. *Simplicity*. Harmondsworth: Penguin Books, 1998.

de Mello, Anthony. *The Way to Love*. New York: Doubleday, 1991.

D'Israeli, Isaac. *Curiosities of Literature*. London: J. Murray, 1791–1834.

Donleavy, J. P. *The Ginger Man*. Paris: The Olympia Press, 1955.

Dornbusch, Rudi. "Euro Fantasies." *Foreign Affairs* 75, no. 5 (September/October 1996): 110–24.

Dornbusch, Rudi. "Growth Forever." *Wall Street Journal*, July 30, 1998.

Dreman, David. "Ben Graham Was Right—Again." *Forbes*, May 5, 1996.

Dreman, David. *Contrarian Investment Strategies: The Next Generation*. New York: Simon & Schuster, 1998.

Dreman, David. "The Not-So-Expert Expert." In *Classics: An Investor's Anthology*, ed. Charles D. Ellis with James R. Vertin. Homewood, IL: Business One Irwin, 1989.

Drucker, Peter. *Management: Tasks, Responsibilities, Practices*. New York: Harper & Row, 1973.

Duffy, Jonathan. "The Right to Be Downright Offensive." *BBC News Magazine*, December 21, 2004.

Dunlap, Albert J., and Bob Andelman. *Mean Business: How I Save Bad Companies and Make Good Companies Great*. New York: Fireside, 1997.

Durant, Will. *The Greatest Minds and Ideas of All Time*. Compiled and edited by John Little. New York: Simon & Schuster, 2002.

Durant, Will. *The Story of Civilization, Volume 1: Our Oriental Heritage*. Norwalk: Easton Press, 1992. First published in 1935 by Simon & Schuster (New York).

Durant, Will. *The Story of Civilization, Volume 4: The Age of Faith*. Norwalk: Easton Press, 1992. First published in 1950 by Simon & Schuster (New York).

Durant, Will. *The Story of Civilization, Volume 5: The Renaissance*. Norwalk: Easton Press, 1992. First published in 1953 by Simon & Schuster (New York).

Durant, Will. *The Story of Civilization, Volume 6: The Reformation*. Norwalk: Easton Press, 1992. First published in 1957 by Simon & Schuster (New York).

Durant, Will. *The Story of Civilization, Volume 7: The Age of Reason Begins*. Norwalk: Easton Press, 1992. First published in 1961 by Simon & Schuster (New York).

Durant, Will. *The Story of Civilization, Volume 9: The Age of Voltaire*. Norwalk: Easton Press, 1992. First published in 1965 by Simon & Schuster (New York).

Durant, Will. *The Story of Philosophy*. New York: Simon & Schuster, 2006. First published in 1926 by Simon & Schuster (New York).

Durant, Will, and Ariel Durant. *The Lessons of History*. New York: Simon & Schuster, 2010. First published in 1968 by Simon & Schuster (New York).

Edwards, Albert. "Forget Equities. Forget Smart Beta. Buy JGBs for the long run!" *Global Strategy Weekly*, February 25, 2016. Société Générale, Cross Asset Research.

Ehrlich, Paul R. *The Population Bomb*. New York: Ballantine Books/Sierra Club, 1968.

Einstein, Albert. "What Life Means to Einstein: An Interview by George Sylvester Viereck." *The Saturday Evening Post*, October 26, 1929.

Ellis, Charles D. "The Loser's Game." *Financial Analyst Journal* 31, no. 4 (July–August 1975): 19–26.

Evans, Richard J. *In Defence of History*. London: Granta Books, 1997.

Fehrman, Carl. *Poetic Creation: Inspiration or Craft.* Minneapolis: University of Minnesota Press, 1980.

Feynman, Richard. "Report of the Presidential Commission on the Space Shuttle Challenger Accident." Vol. 2, appendix F. Washington: U.S. Government Printing Office (June 6, 1986).

Fiedler, Edgar. "Commentary." *Across the Board* 14 (June 1977): 62–63.

Fischer, Martin H. "Fischerisms." Edited by Dent Smith. Encore: a Continuing Anthology 2, no. 2 (July–December, 1942): 309.

Forelle, Charles. "Luxembourg Lies on Secret Meeting." *Wall Street Journal,* May 9, 2011.

Foster, Elon. *New Cyclopædia of Prose Illustrations.* New York: Funk & Wagnalls, 1877.

Fowler, Cary. "Of Pandas and Peas: Saving the Diversity Within Species." *Huffington Post,* June 11, 2010.

Frankfurt, Harry. "How to Spot Bullshit: A Primer by Princeton Philosopher Harry Frankfurt." *Open Culture.* May 30, 2016.

Frankfurt, Harry. *On Bullshit.* Princeton, NJ: Princeton University Press, 2005. First published in 1986 as an essay.

Franklin, Benjamin. *Poor Richard's Almanack.* Philadelphia: B. Franklin, 1732 to 1758.

Freedman, David H. *Wrong: Why Experts* Keep Failing Us—And How to Know When Not to Trust Them *Scientists, Finance Wizards, Doctors, Relationship Gurus, Celebrity CEOs, High-powered Consultants, Health Officials and More.* New York: Little, Brown and Company, 2010.

Freehan, Bill. *Behind the Mask: An Inside Baseball Diary.* Mountain View, CA: World Publications, 1970.

Freud, Sigmund. *Civilization and Its Discontents.* New York: Jonathan Cape & Harrison Smith, 1930.

Friedman, Thomas. *The World Is Flat: A Brief History of the Globalized World in the 21st Century.* New York: Penguin Group, 2005.

Fromm, Erich. "Der Kreative Mensch." In *Gesamtausgabe. Vol. 9: Sozialistischer Humanismus und humanistische Ethik*, edited by Rainer Funk, 399–407. Stuttgart: Deutsche Verlags-Anstalt, 1980–81. Originally published in 1959.

Gaddis, William. *Carpenter's Gothic.* New York: Viking, 1985.

Galbraith, John Kenneth. *Money: Whence it Came, Where it Went.* Harmondsworth: Penguin Books, 1975.

Galbraith, John Kenneth. *A Short History of Financial Euphoria.* London: Penguin Books, 1994. First published in 1990 by Whittle Books.

Galt, John. *Dreams Come Due: Government and Economics as If Freedom Mattered.* New York: Simon & Schuster, 1986.

Gandhi, Mohandas K. *Harijan*, February 17, 1940.

Gandhi, Mohandas K. *Young India*, March 12, 1931.

George, Henry. *A Perplexed Philosopher.* New York: Charles L. Webster and Co., 1892.

Gibran, Khalil. *Sand and Foam.* New York: Alfred A. Knopf, 1926.

Gide, André. *Ainsi soit-il; ou, Les Jeux sont faits Texte imprimé.* Paris: Gallimard, 1952.

Gigerenzer, Gerd. *Risk Savvy: How to Make Good Decisions.* New York: Viking, 2014.

Glick, Bryan. "Timing is Everything in Steve Ballmer's Departure—Why Microsoft Needs a New Vision." *Computer Weekly Editors Blog,* August 27, 2013.

Goetzmann, William N. "Will History Rhyme?—The Past as Financial Future." *Journal of Portfolio Management* 30, no. 5 (2004): 34–41.

Goldman, Robert, and Stephen Papson. *Nike Culture: The Sign of the Swoosh.* Thousand Oaks, CA: Sage Publications, 1998.

Gonzales, Laurence. *Deep Survival: Who Lives, Who Dies, and Why.* New York: W. W. Norton, 2003.

Gracián, Baltasar. *The Art of Worldly Wisdom.* N.p., 1647.

Graham, Benjamin. *The Intelligent Investor.* Rev. ed. New York: HarperCollins, 2003. First published in 1949, Harper & Brothers (New York).

Grinold, Richard C. "The Fundamental Law of Active Management." *Journal of Portfolio Management* 15, no. 3 (Spring 1989): 30–37.

Grinold, Richard C., and Ronald N. Kahn. *Active Portfolio Management: A Quantitative Approach for Producing Superior Returns and Controlling Risk.* 2nd ed. New York: McGraw-Hill, 2000. First published in 1995 under the title *Active Portfolio Management: Quantitative Theory and Applications*, by Probus, a Chicago publisher that no longer exists.

Grove, Andrew S. *Only the Paranoid Survive.* New York: Currency/Doubleday, 1996.

Gutierrez, Carl. "Fannie and Freddie Are Fine, Bernanke Says." *Forbes,* July 16, 2008.

Haedrich, Marcel. *Coco Chanel: Her Life, Her Secrets.* London: Hale, 1971.

Hagstrom, Robert G., Jr. *The Warren Buffett Way: Investment Strategy of the World's Greatest Investor.* New York: John Wiley & Sons, 1994.

Haldane, Andrew G. "The Dog and the Frisbee." Speech at the Federal Reserve Bank of Kansas City's thirty-sixth economic policy symposium, "The Changing Policy Landscape," August 31, 2012, Jackson Hole, WY.

Harari, Yuval Noah. *21 Lessons for the 21st Century*. London: Jonathan Cape, 2018.

Hardcastle, Ephraim. *Daily Mail*, July 22, 2003.

Harding, David. "Black Monday and the Role of Professors Toting Algorithms." *Financial Times*, October 18, 2017.

Harris, Sydney J. *Pieces of Eight*. Boston: Houghton Mifflin Harcourt, 1982.

Hasan, Mehdi. "The NS Interview: Nassim Nicholas Taleb." *NewStatesman*, June 18, 2010.

Hawking, Stephen. *Brief Answers to the Big Questions*. London: John Murray Publishers, 2018.

Hayek, F. A. *The Constitution of Liberty*. Chicago: University of Chicago Press, 1960.

Hayek, F. A. *The Fatal Conceit: The Errors of Socialism*. London: Routledge, 1988.

Hayek, F. A. *The Road to Serfdom*. New York: Routledge Classics, 2006. First published in 1944 by George Routledge Sons.

Heinlein, Robert A. *Assignment in Eternity*. Reading, PA: Fantasy Press, 1953.

Heinlein, Robert A. *Time Enough for Love*. New York: G. P. Putnam's Sons, 1973.

Henderson, Bobby. *The Gospel of the Flying Spaghetti Monster*. London: Harper Collins, 2006.

Hewitt, Jennifer. "Holocaust Truth Set Frank Lowy Free." *The Australian*, November 13, 2010.

Hintze, Michael. "Global Review." *HedgeFund Intelligence*, Autumn 2013.

Housel, Morgan. *The Psychology of Money: Timeless Lessons on Wealth, Greed, and Happiness*. Petersfield, England: Harriman House, 2020.

Hoyt, J. K. *New Cyclopedia of Practical Quotations*. New York: Funk & Wagnalls, 1922.

Hubbard, Elbert. *The Roycroft Dictionary and Book of Epigrams*. New York: Roycrofters, 1923.

Huxley, Aldous. *Do What You Will*. London: Chatto & Windus, 1929.

Huxley, Aldous. *Music at Night and Other Essays*. Garden City, NY: Doubleday, 1931.

Iles, George. *Canadian Stories*. New York: George Iles, 1918.

Ineichen, Alexander M. "20th Century Volatility—A Review of the Stock and Derivatives Markets in the 20th Century." Warburg Dillon Read, December 1999.

Ineichen, Alexander M. *Absolute Returns: Risk and Opportunities of Hedge Fund Investing*. New York: John Wiley & Sons, 2003.

Ineichen, Alexander M. *Asymmetric Returns: The Future of Active Asset Management*. New York: John Wiley & Sons, 2007.

Ineichen, Alexander M. "Nowcasting and Financial Wizardry." IR&M, January 2015.

Ineichen, Alexander M. "Wriston's Law of Capital." IR&M, July 10, 2012.

James, William. *The Principles of Psychology*. New York: Henry Holt and Company, 1890.

Jenks, Philip. *500 of the Most Witty, Acerbic, and Erudite Things Ever Said about Money*. Petersfield, England: Herriman House, 2002.

Kahn, Irving, and Robert D. Milne. "Benjamin Graham, the Father of Financial Analysis." Financial Analysts Research Foundation, 1977.

Kahneman, Daniel. *Thinking, Fast and Slow*. New York: Farrar, Straus and Giroux, 2011.

Kahneman, Daniel, and Amos Tversky. "Prospect Theory: An Analysis of Decision under Risk." *Econometrica* 47, no. 2 (1979): 263–91.

Kamin, Dan. *Charlie Chaplin's One-man Show*. Lanham, MD: Scarecrow Press, 1984.

Kannings, Ann. *Nelson Mandela: His Words*. Morrisville, NC: Lulu Press, 2014.

Karlgaard, Rich. "Predicting the Future: Part II." *Forbes*, February 13, 2006.

Kaufman, Henry. *On Money and Markets: A Wall Street Memoir*. New York: McGraw Hill, 2000.

Kay, John. "Cracks in the Crystal Ball," *Financial Times*, September 29, 1995.

Kay, John. "Economics—Rituals of Rigour." *Financial Times*, August 25, 2011.

Kay, John. "Why the 'Happiest' Cities Are Boring." *Financial Times*, September 9, 2015.

Kerr, Walter. *Journey to the Center of the Theater*. New York: Alfred A. Knopf, 1979.

Keyes, Ralph. *Nice Guys Finish Seventh: False Phrases, Spurious Sayings, and Familiar Misquotations*. New York: HarperCollins Publishers, 1992.

Keyes, Ralph. *The Quote Verifier*. New York: St. Martin's Griffin, 2006.

Keynes, John Maynard. *The General Theory of Employment Interest and Money*. New York: Harcourt, Brace & World, 1936.

Kierkegaard, Søren. *The Sickness Unto Death.* N.p., 1849.

Klarman, Seth A. *Margin of Safety: Risk-Averse Value Investing Strategies for the Thoughtful Investor.* New York: HarperCollins, 1991.

Klein, Michael. "Alternative Investment Summit: Fresh Prince Rocks the Kimpton." *Cayman Compass,* February 11, 2018.

Knecht, Natascha. "Ein kleiner Stein reicht." Interview with Reinhold Messner. *Schweizer Illustrierte,* May 5, 2017.

Knight, Frank H. *Risk, Uncertainty, and Profit.* New York: Sentry Press, 1964. First published in 1921 by Houghton Mifflin (Boston).

Kruger, Justin, and David Dunning. "Unskilled and Unaware of It: How Difficulties in Recognizing One's Own Incompetence Lead to Inflated Self-Assessments." *Journal of Personality and Social Psychology* 77, no. 6 (1999): 1121–34.

Krugman, Paul. "Why Most Economists' Predictions Are Wrong." *The Red Herring,* June 10, 1998.

Lau, Matthew. "Ontario's Minimum Wage Hike Has Been Disastrous, Especially for Disabled Workers." *Foundation for Economic Education,* July 2, 2018.

Lawson, Dominic. "Flip-flop Phil Gets His Spreadsheets in a Twist." *The Times,* October 15, 2017.

Le Bon, Gustave. *The Crowd: A Study of the Popular Mind.* 2nd ed. Atlanta: Cherokee Publishing Company, 1982. First published in 1895 in French (*Psychologie des Foules).*

Lefèvre, Edwin. *Reminiscences of a Stock Operator.* Investment Classics. New York: John Wiley & Sons, 1993. First published in 1923 by George H. Doran and Company (New York).

Lette, Kathy. *The Boy Who Fell to Earth.* London: Transworld Publishers, 2012.

Levy, Leon, with Eugene Linden. *The Mind of Wall Street: A Legendary Financier on the Perils of Greed and the Mysteries of the Market.* New York: Public Affairs, 2002.

Lewis, Michael. *Liar's Poker: Rising through the Wreckage on Wall Street.* New York: Penguin Books, 1989.

Lindbergh, Anne Morrow. *The Wave of the Future, a Confession of Faith.* New York: Harcourt, Brace & Co., 1940.

Lo, Andrew. "The Adaptive Market Hypothesis—Market Efficiency From an Evolutionary Perspective." *Journal of Portfolio Management* 30, no. 5 (2004): 15–29.

Locke, John. *An Essay Concerning Human Understanding, Book IV.* London: Tho. Basset, 1689.

Loomis, Carol. "The Jones Nobody Keeps Up With." *Fortune,* April 1966.

Lovelock, James. *Novacene: The Coming Age of Hyperintelligence.* London: Allen Lane, 2019.

Lowenstein, Roger. *When Genius Failed: The Rise and Fall of Long-Term Capital Management.* New York: Random House, 2000.

Lucas, Robert E., Jr. "Understanding Business Cycles." *Carnegie-Rochester Conference Series on Public Policy* 5 (1977): 7–29.

Lux, Hal. "The Secret World of Jim Simons." *Institutional Investor* 25, no. 11 (November 2000): 38.

Lynch, Peter, with John Rothschild. *Beating the Street.* New York: Fireside, 1993.

Lynch, Peter, with John Rothschild. *One Up on Wall Street: How to Use What You Already Know to Make Money in the Market.* New York: Simon & Schuster, 1989.

Lyons, Dan. *Disrupted: My Misadventure in the Start-Up Bubble.* New York: Hachette Books, 2016.

Machiavelli, Niccolò. *The Prince.* Translated by Wayne A. Rebhorn. New York: W. W. Norton, 2020. Originally published 1513.

Mackay, Charles. *Extraordinary Popular Delusions and the Madness of Crowds.* New York: Harmony Books, 1980. First published in 1841.

Malkiel, Burton G. *A Random Walk Down Wall Street.* New York: W. W. Norton, 1990. First published in 1973 by Irish Booksellers (Portland).

Malthus, Thomas. *An Essay on The Principle of Population.* London: J. Johnson, 1798.

Mandelbrot, Benoit, and Richard L. Hudson. *The (Mis)behavior of Markets: A Fractal View of Risk, Ruin, and Reward.* New York: Basic Books, 2004.

Mander, Benedict. "Trouble in Venezuela Brings Benefits to Its Neighbour." *Financial Times,* May 8, 2012.

Marks, Howard. "Expert Opinion." *Memo to Oaktree Clients,* January 10, 2017.

Marks, Howard. *The Most Important Thing: Uncommon Sense for the Thoughtful Investor.* New York: Columbia University Press, 2011.

Marx, Karl, and Friedrich Engels. *Manifesto of the Communist Party.* Originally a thirty-page pamphlet published in German as *Manifest der Kommunistischen Partei* (London: Kommunistischer Arbeiterbildungsverein and J. C. Burghard, 1848). First translated into English by Helen Macfarlane and published in serial fashion in the periodical, *The Red Republican* (1850). Commonly referred to as *The Communist Manifesto*, a popular English version is *The Communist Manifesto*. Introduction by Francis B. Randall, translated by Samuel Moore, and edited by Joseph Katz. New York: Pocket Books, 1965.

Mauldin, John, and Johnathan Tepper. *Code Red: How to Protect Your Savings from the Coming Crisis*. Hoboken: John Wiley & Sons, 2014.

Maxey, Daisy. "New Index Trackers Use Hedge Funds as Investing Guide." *Wall Street Journal,* December 27, 2006.

McCloskey, Deirdre N. "How Piketty Misses the Point." *Cato Policy Report* 37, no. 4 (July/August 2015).

McConaughey, Matthew. *Greenlights*. New York: Crown Publishing, 2020.

McMaster Bujold, Lois. *Brothers in Arms*. Riverdale, NY: Baen Books, 1989.

Mencken, H. L. *Damn! A Book of Calumny*. New York: Philip Goodman, 1918.

Mencken, H. L. *A Mencken Chrestomathy*. New York: Alfred A. Knopf, 1949.

Minsky, Hyman P. "The Financial Instability Hypothesis." The Jerome Levy Economics Institute Working Paper 74, May 1992.

Minsky, Hyman P. *John Maynard Keynes*. New York: Columbia University Press, 1975.

Mintz, Steven L. *Five Eminent Contrarians: Careers, Perspectives and Investment Tactics*. Burlington, VT: Fraser Publishing Company, 1995.

Mishra, Stuti. "Democrat Lawmaker's Gender Inclusive 'Amen and Awoman' Congressional Prayer Causes Stir." *The Independent,* January 4, 2021.

Montier, James. "The Seven Immutable Laws of Investing." White Paper, GMO, March 2011.

Montier, James, and Philip Pilkington. "The Stock Market as Monetary Policy Junkie: Quantifying the Fed's Impact on the S&P 500." White Paper, GMO (March 2016).

Morley, Ian. *Morley's Laws of Business and Fund Management*. Trowbridge, England: Paragon Publishing, 2016.

Morris, Tom. *Philosophy for Dummies*. New York: Wiley Publishing, 1999.

Munger, Charles T. *Poor Charlie's Almanack: The Wit and Wisdom of Charles T. Munger*. Expanded 3rd ed. Edited by Peter D. Kaufman. Virginia Beach: The Donning Company Publishers, 2008.

Neill, Humphrey B. *The Art of Contrary Thinking: It Pays to be Contrary!* 5th and enlarged ed. Caldwell, ID: Caxton Press, 2001. First published in 1954 by Caxton Press.

Nicholas, James. *A Book of Wisdom and Delight: How to Fall in Love With Life.* Bloomington, IN: iUniverse, 2008.

Nietzsche, Friedrich Wilhelm. *Beyond Good and Evil: Prelude to a Philosophy.* Translated by Walter Kaufman. New York: Vintage Books, 1966.

Noonan, Peggy. "The Unwisdom of Barack Obama." *Wall Street Journal,* September 18, 2014.

O'Brian, P. J. *Will Rogers, Ambassador of Good Will, Prince of Wit and Wisdom.* Philadelphia: John C. Winston, 1935.

O'Dea, Clare. *The Naked Swiss: A Nation Behind 10 Myths.* Basel, Switzerland: Bergli Books, 2016.

Ormerod, Paul. *Why Most Things Fail . . . And How to Avoid It: Evolution, Extinction, and Economics.* London: Faber & Faber, 2005.

O'Rourke, P. J. *Holidays in Hell.* New York: Atlantic Monthly Press, 1988.

Parris, Matthew. *Scorn: The Wittiest and Wickedest Insults in Human History.* London: Profile Books, 2016.

Péguy, Charles. *Basic Verities, Prose and Poetry.* London: Kegan Paul, 1943.

Perrow, Charles. *Normal Accidents: Living with High-Risk Technologies.* Princeton, NJ: Princeton University Press, 1999. First published in 1984 by Basic Books (New York).

Pestalozzi, Johann Heinrich. *Schwanengesang (Swan Song).* Stuttgart und Tübingen: J. G. Cotta'schen Buchhandlung, 1826.

Peter, Laurence J. *Peter's Quotations: Ideas for Our Time.* New York: William Morrow, 1977.

Peters, Tom. "Sound Off: Tell Us What You Think." *Fast Company,* February 28, 2001.

Phillips, Wally. *Way to Go: Surviving in this World until Something Better Comes Along.* New York: William Morrow, 1985.

Picerno, James. *Nowcasting The Business Cycle: A Practical Guide For Spotting Business Cycle Peaks Ahead of the Crowd.* N.p.: Beta Publishing, 2014.

Pierce, Andrew. "The Queen Asks Why No One Saw the Credit Crunch Coming." *The Telegraph,* November 5, 2008.

Poe, Edgar Allan. *Marginalia.* New York: Harper & Brothers, 1838.

Popper, Karl. *Unended Quest: An Intellectual Autobiography.* Glasgow: HarperCollins Distribution Services, 1976.

Price, Steven D. *1001 Dumbest Things Ever Said.* Guilford, CT: Lyons Press, 2004.

Rand, Ayn. *Capitalism: The Unknown Ideal.* New York: New American Library, 1966.

Rand, Ayn. *The Virtue of Selfishness*. New York: New American Library, 1964.

Rasmussen, Jim. "Buffett Talks Strategy With Students." *Omaha World-Herald*, January 2, 1994.

Read, Carveth. *Logic*. London: Grant Richards, 1898.

Redleaf, Andrew, and Richard Vigilante. *Panic: The Betrayal of Capitalism by Wall Street and Washington*. Minneapolis: Richard Vigilante Books, 2010.

Regies, Ed. "The Doomslayer." *Wired*, Issue 5.02, February 1997.

Reid, Margaret. *The Secondary Banking Crisis 1973–1975; The Inside Story of Britain's Biggest Banking Upheaval*. New York: Macmillan Press, 1982.

Renard, Jules. "Cherchez le Ridicule en Tout, Vous le Trouverez." *Journal*, February 17, 1890.

Ridley, Matt. *The Rational Optimist: How Prosperity Evolves*. New York: HarperCollins, 2011.

Robson, David. *The Intelligence Trap: Revolutionise Your Thinking and Make Wiser Decisions*. London: Hodder & Stoughton, 2019.

Rogers, Jim. *Investment Biker: Around the World with Jim Rogers*. Chichester: John Wiley & Sons, 2000. First published in 1994 by Beeland Interest (Miami).

Rogers, Will. "From Nuts to the Soup." *New York Times*, August 31, 1924.

Ronay, Barney. *The Manager: The Absurd Ascent of the Most Important Man in Football*. London: Sphere, 2009.

Rosenzweig, Phil. *The Halo Effect: How Managers Let Themselves Be Deceived*. London: Simon & Schuster, 2007.

Rothbard, Murray. *For a New Liberty: The Libertarian Manifesto*. London: Macmillan, 1973.

Roux, Joseph. *Meditations of a Parish Priest: Thoughts*. New York: Thomas Cromwell, 1866.

Russell, Bertrand. *Marriage and Morals*. New York: H. Liveright, 1929.

Russell, Bertrand. *Mortals and Others. Vol 2, Bertrand Russell's American Essays, 1931–1935*. Edited by Harry Ruja. London: Routledge, 1998.

Russell, Bertrand. *Unpopular Essays*. London: George Allen and Unwin, 1950.

Russo, J. Edward, and Paul J. H. Schoemaker. *Decision Traps: The Ten Barriers to Brilliant Decision-Making and How to Overcome Them*. New York: Simon & Schuster/Fireside, 1989.

Sagan, Carl. *Cosmos*. New York: Random House, 1980.

Sagan, Carl. *The Demon-Haunted World: Science as a Candle in the Dark*. New York: Random House, 1996.

Samuelson, Paul A., and William D. Nordhaus. *Economics*. 13th ed. New York: McGraw-Hill, 1989.

Santayana, George. *The Life of Reason, Volume 1*. Westminster: Archibald Constable & Co., 1905.

Schwager, Jack. *Market Sense and Nonsense: How the Markets Really Work (and How They Don't)*. Hoboken: John Wiley & Sons, 2013.

Schwager, Jack. *Market Wizards: Interviews with Top Traders*. New York: CollinsBusiness, 1993. First published in 1989 by the New York Institute of Finance.

Schwager, Jack. *The New Market Wizards: Conversations with America's Top Traders*. New York: HarperCollins, 1992.

Sen, N. B. *Wit and Wisdom of Socrates, Plato, Aristotle*. New Delhi: New Book Society of India, 1967.

Shakespeare, William. *As You Like It* (1603).

Shaw, George Bernard. *Androcles and the Lion*, preface. New York: Brentano's, 1910.

Shaw, George Bernard. *Back to Methuselah*. New York: Brentano's, 1921.

Shaw, George Bernard. *Man and Superman. A Comedy and a Philosophy*. Westminster: Archibald Constable & Co., 1903.

Sherden, William A. *The Fortune Sellers: The Big Business of Buying and Selling Predictions*. New York: John Wiley & Sons, 1998.

Shilling, A. Gary. "A. Gary Shilling's Insight." *Forbes*, February 1993.

Simon, Herbert. *Models of Man: Social and Rational*. New York: John Wiley & Sons, 1957.

Simon, Herbert. "Theories of Decision Making in Economics and Behavioral Sciences." *American Economic Review* 49, no. 2 (June 1959): 253–83.

Skousen, Mark. *The Maxims of Wall Street*. 5th ed. Washington, DC: Capital Press, 2017. First published in 2011 with Skousen Publishing (Winter Park, FL).

Smit, P. J. *Strategy Implementation: Readings*. Kenwyn: Juta Academic, 2000.

Smollett, Tobias. *The Adventures of Roderick Random*. London: J. Osborn, 1748.

Sommerfeld, Arnold. "To Albert Einstein's Seventieth Birthday." In *Albert Einstein: Philosopher-Scientist*, ed. Paul A. Schilpp, Library of Living Philosophers, vol. 7, 102. La Salle, IL: Open Court, 1949. The essay, originally published as "Zum Siebzigsten Geburtstag Albert Einsteins" in *Deutsche Beiträge* (Eine Zweimonatsschrift) 3, no. 2 (1949).

Sornette, Didier. *Why Stock Markets Crash: Critical Events in Complex Financial Systems*. Princeton, NJ: Princeton University Press, 2003.

Soros, George. *The Alchemy of Finance: Reading the Mind of the Market*. New York: John Wiley & Sons, 2003. First published in 1987 by Simon & Schuster (New York).

Soros, George. "Fallibility, Reflexivity, and the Human Uncertainty Principle." *Journal of Economic Methodology* 20, no. 4 (2013): 309–29.

Soros, George. *Soros on Soros: Staying Ahead of the Curve*. New York: John Wiley & Sons, 1995.

Sowell, Thomas. *Applied Economics: Thinking Beyond Stage One*. New York: Basic Books, 2004.

Sowell, Thomas. *Barbarians inside the Gates and Other Controversial Essays*. Stanford: Hoover Institution Press, 1999.

Sowell, Thomas. "A Childish Letter." *Jewish World Review*, August 17, 1998.

Sowell, Thomas. *Controversial Essays*. Stanford: Hoover Institution Press Publication, 2002.

Sowell, Thomas. "A Defining Moment." *Real Clear Politics*, February 7, 2012.

Sowell, Thomas. *Ever Wonder Why? and Other Controversial Essays*. Stanford: Hoover Institution Press, 2006.

Sowell, Thomas. *The Thomas Sowell Reader*. New York: Basic Books, 2011.

Spencer, Herbert. *Essays on Education and Kindred Subjects*. London: Everyman's Library, 1861.

Spencer, Herbert. *Social Statics*. London: John Chapman, 1851.

Spitznagel, Mark. *The Dao of Capital: Austrian Investing in a Distorted World*. Hoboken: John Wiley & Sons, 2013.

Stein, Herbert. "Herb Stein's Unfamiliar Quotations: On Money, Madness, and Making Mistakes." *Slate*, May 15, 1997.

Steinbach Tarnutzer, Karin. "Tod eines Ausnahmebergsteigers." *Neue Zürcher Zeitung (NZZ)*, May 2, 2017.

Stinnett, Caskie. *Out of the Red*. New York: Random House, 1960.

Stothard, Michael. "Spring Arrives for Mélenchon Far-left Crusade." *Financial Times*, April 5, 2017.

Surowiecki, James. *The Wisdom of Crowds*. New York: Doubleday, 2004.

Suzuki, Shunryu. *Zen Mind, Beginner's Mind*. New York: Weatherhill, 1970.

Taleb, Nassim Nicholas. *Antifragile: Things That Gain from Disorder*. New York: Random House, 2012.

Taleb, Nassim Nicholas. *The Black Swan: The Impact of the Highly Improbable.* New York: Random House, 2007.

Taleb, Nassim Nicholas. *Fooled by Randomness: The Hidden Role of Chance in Markets and in Life.* New York: Thomson/Texere, 2001. 2nd ed. 2004. Now part of the Incerto series, which includes *The Black Swan, Antifragil, Skin in the Game,* and *The Bed of Procrustes.*

Taleb, Nassim Nicholas. *Skin in the Game: Hidden Asymmetries in Daily Life.* New York: Penguin Books, 2017.

Tetlock, Philip E. *Expert Political Judgment: How Good Is It? How Can We Know?* Princeton, NJ: Princeton University Press, 2005.

Tetlock, Philip E., and Dan Gardner. *Superforecasting: The Art and Science of Prediction.* New York: Crown Publishers, 2015.

Thatcher, Margaret. *Statecraft: Strategies for a Changing World.* New York: HarperCollins, 2002.

Thiel, Andreas. *Humor: Das Lächeln des Henkers.* Thun: Werd Verlag, 2015.

Thiel, Peter. *Zero to One: Notes on Start Ups, or How to Build the Future.* London: Virgin Books, 2014.

Thompson, Joseph Wilmer. *Selling: A Behavioral Science Approach.* New York: McGraw Hill, 1966.

Thurber, James. "The Fairly Intelligent Fly." *The New Yorker,* February 4, 1939.

Tier, Mark. *The Winning Investment Habits of Warren Buffett and George Soros.* New York: St. Martin's Griffin, 2006.

Tinbergen, Jan. "The Role of Errors in Scientific Development." *Review of Social Economy* 46 (1998): 225–30.

Tinsley, Catherine H., Robin L. Dillon, and Peter M. Madsen. "How to Avoid Catastrophe." *Harvard Business Review,* April 2011.

Tolstoy, Leo. *War and Peace.* Translated by Anthony Briggs. New York: Penguin Classics, 2005. Originally published in Russian in 1869.

Tripp, Rhoda Thomas. *The International Thesaurus of Quotations.* New York: Thomas Y. Crowell Co., 1970.

Turner, Adair. "Banks Are Safer but Debt Remains a Danger." *Financial Times,* September 11, 2018.

Tversky, Amos, and Daniel Kahneman. "Judgment under Uncertainty: Heuristics and Biases." *Science,* New Series 185, no. 4157 (September 1974): 1124–31.

Twain, Mark. *Following the Equator.* N.p., 1897.

Twain, Mark. *Mark Twain's Notebook*. Edited by Albert Bigelow Paine. New York: Harper & Bros., 1935.

Twain, Mark. *Tom Sawyer Abroad*. New York: Charles L. Webster & Co., 1894.

Ueshiba, Morihei. *The Art of Peace*. Translated by John Stevens. Boston: Shambhala Publications, 1992.

Veres, Robert N. "The Vision Thing." *Investment Advisor*, June 1997.

Voehl, Frank. *Deming: The Way We Knew Him*. Boca Raton: St. Lucie Press, 1995.

von Ebner-Eschenbach, Marie. *Aphorisms*. Translated by D. Scrase and W. Mieder. Riverside, CA: Ariadne Press, 1994. German original, *Aphorismus*, published 1880, and republished in a collected works edition, *Gesammelte Schriften, Erste Band*. Berlin: Verlag von Gebrüder Paetel, 1893.

von Goethe, Johann Wolfgang. *Goethe, Maximen und Reflexionen. Aphorismen und Aufzeichnungen. Nach den Handschriften des Goethe-und Schiller-Archivs hg. von Max Hecker*. Weimer: Verlag der Goethe-Gesellschaft, 1907.

von Mises, Ludwig. *Epistemological Problems of Economics*. Translated by George Reisman. Edited and with a foreword by Bettina Bien Greaves and Introduction by Jörg Guido Hülsmann. 3rd ed. Indianapolis: Liberty Fund, 2013. Originally published in German as *Grundprobleme der Nationalökonomie*. Jena: Verlag von Gustav Fischer, 1933.

von Mises, Ludwig. *Human Action: A Treatise on Economics*. 4th ed. San Francisco: Fox & Wilkes, 1996. First published in 1949 by Yale University Press.

von Mises, Ludwig. "Lord Keynes and Say's Law." *The Freeman*, October 30, 1950.

von Mises, Ludwig. *Omnipotent Government: The Rise of the Total State and Total War*. Auburn: Mises Institute, 2010. First published in 1944 by Yale University Press.

von Oech, Roger. *A Whack on the Side of the Head*. New York: Grand Central, 2002.

Voltaire. *Le Dîner du Comte de Boulainvilliers*. N.p., 1767.

Voltaire. Letter to Frederick William, Prince of Prussia, November 28, 1770.

Voltaire. *Questions Sur Les Miracles*. Genève: n.p., 1765.

Vonnegut, Kurt. *Player Piano*. New York: Macmillan, 1952.

Webster, John. "The Alternative Balancing Act." *Greenwich Associates*, December 2003.

Weekes, Karen. *Women Know Everything!* Philadelphia: Quirk Books, 2007.

Weil, Johnathan. "Geithner Downgrades His Own Credibility to Junk." *Bloomberg,* April 21, 2011.

Weis, Daniel. *Everlasting Wisdom.* Trowbridge, England: Paragon Publishing, 2010.

West, Jessamyn. *To See the Dream.* New York: Harcourt, Brace and Company, 1957.

Whitehead, Alfred North. *The Concept of Nature.* Cambridge: Cambridge University Press, 1919.

Whitehead, Alfred North. *Process and Reality: An Essay in Cosmology.* Cambridge: Cambridge University Press, 1929.

Wilde, Oscar. *An Ideal Husband.* London: Leonard Smithers and Company, 1899.

Wilde, Oscar. *Lady Windermere's Fan.* N.p., 1892.

Wilde, Oscar. *The Illustrated Oscar Wilde.* Edited by Roy Gasson. Poole, Dorset: New Orchard Editions, 1977.

Wilde, Oscar. *The Model Millionaire.* New York: Dodd Mead and Company, 1891.

Wilder, Thornton. *The Eighth Day.* New York: Harper & Brothers, 1967.

Wilmott, Paul, and David Orrell. *The Money Formula: Dodgy Finance, Pseudo Science, and How Mathematicians Took Over the Markets.* Chichester: John Wiley & Sons, 2017.

Wilson, Robert Anton. *The Illuminati Papers.* San Francisco: And/Or Press, 1980.

Winkler, Rolfe, and Justin Lahart. "How Do Pundits Never Get It Wrong? Call a 40% Chance." *Wall Street Journal,* February 26, 2018.

Wittgenstein, Ludwig. *Culture and Value.* Translated by Peter Winch. Chicago: Chicago Press, 1980. German original, *Vermischte Bemerkungen.* Oxford: Basil Blackwell, 1977.

Wohlstetter, Charles. *The Right Time, The Right Place.* New York: Applause, 1997.

Wollstonecraft, Mary. *The Female Reader.* London: Gale and the British Library, 1789.

Woods, Ralph Louis. *The Modern Handbook of Humor.* New York: McGraw Hill, 1967.

Yglesias, Matthew. "The Bullshitter-in-Chief." *Vox,* May 30, 2017.

Young, Edward. *Love of Fame.* London: J. Tonson in the Strand, 1728.

Zakaria, Fareed. "Culture Is Destiny: A Conversation with Lee Kuan Yew." *Foreign Affairs* 73, no. 2 (Mar.–Apr. 1994): 109–26.

Zappa, Frank, and Peter Occhiogrosso. *The Real Frank Zappa Book*. New York: Poseidon Press, 1989.

Zeikel, Arthur. "On Thinking." *Financial Analyst Journal* 44, no. 3 (May–June 1988): 11–17.

Zweig, Jason. *The Devil's Financial Dictionary*. New York: PublicAffairs, 2015.

Zweig, Jason "Inefficient Markets Are Still Hard to Beat," *Wall Street Journal,* January 9, 2010.

Zweig, Martin. *Winning on Wall Street*. New York: Warner Business Books, 1986.

ENDNOTES

1　Quoted in Daniel Weis, *Everlasting Wisdom* (Trowbridge, England: Paragon Publishing, 2010).

2　Original: "Un sot savant est sot plus qu'un sot ignorant." *Les Femmes Savantes* (1672), Act IV, sc. iii.

3　David Robson, *The Intelligence Trap: Revolutionise Your Thinking and Make Wiser Decisions* (London: Hodder & Stoughton, 2019), 3.

4　Will Durant, *The Story of Philosophy* (New York: Simon & Schuster, 2006), 7. First published 1926 by Simon & Schuster (New York).

5　Peggy Noonan, "The Unwisdom of Barack Obama," *Wall Street Journal*, September 18, 2014.

6　Mark Twain, *Following the Equator* (1897). There are capacity constraints in active asset management. The investment opportunities are directly related, as Twain implies, to the scale of investor folly in the marketplace. From the perspective of the active manager: the more folly, the merrier.

7　From Benoit Mandelbrot and Richard L. Hudson, *The (Mis)behavior of Markets: A Fractal View of Risk, Ruin, and Reward* (New York: Basic Books, 2004), 14.

8　From Jason Zweig, *The Devil's Financial Dictionary* (New York: PublicAffairs, 2015), 81. Quotation is in relation to the efficient market hypothesis. Originally in Jason Zweig "Inefficient Markets Are Still Hard to Beat," *Wall Street Journal*, January 9, 2010.

9　Robert A. Heinlein, *Assignment in Eternity* (Reading, PA: Fantasy Press, 1953).

10　Burton G. Malkiel, *A Random Walk Down Wall Street* (New York: W. W. Norton, 1990), 31–32. First published in 1973.

11　Seth A. Klarman, *Margin of Safety: Risk-Averse Value Investing Strategies for the Thoughtful Investor* (New York: HarperCollins, 1991).

12　Caltech commencement address, 1974.

13　Howard Marks, *The Most Important Thing: Uncommon Sense for the Thoughtful Investor* (New York: Columbia University Press, 2011), 28.

14　Thomas Aquinas, *Summa contra Gentiles*, i, 1. From Will Durant, *The Story of Civilization, Volume 4: The Age of Faith* (Norwalk: Easton Press, 1992). First published in 1950 with Simon & Schuster (New York). An alternative translation reads: "The pursuit of wisdom is more perfect, more noble, more useful, and more full of joy."

15   Whitney Tilson's 2007 Wesco Annual Meeting Notes.

16   Berkshire Hathaway, *Financial Review*, 1985.

17   Originally in *Maximes et Pensées* (1795) published posthumously by his friend Pierre-Louis Ginguené.

18   On a trip to Asia in 2014, the president used a baseball analogy to explain his foreign policy as one that is more focused on "singles and doubles" than home runs. Jeffrey Goldberg from *The Atlantic* called the quotation the "Obama Doctrine." "Shit" is often softened to "stuff" when referred to the Obama Doctrine.

19   I use a variant of this quote. Original: "*Virtus est vitium fugere et sapientia prima stultitia caruisse.*" Literally: "To flee vice is the beginning of virtue, and to have got rid of folly is the beginning of wisdom." Wikiquote contributors, "Horace," Wikiquote.

20   Isaac D'Israeli, *Curiosities of Literature* (London: J. Murray, 1791–1834).

21   Charles T. Munger, *Poor Charlie's Almanack: The Wit and Wisdom of Charles T. Munger*, ed. Peter D. Kaufman, expanded 3rd ed. (Virginia Beach: Donning Company Publishers, 2008).

22   Herbert Stein, "Herb Stein's Unfamiliar Quotations: On Money, Madness, and Making Mistakes," *Slate*, May 15, 1997.

23   Albert Edwards, "Forget Equities. Forget Smart Beta. Buy JGBs for the Long Run!" *Global Strategy Weekly*, Société Générale, Cross Asset Research, February 25, 2016.

24   Jonathan Burton, "Ten Rules to Remember about Investing in the Stock Market," *Marketwatch*, June 11, 2008. The other nine rules are: 1. Markets tend to return to the mean over time. 2. Excesses in one direction will lead to an excess in the other direction. 3. There are no new eras—excesses are never permanent. 4. Exponential rising and falling markets usually go further than you think. 5. The public buys the most at the top and the least at the bottom. 6. Fear and greed are stronger than long-term resolve. 7. Markets are strongest when they are broad and weakest when they narrow to a handful of blue chips. 8. Bear markets have three stages. 10. Bull markets are more fun than bear markets. Hat tip to David Rosenberg.

25   Mark Twain, *Mark Twain's Notebook*, ed. Albert Bigelow Paine (New York: Harper & Bros., 1935), 393. First published 1922. Spelling and punctuation in the original.

26   Søren Kierkegaard, *The Sickness Unto Death* (n.p., 1849).

27   Gustave Le Bon, *The Crowd: A Study of the Popular Mind*, 2nd ed. (Atlanta: Cherokee Publishing Company, 1982), 123 and 125. First published in 1895 in French (*Psychologie des Foules*). I read *The Crowd* very early in investment life and, when flicking through it thirty years later, I found it amazing how well it is applicable to finance, given that it was written in 1895 and not at all intended for an investment audience. On my "top ten" list of twenty-five books (I maintain such a list because I am occasionally asked to provide such a list of books related to investments and risk

management) it ranks second after the Durants's *The Lessons of History* (1968). The twenty-five books of my top ten list are mentioned in the closing remarks of this book.

28   *Poor Richard's Almanack* (1747). A variant reads: "A mob has heads enough but no brains."

29   From Friedrich Wilhelm Nietzsche, *Beyond Good and Evil: Prelude to a Philosophy*, trans. Walter Kaufmann (New York: Random House, 1966). Originally published in German (1866) as, *Jenseits von Gut und Böse: Vorspiel einer Philosophie der Zukunft*. There are many variations of this quote.

30   From Charles Mackay, *Memoirs of Extraordinary Popular Delusions* (London: Richard Bentley, 1841). The full passage is worth an endnote: "We find that whole communities suddenly fix their minds upon one object, and go mad in its pursuit, that millions of people become simultaneously impressed with one delusion, and run after it, till their attention is caught by some new folly more captivating than the first. Men, it has been well said, think in herds, it will be seen that they go mad in herds, while they only recover their senses slowly, and one by one." This is, of course, broadly applicable beyond just finance.

31   As quoted by Bernard Baruch in his foreword to the 1932 edition of Charles Mackay, *Extraordinary Popular Delusions and the Madness of Crowds* (New York: Harmony Books, 1980). See endnote 30 above.

32   As quoted, for example, in Henry Cohen, *Talmudic Sayings: Selected and Arranged Under Appropriate Headings* (New York: Bloch Publishing Company, 1910).

33   From John Maynard Keynes, *The General Theory of Employment, Interest, and Monday* (New York: Harcourt, Brace & World, 1936), chapter twelve. The full quotation is worth the reader's attention because nothing has changed. The reference is still applicable, and understanding the incentives of the principal's agent is important: "The game of professional investment is intolerably boring and over-exacting to anyone who is entirely exempt from the gambling instinct; whilst he who has it must pay to this propensity the appropriate toll. Furthermore, an investor who proposes to ignore near-term market fluctuations needs greater resources for safety and must not operate on so large a scale, if at all, with borrowed money—a further reason for the higher return from the pastime to a given stock of intelligence and resources. Finally, it is the long-term investor, he who most promotes the public interest, who will in practice come in for most criticism, wherever investment funds are managed by committees or boards or banks. For it is in the essence of his behaviour that he should be eccentric, unconventional and rash in the eyes of average opinion. If he is successful, that will only confirm the general belief in his rashness; and if in the short run he is unsuccessful, which is very likely, he will not receive much mercy. Worldly wisdom teaches that it is better for reputation to fail conventionally than to succeed unconventionally."

34   David Rosenberg, *Breakfast with Dave*, Gluskin Sheff, July 27, 2015.

35   Quoted from *The Week*, February 24, 2018, originally in *The Sunday Telegraph*.

36   As quoted in Philip Jenks, *500 of the Most Witty, Acerbic, and Erudite Things Ever Said about Money* (Petersfield, England: Herriman House, 2002).

37   As quoted in Marcel Haedrich, *Coco Chanel: Her Life, Her Secrets* (London: Hale, 1971).

38   Barton Biggs, *Hedgehogging* (Hoboken: John Wiley & Sons, 2006), 143.

39   Steven L. Mintz, *Five Eminent Contrarians: Careers, Perspectives and Investment Tactics* (Burlington, VT: Fraser Publishing Company, 1995), 3.

40   This quotation is listed under Voltaire on Wikiquote (February 4, 2017), but the original source was not found. A similar quotation is also attributed to Maximilien Robespierre.

41   Attributed to Maynard Keynes. The quotation fits Keynes's investment style when he was running King's College's endowment in Cambridge.

42   Quoted in Henry Kaufman, *On Money and Markets: A Wall Street Memoir* (New York: McGraw Hill, 2000), 292, making reference to Barton M. Biggs's *Groupthink* in the US and the Americas Investment Perspectives, *Morgan Stanley Dean Witter Newsletter*, April 7, 1999.

43   Ray Dalio, "Unconventional Wisdom," *Institutional Investor*, March 6, 2015.

44   Nassim Nicholas Taleb, *Fooled by Randomness: The Hidden Role of Chance in Markets and in Life*, 2nd ed. (New York: Thomson/Texere, 2004), xxv. *Fooled by Randomness* was ranked ninth in my "top ten" list related loosely to finance and risk management.

45   Jean-Jacques Rousseau, *Emile, or On Education* (The Hague: Jean Néaulme, 1762).

46   Humphrey B. Neill, *The Art of Contrary Thinking: It Pays to Be Contrary!* 5th and enlarged ed. (Caldwell, ID: Caxton Press, 2001), 16. Emphasis in the original. First published in 1954 by Caxton Press.

47   Mark Buchanan, "The (un)Wisdom of Crowds," *Physics Perspective*, July 10, 2016, making reference to Mirta Galesic, Daniel Barkoczi, and Konstantinos Katsikopoulos (2015) "Can Small Crowds Be Wise? Moderate-Sized Groups Can Outperform Large Groups and Individuals Under Some Task Conditions," Santa Fe Institute working paper.

48   Ludwig von Mises, *Omnipotent Government: The Rise of the Total State and Total War* (Auburn: Mises Institute, 2010), 121. First published in 1944 by Yale University Press. The subchapter in which the quotation appears is called *Misapprehended Darwinism*. Full quote: "Reason is the main resource of man in his struggle for survival. It is foolish to view human reason as something unnatural or even contrary to nature. Reason fulfills a fundamental biological function in human life. It is the specific feature of man. When man fights he nearly always makes use of it as his most efficient weapon. Reason guides his steps in his endeavors to improve the external conditions of his life and well-being. Man is the reasonable animal, homo sapiens."

49   There are many variants of this saying. Some quote it, or a variant, as a proverb. The quotation is sometimes attributed to Carl Mayer von Rothschild (1788–1855).

50   Benjamin Graham, *The Intelligent Investor*, rev. ed. (New York: HarperCollins, 2003), xii. First published in 1949 by Harper & Brothers (New York).

51   Warren Buffett has been using this quotation his whole life. There are many variations. Full quote: "I will tell you how to become rich. Close the doors. Be fearful when others are greedy. Be greedy when others are fearful." According to Wikiquote (wikiquote.org), retrieved December 26, 2016, he said this when lecturing a group of students at Columbia University when he was twenty-one.

52   George W. Bush, "President Hosts Conference on Minority Homeownership," George Washington University (October 15, 2002).

53   Ben Bernanke, "The Subprime Mortgage Market," Speech, Federal Reserve Bank of Chicago's 43rd Annual Conference on Bank Structure and Competition, Chicago (May 17, 2007).

54   Ian Morley, *Morley's Laws of Business and Fund Management* (Trowbridge, England: Paragon Publishing, 2016) 23.

55   Peter Thiel, *Zero to One: Notes on Start Ups, or How to Build the Future* (London: Virgin Books, 2014), 22.

56   As quoted in Irving Kahn and Robert D. Milne, "Benjamin Graham, the Father of Financial Analysis," Financial Analysts Research Foundation (1977), 41.

57   Humphrey B. Neill, *The Art of Contrary Thinking: It Pays to Be Contrary!* 5th and enlarged ed. (Caldwell, ID: Caxton Press, 2001), 60. First published in 1954 by Caxton Press.

58   Quoted in Katherine Burton, "Druckenmiller to Shut Fund After 30 Years as Stress Takes Toll," *Bloomberg*, August 19, 2010. I have used the quotation slightly out of context to support my point. Full quote: "When you're sure you're right, no trade is too big. And the bigger your gains in a year, the more aggressive you can be. It takes courage to be a pig." This is Stanley Druckenmiller's motto, and he has a yellow porcelain pig named Jerome on his desk to remind him of it.

59   The big crunch anecdote is from Stephen Hawking, *Brief Answers to the Big Questions* (London: John Murray Publishers, 2018), 63–64.

60   Will Durant, *The Story of Civilization, Volume 1: Our Oriental Heritage* (New York: Simon & Schuster, 1935). The full quotation is worth your consideration, suggesting, of course, that it is global cooling, not global warming, that is the big killer: "Certain factors condition civilization, and may encourage or impede it. First, geological conditions. Civilization is an interlude between ice ages: at any time the current of glaciation may rise again, cover with ice and stone the works of man, and reduce life to some narrow segment of the earth."

61   I have been applying Ormerod's iron law of failure to finance since around 2007. Some of the material in this chapter draws on earlier work.

62   Paul Ormerod, *Why Most Things Fail . . . And How to Avoid It: Evolution, Extinction, and Economics* (London: Faber & Faber, 2005), x.

63   He then adds: "The other thing I've learned is that even when all the wealth is gone, life goes on." From Jim Rogers, *Investment Biker: Around the World with Jim Rogers* (Chichester: John Wiley & Sons, 2000), 381. First published in 1994 by Beeland Interest (Miami).

64   Gustave Le Bon, *The Crowd: A Study of the Popular Mind*, 2nd ed. (Atlanta: Cherokee Publishing Company, 1982), last paragraph of book, 219. First published in 1895 in French (*Psychologie des Foules*).

65   Paul Ormerod, *Why Most Things Fail . . . And How to Avoid It: Evolution, Extinction, and Economics* (London: Faber & Faber, 2005), xi.

66   Parliamentary Debates: House of Commons Official Report, vol. 317 (1936), 423.

67   Edwin Lefèvre, *Reminiscences of a Stock Operator*, Investment Classics (New York: John Wiley & Sons, 1993), 228. First published in 1923 by George H. Doran and Company (New York).

68   F. A. Hayek, *The Constitution of Liberty* (Chicago: University of Chicago Press, 1960), The Common Sense of Progress (Ch. 3).

69   As quoted in John Little, *Striking Thoughts: Bruce Lee's Wisdom for Daily Living* (Clarendon: Tuttle Publishing, 2000).

70   Tom Morris, *Philosophy for Dummies* (New York: Wiley Publishing, 1999), 307.

71   Charles Perrow, *Normal Accidents: Living with High-Risk Technologies* (Princeton, NJ: Princeton University Press, 1999), 5. Emphasis in the original. First published in 1984 by Basic Books (New York).

72   Charles Perrow, *Normal Accidents*, 7.

73   From Cicero, *De Finibus Bonorum et Malorum* (45 BC), book V, chapter 58. Variant translation: "Everything has a small beginning." Another variant, sourced from Orationes Philippicae V, reads: "The most important events are often determined by very trivial causes."

74   Blaise Pascal, *Pensées* (1658), no. 32.

75   Richard Bookstaber, *A Demon of Our Own Design: Markets, Hedge Funds, and the Perils of Financial Innovation* (Hoboken: John Wiley & Sons, 2007), 155.

76   "Ignorance is bliss" is a proverb. It means the lack of knowledge results in happiness; it is more comfortable not to know certain things. A Hungarian proverb, somewhat related, states: "The believer is happy; the doubter is wise."

77   Andrew G. Haldane, "The Dog and the Frisbee," speech at the Federal Reserve Bank of Kansas City's thirty-sixth economic policy symposium, "The Changing Policy Landscape," August 31, 2012, Jackson Hole, WY.

78   The quotation used here is a variant or a derivative from a 1961 speech Ayn Rand gave at a symposium titled "Ethics in Our Time" held at the University of Wisconsin in Madison. The original reads as follows: "He is free to make the wrong choice, but not free to succeed with it. He is free to evade reality, he is free to unfocus his mind and stumble blindly down any road he pleases, but not free to avoid the abyss he refuses to see. Knowledge, for any conscious organism, is the means of survival; to

a living consciousness, every 'is' implies an 'ought.' Man is free to choose not to be conscious, but not free to escape the penalty of unconsciousness: destruction." From Quote Investigator (May 15, 2017). Sometimes the quotation I use is paraphrased as "You can ignore reality, but you cannot ignore the consequences of ignoring reality." This is from her interestingly titled book *The Virtue of Selfishness* (New York: New American Library, 1964).

79   There are variations to this quote. Wikiquote (December 1, 2016) quotes the original as "Dans les champs de l'observation le hasard ne favorise que les esprits prepares," translates this to "in the fields of observation chance favors only the prepared mind," and references the quotation to a lecture at the University of Lille on December 7, 1854.

80   Cary Fowler, "Of Pandas and Peas: Saving the Diversity Within Species," *Huffington Post*, June 11, 2010.

81   Aristotle, *Poetics* (c. 335 BC).

82   Oscar Wilde, *Lady Windermere's Fan*, Mr. Dumby, Act III (n.p., 1892).

83   I herein use a popular variant. Original is from *Tom Sawyer Abroad* (1894) and reads: ". . . the person that had took a bull by the tail once had learnt sixty or seventy times as much as a person that hadn't, and said a person that started in to carry a cat home by the tail was getting knowledge that was always going to be useful to him, and warn't ever going to grow dim or doubtful."

84   Burton G. Malkiel, *A Random Walk Down Wall Street* (New York: W. W. Norton, 1990), 25. First published in 1973 by Irish Booksellers (Portland).

85   Laurence Gonzales, *Deep Survival: Who Lives, Who Dies, and Why* (New York: W. W. Norton, 2003), 37.

86   Yuval Noah Harari, *21 Lessons for the 21st Century* (London: Jonathan Cape, 2018), 47.

87   Morgan Housel, *The Psychology of Money: Timeless Lessons on Wealth, Greed, and Happiness* (Petersfield, England: Harriman House, 2020) 59.

88   Jennifer Hewitt, "Holocaust Truth Set Frank Lowy Free," *The Australian*, November 13, 2010.

89   Jack Schwager, *Market Wizards: Interviews with Top Traders* (New York: CollinsBusiness, 1993). First published in 1989 by the New York Institute of Finance.

90   Tom Peters, "Sound Off: Tell Us What You Think," *Fast Company*, February 28, 2001.

91   From Laurence Gonzales, *Deep Survival: Who Lives, Who Dies, and Why* (New York: W. W. Norton, 2003), 64.

92   As quoted in Paul Beatty, *Hokum: An Anthology of African-American Humor* (New York: Bloomsbury, 2006), 101.

93   *The Notebooks of Leonardo da Vinci*, trans. Jean Paul Richter. New York: Scribner and Welford, 1880.

94   As quoted in Robert S. Allen, *Drive to Victory* (New York: Berkley, 1947), 27. Originally published as *Lucky Forward*, vol. 3, part 4.

95   Berkshire Hathaway, *Annual Report*, 2005.

96   As quoted in Joseph Wilmer Thompson, *Selling: A Behavioral Science Approach* (New York: McGraw Hill, 1966), 197.

97   Will Durant, *The Story of Civilization, Volume 6: The Reformation* (New York: Simon & Schuster, 1957). In a letter from May 30, 1519 to Luther. Passage in which quote occurs: ". . . It might be wiser of you to denounce those who misuse the Pope's authority than to censure the Pope himself. So also with kings and princes. Old institutions cannot be rooted up in an instant. Quiet argument may do more than wholesale condemnation. Avoid all appearance of sedition. Keep cool. Do not get angry. Do not hate anybody. Do not be excited over the noise you have made . . ."

98   As presented at the 2000 Hedge Fund Symposium in April 2000 in London. The other four red flags were: too much money, too much leverage, issues with funding, and, interestingly, too much transparency. This latter point is interesting as investors want a lot of transparency. The regulator too wants money managers to show their hand. However, when in distress, the market knowing your positions is a negative. He used the Hunt brothers and their position in silver as an example. See chapter two of Alexander Ineichen, *Absolute Returns: Risk and Opportunities of Hedge Fund Investing* (New York: John Wiley & Sons, 2003) for more detail.

99   Albert J. Dunlap and Bob Andelman, *Mean Business: How I Save Bad Companies and Make Good Companies Great* (New York: Fireside, 1997), 7.

100   Epictetus, *The Discourses*, book II, chapter 17.

101   *A Fish Called Wanda* (1988), British American heist comedy film directed by Charles Crichton and written by John Cleese. It stars John Cleese, Jamie Lee Curtis, Kevin Kline, and Michael Palin. I probably saw the film in 1988. And I'm still chuckling from some of the memorable scenes when reflecting.

102   From Laurence Gonzales, *Deep Survival: Who Lives, Who Dies, and Why* (New York: W. W. Norton, 2003), 60.

103   Minna Antrim, *Naked Truth and Veiled Allusions* (Philadelphia: Henry Altemus Company, 1901). Antrim was paraphrasing Heinrich Heine (1797–1856), the German poet, author, and literary critic. There are many variants of experience being costly.

104   Original: "La vie et la mort font partie de la même cordée." Author's own translation. Source of the quotation and 2013 interview reference are from Karin Steinbach Tarnutzer, "Tod eines Ausnahmebergsteigers," *Neue Zürcher Zeitung (NZZ)*, May 2, 2017. In the days after Steck's death, some letters to the editors showed compassion. Others suggested that he had it coming, Steck being broadly perceived as suicidal. In essence, Stein's Law, Murphy's Law, and the iron law of failure all applied.

105   "Mountains," *Planet Earth II*, episode 2 (BBC, 2016). Quotation is from section where Attenborough discusses the highest colony of flamingos in the world, who live above fourteen thousand feet; and there's a lot of ice. Full quote: "Walking on thin ice is always risky. And it's hard to retain one's dignity especially when you're wearing stilts."

106   Natascha Knecht, "Ein kleiner Stein reicht," Interview with Reinhold Messner, *Schweizer Illustrierte*, May 5, 2017. Translation is my own.

107   "Mountains," *Planet Earth II,* episode 2 (BBC, 2016). Quotation refers to snow leopards' ordeal to survive at high altitudes with little prey. Whether snow leopards, like elite rock climbers, rely much on luck when trolling around in the mountains, I do not know; I doubt it. They seem risk savvier or less suicidal or both.

108   As quoted in Michael Blastland and David Spiegelhalter, *The Norm Chronicles: Stories and Numbers about Danger* (London: Profile Books, 2013), 176.

109   I assumed a five-day hospital stay, implying three hundred and eighty MicroMorts. In this section, I also ignored that going to hospital most often isn't an option, while skydiving and mountaineering are. Furthermore, I also ignored all the good aspects of modern medicine and hospitalization, as I focus on danger and risk only.

110   Blastland and Spiegelhalter, *The Norm Chronicles*, 179–80.

111   Jennifer Peedom, *Mountain* (2017), documentary film narrated by William Dafoe.

112   Reinhold Messner, *Stuttgarter Zeitung*, August 6, 2008. Original: "Wir gehen immer mit dem Jung-Siegfried-Gefühl los. Wir denken, wir seien unverwundbar. Das ist natürlich völlig naiv und falsch." Translation is my own.

113   Edgar Allan Poe, *Marginalia* (New York: Harper & Brothers, 1838).

114   Will Rogers, "From Nuts to the Soup," *New York Times*, August 31, 1924.

115   Yoda speaking to Luke when the latter seems to be having a juvenile tantrum. George Lucas, *Star Wars: Episode VIII—The Last Jedi* (Burbank, CA: Lucasfilm, 2017).

116   Morihei Ueshiba, *The Art of Peace*, trans. John Stevens (Boston: Shambhala Publications, 1992).

117   Alfred North Whitehead, *Process and Reality: An Essay in Cosmology* (Cambridge: Cambridge University Press, 1929).

118   Arnold Schwarzenegger, "Winning According to Schwarzenegger," interview by Marian Christy, *Boston Globe*, May 9, 1982. Full quote: "Strength does not come from winning. Your struggles develop your strengths. When you go through hardships and decide not to surrender, that is strength. When you make an impasse passable, that is strength. But you must have ego, the kind of ego which makes you think of yourself in terms of superlatives. You must want to be the greatest. We are all starved for compliments. So we do things that get positive feedback."

119   Jack Schwager, *Market Wizards: Interviews with Top Traders* (New York: CollinsBusiness, 1993), 123. First published in 1989 by the New York Institute of Finance.

120   Gerd Gigerenzer, *Risk Savvy: How to Make Good Decisions* (New York: Viking, 2014), 29.

121   Gerd Gigerenzer, *Risk Savvy*, 31.

122   As quoted in Robert Goldman and Stephen Papson, *Nike Culture: The Sign of the Swoosh* (Thousand Oaks, CA: Sage Publications, 1998), 49.

123   Michael Klein, "Alternative Investment Summit: Fresh Prince Rocks the Kimpton," *Cayman Compass*, February 11, 2018. The quotes are from Will Smith's YouTube channel.

124   As quoted in Ann Kannings, *Nelson Mandela: His Words* (Morrisville, NC: Lulu Press, 2014).

125   Garson O'Toole at Quote Investigator (December 23, 2020) has some reservations to sourcing the quote to Confucius. He credits Irish author Oliver Goldsmith in the 1760s as the earliest appearance of the content of the quote. Goldsmith wrote a series of letters under the pseudonym of an imaginary Chinese traveler based in London named Lien Chi Altangi in the *Public Ledger* magazine of London.

126   As quoted in Wally Phillips, *Way to Go: Surviving in This World until Something Better Comes Along* (New York: William Morrow, 1985), 200.

127   Nassim Nicholas Taleb, *Antifragile: Things That Gain from Disorder* (New York: Random House, 2012) 180. Emphasis in the original.

128   George Soros, *Soros on Soros: Staying Ahead of the Curve* (New York: John Wiley & Sons, 1995), 11.

129   Kurt Vonnegut, *Player Piano* (New York: Macmillan, 1952).

130   Average from 2000 to 2019, from Wikipedia, https://en.wikipedia.org/wiki/Aviation_accidents_and_incidents, retrieved December 23, 2020.

131   Matt Austin and Jordan Derk, "Lives Lost, Lives Saved: An Updated Comparative Analysis of Avoidable Deaths at Hospitals Graded by the Leapfrog Group," Armstrong Institute for Patient Safety and Quality Johns Hopkins Medicine (May 2019).

132   Gerd Gigerenzer, *Risk Savvy: How to Make Good Decisions* (New York: Viking, 2014), 51.

133   Richard Branson, @richardbranson, Twitter (June 20, 2017).

134   Charles T. Munger, *Poor Charlie's Almanack: The Wit and Wisdom of Charles T. Munger*, ed. Peter D. Kaufman, expanded 3rd ed. (Virginia Beach: The Donning Company Publishers, 2008), 320.

135   My own translation from the original: "Ihr seid alle Idioten zu glauben, aus Eurer Erfahrung etwas lernen zu können, ich ziehe es vor, aus den Fehlern anderer zu lernen, um eigene Fehler zu vermeiden." From Wikiquote, de.wikiquote.org (December 2, 2016), referencing the preface of Robert D. Buzzell and Bradley T. Gale, *Das PIMS-Programm. Strategien und Unternehmenserfolg* (Wiesbaden: Gabler Verlag, 1989). There are some variations to this quote. Gerd Gigerenzer, *Risk Savvy: How to Make Good Decisions* (New York: Viking, 2014) references the following variation to Bismarck: "Only a fool learns from his own mistakes. The wise man learns from the mistakes of others."

136   Russell Napier, "Why We Can Learn More from Stupid People Than from Smart People: The Uses and Abuses of Financial History," Dinner presentation, 62nd Annual CFA Institute Financial Analysts Seminar, Chicago (July 24, 2017).

137   Benjamin Franklin, *Poor Richard's Almanack* (1749).

138   Pliny the Elder, *Naturalis Historia*, book XVIII, sec. 31.

139   Aesop, "The Lion, the Ass, and the Fox Hunting." *Aesop's Fables.*

140   Douglas Adams, *Last Chance to See* (London: Heinemann, 1979), chapter 4.

141   Joseph Roux, *Meditations of a Parish Priest: Thoughts* (New York: Thomas Cromwell, 1866).

142   Richard Feynman, "Report of the Presidential Commission on the Space Shuttle Challenger Accident," vol. 2, appendix F (June 6, 1986). The IQ remark in the text is from David Robson, *The Intelligence Trap: Revolutionise Your Thinking and Make Wiser Decisions* (London: Hodder & Stoughton, 2019), who makes the point that Feynman's curiosity and persistency to learn are much more important for success than IQ. Feynman once referred to himself as having "limited intelligence."

143   Catherine H. Tinsley, Robin L. Dillon, and Peter M. Madsen, "How to Avoid Catastrophe," *Harvard Business Review Magazine*, April 2011.

144   Or, as Barton Biggs once must have put it: "Bull markets are like sex. It feels best just before it ends." (This quotation is often attributed to Warren Buffett who quoted the late Barton Biggs in the *2013 Annual Report* of Berkshire Hathaway.)

145   As quoted in Charles Wohlstetter, *The Right Time, the Right Place* (New York: Applause, 1997), 64.

146   George Lucas, *Star Wars: Episode V—The Empire Strikes Back* (Burbank, CA: Twentieth Century Fox, 1980).

147   John Kenneth Galbraith, *A Short History of Financial Euphoria* (London: Penguin Books, 1994), 17. First published in 1990 by Whittle Books.

148   Edwin Lefèvre, *Reminiscences of a Stock Operator*, Investment Classics (New York: John Wiley & Sons, 1993), 70. First published in 1923 by George H. Doran and Company (New York).

149   Johann Heinrich Pestalozzi, *Schwanengesang (Swan Song)* (Stuttgart und Tübingen: J. G. Cotta'schen Buchhandlung, 1826), Pestalozzi's memoir, written in the last two years of his life.

150   Matthew McConaughey, *Greenlights* (New York: Crown Publishing, 2020), 3.

151   Jonas Salk, Academy of Achievement interview, May 16, 1991.

152   I wasn't spending too much time on my own investments then. I was invested in capital guaranteed structured products on the hot sectors, i.e., media, telecom, and technology. This means I had positive returns on the way up; underperforming my comrades in their twenties while the losses were limited to around 10 percent, with the last tranche in the early 2000s. See Alexander Ineichen, *Asymmetric Returns: The Future of Active Asset Management* (New York: John Wiley & Sons, 2007) for details. How did I do in 2008? I'd rather not talk about it.

153   Jack Schwager, *The New Market Wizards: Conversations with America's Top Traders* (New York: CollinsBusiness, 1992).

154   Roger von Oech, *A Whack on the Side of the Head* (New York: Grand Central, 2002).

155   "The Milkmaid and Her Pail," *Aesop's Fables*.

156   James Montier and Philip Pilkington, "The Stock Market as Monetary Policy Junkie: Quantifying the Fed's Impact on the S&P 500," GMO White Paper, March 2016. From the introduction: "Jeremy Grantham has a lovely saying that resonates deeply with us, and it is, 'Always cry over spilled milk.' Analyzing past errors and mistakes is crucial to improving our understanding, and vital if we are to stand any chance of avoiding making similar errors in the future. Indeed, 'Always Cry Over Spilled Milk' was the title of an internal investment conference we held at GMO toward the end of last year. The deeper subject was seeking to understand why our forecast for the S&P 500 had been too pessimistic over the last two decades or so."

157   Gerd Gigerenzer, *Risk Savvy: How to Make Good Decisions* (New York: Viking, 2014), 48.

158   From quora.com (December 7, 2016): "The *Yale Book of Quotations* attributes the quotation 'If you think education is expensive, try ignorance' to the former president of Harvard University Derek Bok, but it includes another note stating that the quotation appeared in the *Washington Post* on October 6, 1975. However, when you search for the quotation in Google Newspaper archive, the earliest appearance of the quotation is on October 6, 1975, but it was not written by Derek Bok. Instead, the quotation appears in context in an Ann Landers column. For this reason, I think the definitive attribution to the quotation must go to Eppie Lederer, the woman who wrote under the 'Ann Landers' pseudonym in 1975." Ralph Keyes, *The Quote Verifier* (New York: St. Martin's Griffin, 2006) argues that Ann Landers got the idea from Sir Claus Moser (1922–2015, British statistician): "Education costs nothing. But then, so does ignorance." According to the Quote Investigator (April 24, 2017) both Derek Bok and Ann Landers have both disclaimed credit for the quote. QI credits Robert Orben (b. 1927) with the exact wording of the quote. "Orben was a very successful comedy writer who supplied jokes to others via books and a newsletter. He also wrote material contractually for other comedians, business executives and politicians. QI conjectures that Orben constructed this precise formulation; however, the remark was not particularly novel. A variety of statements using the same keywords and expressing the same idea have been circulating since the early 1900s. For example, in 1902 an advertisement for a Conservatory of Music in Ottumwa, Iowa contained the following: "Education is expensive but ignorance is more so."

159   From the Quote Investigator (December 26, 2020): "This statement was placed in an appendix called 'Red Herrings: False Attributions' in the book *Churchill By Himself*, which presented a comprehensive collection of quotations from the prominent statesman edited by Richard M. Langworth who is the top expert in this domain. Langworth noted that the expression has also been attributed to Abraham Lincoln. In the realm of quotations the names of Churchill and Lincoln both attract a profusion of spurious ascriptions: Success is going from failure to failure without losing your

enthusiasm. Broadly attributed to Churchill, but found nowhere in his canon. An almost equal number of sources credit this saying to Abraham Lincoln; but none of them provides any attribution."

160   Cat on the Scent (Mrs. Murphy #7). Farrah Fawcett (1947–2009), an American actress, on a related topic: "God made man stronger but not necessarily more intelligent. He gave women intuition and femininity. And, used properly, that combination easily jumbles the brain of any man I've ever met." This was not lost on the writers of *Game of Thrones*, as the somewhat scary Cersei Lannister, overwhelmingly portrayed by Lena Headey, put it: "You are as big a fool as every other man. That little worm between your legs does half your thinking." (She was talking to a midget.) Will Durant got all this. When discussing the Renaissance, he speculated what Mona Lisa is smiling about: "What is she smiling at? The efforts of the musicians to entertain her? The leisurely diligence of an artist who paints her through a thousand days and never makes an end? Or is it not just Mona Lisa smiling, but woman, all women, saying to all men: 'Poor impassioned lovers! A Nature blindly commanding continuance burns your nerves with an absurd hunger for our flesh, softens your brains with a quite unreasonable idealization of our charms, lifts you to lyrics that subside with consummation—and all that you may be precipitated into parentage! Could anything be more ridiculous? But we too are snared; we women pay a heavier price than you for your infatuation. And yet, sweet fools, it is pleasant to be desired, and life is redeemed when we are loved.'" See Will Durant, *The Story of Civilization, Volume 5: The Renaissance* (Norwalk: Easton Press, 1992). First published in 1953 by Simon & Schuster (New York).

161   From the Quote Investigator (December 26, 2020): "The earliest known attribution of a version of this quotation to Twain occurred in 1907 [*The Oxford Mark Twain*]. However, QI believes that credit for this saying should go to the controversial novelist and essayist Grant Allen who published a variant in 1894. Indeed, Grant Allen was so enamored with the maxim that schooling interfered with education that he presented it in an essay and then restated it within at least three of his novels. The four works were published in: 1894, 1895, 1896, and 1899."

       Frank Zappa is quoted having said pretty much the same thing: "If you want to get laid, go to college. If you want an education, go to the library."

162   Aristotle, *Nicomachean Ethics,* trans. David Ross, revised by J. L. Ackrill and J. O. Urmson (Oxford: Oxford University Press, 1980), book II, 1103a.33.

163   From Wikipedia (December 26, 2020).

164   The original source from this quote, one of my favorites, is disputed. No published occurrence of such an attribution has yet been located prior to one in Helen Granat, *Wisdom Through the Ages* (Bloomington, IN: Trafford Publishing, 2003), 225. It was used as an early slogan at Apple Computer in 1984, but the earliest occurrence yet located is in William Gaddis, *The Recognitions* (Corvallis, OR: Studio Books, 1955) on page 457: "Stop being so God Damn humble . . . You know God damn well that . . . that humility

is defiance . . . simplicity today is sophisticated . . . simplicity is the ultimate sophistication today." From Wikiquote (December 26, 2020). The quotation is also attributed to Clare Boothe Luce (1903–87), an American playwright, journalist, editor, ambassador, and political figure.

165 Marilyn Monroe, when asked about her nocturnal habits. Quoted in *Saturday Evening Post*, May 12, 1956.

166 Will Durant, *The Story of Civilization, Volume 9: The Age of Voltaire* (Norwalk: Easton Press, 1992). First published in 1965 with Simon & Schuster (New York). Reference to Georg Brandes, *Voltaire* 2V (New York).

167 As quoted by Dent Smith, see Martin H. Fischer, "Fischerisms," ed. Dent Smith, Encore: a Continuing Anthology 2, no. 2 (July–December, 1942): 309.

168 The proverb appears in *Hamlet*, in the second act where Polonius says, "Since brevity is the soul of wit / And tediousness the limbs and outward flourishes, I will be brief . . ." It is open to debate whether Shakespeare is the original source or whether he just used and popularized it.

169 http://www.ineichen-rm.com/mission-philiosophy.

170 As quoted in Charles D. Ellis, "The Loser's Game," *Financial Analyst Journal* 31, no. 4 (July–August 1975): 19–26.

171 As quoted in *Reader's Digest*, October 1967.

172 William James, *The Principles of Psychology* (New York: Henry Holt and Company, 1890), chapter 22.

173 Full quote: "For us, with the rule of right and wrong given us by Christ, there is nothing for which we have no standard. And there is no greatness where there is not simplicity, goodness, and truth." From Leo Tolstoy, *War and Peace*, bk. XIV, ch. 18. Originally published in Russian by the magazine *The Russian Messenger* (1865–67), then self-published as a book in 1869 (Moscow: By the Author, 1869).

174 Mary Wollstonecraft, *The Female Reader* (London: Gale and the British Library, 1789).

175 Berkshire Hathaway Annual Meeting, Omaha, NE (May 3, 2008).

176 Peter Lynch, with John Rothschild, *Beating the Street* (New York: Fireside, 1993), 27.

177 Dennis Gartman, *The Gartman Letter*, January 29, 2009.

178 Coco Chanel, interview in *Harper's Bazaar*, 1923.

179 Agatha Christie, *The Mysterious Affair at Styles* (New York: John Lane, 1920).

180 Scott Adams, *God's Debris: A Thought Experiment* (Kansas City: Andrews McMeel Publishing, 2001).

181 Edward de Bono, *Simplicity* (Harmondsworth: Penguin Books, 1998), 68.

182 Alfred North Whitehead, *The Concept of Nature* (Cambridge: Cambridge University Press, 1919), chapter 7. Full quote: "The aim of science is to seek the simplest explanations of complex facts. We are apt to fall into the error of thinking that the facts are simple because simplicity is the goal of our quest. The guiding motto in the life of every natural philosopher should be, 'Seek simplicity and distrust it.'"

183   According to one source, this is a fake quote and Alan Blinder never said anything to that effect. A *PBS Nightly Business Report* in 1994 is often quoted as the original source, but an exact date or a transcript cannot be found.

184   Carl Sagan, *The Demon-Haunted World: Science as a Candle in the Dark* (New York: Random House, 1996).

185   Charles Forelle, "Luxembourg Lies on Secret Meeting," *Wall Street Journal*, May 9, 2011.

186   Niccolò Machiavelli, *The Prince: A Revised Translation, Backgrounds, Interpretations*, trans. Wayne A. Rebhorn (New York: W. W. Norton 2020), chapter 18. Originally published 1513.

187   Quoted in Steven D. Price, *1001 Dumbest Things Ever Said* (Guilford, CT: Lyons Press, 2004).

188   *The Notebooks of Leonardo da Vinci*, trans. Jean Paul Richter (New York: Scribner and Welford, 1888). Full quote: "Beyond a doubt truth bears the same relation to falsehood as light to darkness; and this truth is in itself so excellent that, even when it dwells on humble and lowly matters, it is still infinitely above uncertainty and lies, disguised in high and lofty discourses; because in our minds, even if lying should be their fifth element, this does not prevent that the truth of things is the chief nutriment of superior intellects, though not of wandering wits."

189   Harry Frankfurt, "How to Spot Bullshit: A Primer by Princeton Philosopher Harry Frankfurt," *Open Culture*, May 30, 2016. See also his book, Harry Frankfurt, *On Bullshit* (Princeton, NJ: Princeton University Press, 2005).

190   Matthew Yglesias, "The Bullshitter-in-Chief," *Vox*, May 30, 2017.

191   The earliest source found in Google Books dates from 1968, and does not attribute it to W. C. Fields but to a certain "Bill": "I said, 'What do you do, Bill?' He says 'Well, if I can't dazzle them with my brilliance I baffle them with my bull,' and doggone if he doesn't." Not found attributed to W. C. Fields until 2005. From Wikiquote (October 27, 2017). The quotation has been printed on signs and T-shirts since at least the early 1970s. James Boren (1925–2010) and his spoof organization called the International Association of Professional Bureaucrats helped to popularize the flippant one-liner. The saying "If you can't convince them, confuse them" was popularized by US President Harry S. Truman in 1948. From barrypopik.com (October 27, 2017).

192   Voltaire, *Questions Sur Les Miracles* (Genève: n.p., 1765). I herein use a popular variant. Original: Certainement qui est en droit de vous rendre absurde est en droit de vous rendre injuste. (Certainly anyone who has the power to make you believe absurdities has the power to make you commit injustices.)

193   Don King, *Sunday Times*, December 18, 1994.

194   Edward de Bono, *Simplicity* (Harmondsworth: Penguin Books, 1998), 66.

195   John Authers, "Ed Thorp: the Man Who Beat the Casinos, then the Markets, Lunch with the FT," *Financial Times*, February 5, 2017.

196   Alberto Brandolini, @ziobrando, Twitter (January 11, 2013) and Wikipedia (October 27, 2017). Brandolini was inspired by Daniel Kahneman, *Thinking, Fast and Slow* (New York: Farrar, Straus and Giroux, 2011).

197   Quentin Crisp, *Manners from Heaven* (London: Hutchinson, 1984). Full quote: "Of course I lie to people. But I lie altruistically—for our mutual good. The lie is the basic building block of good manners. That may seem mildly shocking to a moralist—but then what isn't?"

198   Dr. Travis Bradberry, "8 Signs You're Being Lied to," *HuffPost*, May 28, 2017. If you are unfamiliar with the research of lie spotting, look up this article. I believe this works in practice, especially signs listed as number one and eight.

199   Michael Crichton, "Environmentalism is a Religion," Remarks to the Commonwealth Club, San Francisco, September 15, 2003.

200   Agatha Christie, *After the Funeral* (New York: Black Dog & Leventhal, 1953). First published 1900.

201   George Soros, *The Alchemy of Finance: Reading the Mind of the Market* (New York: John Wiley & Sons, 2003), 37. First published in 1987 with Simon & Schuster (New York).

202   Paul Ormerod, *Why Most Things Fail . . . And How to Avoid It: Evolution, Extinction, and Economics* (London: Faber & Faber, 2005), 68.

203   Phil Rosenzweig, *The Halo Effect: How Managers Let Themselves Be Deceived* (London: Simon & Schuster, 2014), xii and 101. First published in 2008 with Simon & Schuster (New York).

204   Jack Schwager, *Market Wizards: Interviews with Top Traders* (New York: CollinsBusiness, 1993), 126. First published in 1989 by the New York Institute of Finance. The quotation is a reference to a lesson learned from a big loss early in his career; as in "learning by doing," discussed earlier.

205   There is some uncertainty as to the origin of this quotation. The quotation is attributed to both Mark Twain and Will Rogers. The quotation fits both men's style. According to Wikiquote (December 26, 2020) it is misattributed to Will Rogers. Emphasis is my own.

       I have been using this quote throughout my career to underline the importance of protecting one's principal in active risk management.

206   John Kenneth Galbraith, *A Short History of Financial Euphoria* (London: Penguin Books, 1994), 13. First published in 1990 by Whittle Books. Full quote: "Contributing to and supporting this euphoria are two further factors little noted in our time or in past times. The first is the extreme brevity of the financial memory. In consequence, financial disaster is quickly forgotten. In further consequence, when the same or closely similar circumstances occur again, sometimes in only a few years, they are hailed by a new, often youthful, and always supremely self-confident generation as a brilliantly innovative discovery in the financial and larger economic world. There can be few fields of human endeavor in which history counts for so little as in the world of finance. Past experience, to the extent that it is part of memory at all, is dismissed as the primitive refuge of those who do not have insight to appreciate the incredible wonders of the present." This is pure applied wisdom as far as I can judge. This quote is one of my top ten quotes in this book.

207 Remarks by Mr. Alan Greenspan before a conference sponsored by the Office of the Comptroller of the Currency, Washington, DC (October 14, 1999).

208 Ludwig von Mises, *Human Action: A Treatise on Economics*, 4th ed. (San Francisco: Fox & Wilkes, 1996), 517. First published 1949 by Yale University.

209 See Thomas Sowell, *Ever Wonder Why? and Other Controversial Essays* (Stanford: Hoover Institution Press, 2006), 89.

210 As quoted in Andrew Alexander, "Safe as Houses," *The Spectator*, May 22, 1976. Peter Bauer counted many journalists as his friends, including Andrew Alexander. See also John O'Sullivan, "Peter Bauer and the English Class System," *Cato Journal* 25, no. 3 (Fall 2005): 489–501.

211 Julian Fellowes, *Downton Abbey*, episode #1.1 (ITV Studios, 2010–15). This quotation also depicts well the idea that risk and opportunity are two sides of the same coin, a topic discussed later in the book.

212 Lois McMaster Bujold, *Brothers in Arms* (Riverdale, NY: Baen Books, 1989).

213 The source of this definition is from the education materials of Chicago-based options trading boutique O'Connor that joint ventured with Swiss Bank Corporation, my then employer, in the late 1980s. The definition has stood the test of time. It seems robust. Hat tip to Glenn Satty and Joe Trocollo.

214 Gene Roddenberry, "The Enterprise Incident," episode in *Star Trek* [TV Series], 1968.

215 James Montier, "The Seven Immutable Laws of Investing," White Paper, GMO (March 2011).

216 Quoted from Roger Lowenstein, *When Genius Failed: The Rise and Fall of Long-Term Capital Management* (New York: Random House, 2000), 64.

217 Barton Biggs, *Diary of a Hedgehog: Biggs' Final Words on the Markets* (Hoboken: John Wiley & Sons, 2012), xvii.

218 Tanya Styblo Beder, "VAR: Seductive but Dangerous," *Financial Analyst Journal* 51, no. 5 (September–October 1995): 12–24.

219 Johann Wolfgang von Goethe, *Goethe, Maximen und Reflexionen. Aphorismen und Aufzeichnungen. Nach den Handschriften des Goethe- und Schiller-Archivs hg. von Max Hecker* (Weimer: Verlag der Goethe-Gesellschaft, 1907).

220 David Harding, "Black Monday and the Role of Professors Toting Algorithms," *Financial Times*, October 18, 2017. So called "gap risk" is not the main part of this book. Gap risk and the lack of liquidity are topics tangentially covered throughout the book though.

221 As quoted in the essay "To Albert Einstein's Seventieth Birthday" by Arnold Sommerfeld, in *Albert Einstein: Philosopher-Scientist*, ed. Paul A. Schilpp, Library of Living Philosophers, vol. 7 (La Salle, IL: Open Court, 1949), 102. The essay, originally published as "Zum Siebzigsten Geburtstag Albert Einsteins" in *Deutsche Beiträge* (Eine Zweimonatsschrift) 3, no. 2 (1949), was translated specifically for the book by Schilpp. From Wikiquote (December 7, 2016).

222   Quoted from Howard Marks, "Expert Opinion," *Memo to Oaktree Clients*, January 10, 2017. The "experienced, connected Democrat" and Hillary Clinton supporter, according to Marks, used this one-liner in relation to Sanders, and was proven right. He used it again against Trump. The math was indeed irresistible, as it often is.

223   See Frank H. Knight, *Risk, Uncertainty, and Profit* (New York: Sentry Press, 1964), 19. First published in 1921 by Houghton Mifflin (Boston).

224   Walter Bagehot, *Literary Studies* (London: Longmans, Green, and Company, 1879).

225   Cicero, *De Natura*, 5, 12; reported in J. K. Hoyt, *New Cyclopedia of Practical Quotations* (New York: Funk & Wagnalls, 1922), 634.

226   Paul Wilmott and David Orrell, *The Money Formula: Dodgy Finance, Pseudo Science, and How Mathematicians Took Over the Markets* (Chichester: John Wiley & Sons, 2017), 166.

227   Yuval Noah Harari, *21 Lessons for the 21st Century* (London: Jonathan Cape, 2018), 7.

228   Carveth Read, *Logic* (London: Grant Richards, 1898). A variant of this quotation is often misattributed to Keynes.

229   Wilmott and Orrell, *The Money Formula*, 109–10. "Boffin" is a somewhat derogatory British term for scientist.

230   Wilmott and Orrell, *The Money Formula*, 109.

231   Phil Rosenzweig, *The Halo Effect: How Managers Let Themselves Be Deceived* (London: Simon & Schuster, 2007).

232   Daisy Maxey, "New Index Trackers Use Hedge Funds as Investing Guide," *Wall Street Journal*, December 27, 2006. A cynical investor examining a long-term chart of GE to 2020 might argue that the computer probably would have done a better job running the company post-Welch.

233   Sigmund Freud, *Civilization and Its Discontents* (New York: Jonathan Cape & Harrison Smith, 1930).

234   Peter L. Bernstein, *Against the Gods: The Remarkable Story of Risk* (New York: John Wiley & Sons, 1996), 336.

235   Original: "[Speaking of computers] But they are useless. They can only give you answers." The origin seems to be the article "Pablo Picasso: A Composite Interview" by William Fifield, which appeared in the *Paris Review* 32, Summer–Fall 1964, and collected a number of interviews Fifield had done with Picasso. The variant I use seems to have arisen in the 1980s; the earliest known appearance in a book is in an article by Herman Feshbach, "Reflections on the Microprocessor Revolution: A Physicist's Viewpoint," in *Man and Technology: The Social and Cultural Challenge of Modern Society*, ed. Bruce M. Adkins (Cambridge: Cambridge Information and Research Service, 1983), 100. From Quote Investigator and Wikiquote (January 10, 2017).

236   Jim Rasmussen, "Buffett Talks Strategy with Students," *Omaha World-Herald*, January 2, 1994. The context of the quotation is in relation to buying a business and Mr. Buffett not adding an equity risk premium to the discount rate, which would be finance orthodoxy. The full quotation

reads: "I put a heavy weight on certainty. If you do that, the whole idea of a risk factor doesn't make any sense to me. Risk comes from not knowing what you're doing." From Roberg G. Hagstrom, *The Warren Buffett Way: Investment Strategy of the World's Greatest Investor* (New York: John Wiley & Sons, 1994), 94–95. I believe this risk-comes-from-not-knowing-what-you're-doing to be one of the top ten pieces of wisdom in this book. Top three perhaps.

237   Arthur Ashe, quoted from an advertisement by Barra, Inc., a provider of risk tools.

238   Towers Watson, "The Wrong Type of Snow—Risk Revisited," February 2012. https://www.thinkingaheadinstitute.org/content/uploads/2020/11/TW-EU-2012-26014_The_wrong_type_of_snow_update.pdf.

239   As quoted in an editorial for an early issue of the London Business School's Risk Measurement Service, almost forty years ago. From email correspondence with the author (December 22, 2016).

240   Andreas Thiel, *Humor: Das Lächeln des Henkers* (Thun: Werd Verlag, 2015), 137. Translation is my own.

241   In the 2019 Survey, Switzerland ranked fourth together with Sweden and Singapore, a low rank standing for least corrupt. China was ranked eightieth from one hundred and ninety-eight countries, a rank it shared with Benin, Ghana, India, and Morocco. The mention of Macao in the text is a reference to the policy of bribing government officials by letting them win at the gaming tables of Macao.

242   Which is of course entirely untrue. Switzerland is fourth based on Nobel Prize winners per capita after Faroe Islands, that has one Nobel laureate, Saint Lucia and Luxembourg, that have two each. Furthermore, Switzerland ranked third in patents per capita after South Korea and Japan in 2018. The Swiss are creative: it does actually require a beautiful mind to come up with the idea of stirring pieces of leftover bread on an oversized fork in a pot of melted cheese.

243   Quoted from imdb.com (December 16, 2016). In contrast, this is how one zerohedge.com subscriber put it (in relation to the Swiss referendum to stop the national bank selling its gold reserves): "Blessed are the Swiss cheesemakers, for they make holey cheese."

244   After the defeat at Bibracte, and in exchange for their freedom, the Helvetians agreed to Caesar's demand that they guard the frontier in the north of their territory against Germanic invasions. However, this agreement was broken in 52 BC when eight thousand Helvetians left to support Vercingetorix (chieftain of the Gauls, no relation to Asterix) who was leading the Gallic uprising against Rome. Caesar won against the Gauls, and the Romans occupied all the conquered territories, including Helvetia.

245   Jeremy Bentham, *Panopticon; or, the Inspection House* (Dublin: T. Payne, 1791).

246   Edward R. Pressman, Wall Street: Money Never Sleeps, American drama film directed by Oliver Stone, 2010. The fact that Gordon Gekko was portraying a criminal, I'll leave aside for the moment.

247   Walter Bagehot, "Dull Government," *Saturday Review*, February 16, 1856.

248   True story: It's the mid-2010s, I'm based in Zurich and give a 11 a.m.
      presentation at a conference in Frankfurt, a keynote presentation, if I
      remember correctly. (An entirely regular presentation, if I remember
      incorrectly.) During my presentation, in relation to portfolio volatility,
      I make the reference to the Swiss being perceived as dull and that being
      a good thing from a wealth preservation standpoint; the argument I just
      made earlier. Taking the 6 p.m. flight back to Zurich, heading to the exit
      at Zurich airport, I was overtaken by a Swiss financial professional who,
      locally, was quite famous and herein will remain unnamed. Once this
      bolting Swiss financial professional, who was ten to fifteen years older than
      I was then, overtakes me, he turns back and fumingly yells at me in Swiss
      German: "By the way, not all of us are humorless!" and continues darting
      for the exit, pulling his rolling onboard luggage masculinely behind him.
          Clare O'Dea, the author of *The Naked Swiss: A Nation Behind 10 Myths*
      (Basel, Switzerland: Bergli Books, 2016), has the last word on the subject:
      "The Swiss will never be the wild child of Europe; you only have to look at
      their lovingly tended vegetable patches to see that. But whether they are
      boring or not most likely depends on the eye of the beholder."

249   As quoted in Mark Tier, *The Winning Investment Habits of Warren Buffett
      and George Soros* (New York: St. Martin's Griffin, 2006), 217.

250   1910 data is from William N. Goetzmann, "Will History Rhyme?—The
      Past as Financial Future," *Journal of Portfolio Management* 30, no. 5
      (2004): 34–41, quoting Vladimir Lenin, *Imperialism: The Highest Stage of
      Capitalism* (New York: International Publishing Company Reprint, 1969).
      Originally published in 1917. The chapter draws on material first published
      in Alexander Ineichen, *Asymmetric Returns: The Future of Active Asset
      Management* (New York: John Wiley & Sons, 2007). The following indices
      were used to calculate market capitalization in Swiss Francs (CHF) as of
      December 23, 2020: Swiss Performance Index, FTSE All-Share Index,
      Vienna Stock Exchange Share Index, and Budapest Stock Exchange Stock
      Index. The market capitalizations were: CHF1.67 trillion (tr), CHF2.87tr,
      CHF0.11tr, and CHF0.01tr, rounded to two decimals. Raw data was from
      Bloomberg. Calculations are my own.

251   Oscar Wilde, *The Model Millionaire* (New York: Dodd Mead and Company,
      1891).

252   John Kay, "Why the 'Happiest' Cities Are Boring," *Financial Times*,
      September 9, 2015.

253   F. A. Hayek, *The Fatal Conceit: The Errors of Socialism* (London: Routledge,
      1988), 76. Full quote: "The curious task of economics is to demonstrate
      to men how little they really know about what they imagine they can
      design. To the naive mind that can conceive of order only as the product
      of deliberate arrangement, it may seem absurd that in complex conditions
      order, and adaptation to the unknown, can be achieved more effectively by
      decentralizing decisions and that a division of authority will actually extend

the possibility of overall order. Yet that decentralization actually leads to more information being taken into account."

254   Will Durant, *The Story of Philosophy* (New York: Simon & Schuster, 2006), xxviii. Originally published in 1926 by Simon & Schuster (New York). The quotation is from the introduction. A larger part of the quotation reads as follows: "Science is analytical description, philosophy is synthetic interpretation. Science wishes to resolve the whole into parts, the organism into organs, the obscure into the known . . . the scientist is as impartial as Nature in Turgenev's poem: he is as interested in the leg of a flea as in the creative throes of a genius. But the philosopher is not content to describe the fact; he wishes to ascertain its relation to experience in general, and thereby to get at its meaning and its worth; he combines things in interpretive synthesis; he tries to put together, better than before, that great universe-watch which the inquisitive scientist has analytically taken apart . . . Science without philosophy, facts without perspective and valuation, cannot save us from havoc and despair. Science gives us knowledge, but only philosophy can give us wisdom." A related quotation from the author's note to the reader, dated 1926, reads: "Analysis belongs to science, and gives us knowledge; philosophy must provide a synthesis for wisdom."

255   Kathy Lette, *The Boy Who Fell to Earth* (London: Transworld Publishers, 2012).

256   The Knowledge Pyramid is most often credited to Russell L. Ackoff, "From Data to Wisdom," *Journal of Applied Systems Analysis* 16 (1989): 3–9. Some versions exclude "understanding." The idea also known as the "Data Information Knowledge and Wisdom Hierarchy" (DIKW) or the "Knowledge Hierarchy."

257   Thomas Alvin Boyd, *Prophet of Progress: Selections from the Speeches of Charles F. Kettering* (New York: E. P. Dutton, 1961).

258   I believe this to be a wonderful quotation by what was arguably a clever chap; Kant, that is. However, it's one of those quotes that are just too convenient. The quotation is fabricated; evolved from different parts over time. The Quote Investigator ("QI"), one of my go-to sources when trying to find the original source of a quote, phrased it as follows: "Immanuel Kant communicated in German, and QI believes that he probably did not write or speak a statement in German that corresponded to the English quotation above. Instead, QI believes that the first part of the expression was crafted by the influential philosopher and sociologist Herbert Spencer. In addition, QI conjectures that the popular historian Will Durant constructed the second part while he was attempting to explain the thoughts of Kant; Durant also combined the two parts. Kant died in 1804, and the earliest evidence of the first phrase was published in an essay titled "The Art of Education" by Spencer in May 1854 . . . Durant explained Kant's philosophical position by discussing a hierarchical sequence of interacting levels. The quotation under examination was part of Durant's elucidation: 'Sensation is unorganized stimulus, perception is organized sensation,

conception is organized perception, science is organized knowledge, wisdom is organized life: each is a greater degree of order, and sequence, and unity.'" From Quote Investigator (June 23, 2017). I attributed the original idea to Kant in the text, despite the reservations.

259   Gustave Le Bon, *The Crowd: A Study of the Popular Mind*, 2nd ed. (Atlanta: Cherokee Publishing Company, 1982), 86. First published in 1895 in French: *Psychologie des Foules*.

260   Jack Schwager, *Market Wizards: Interviews with Top Traders* (New York: CollinsBusiness, 1993), 128. First published in 1989 by the New York Institute of Finance.

261   I thought this was a "saying." Wikiquote (December 7, 2016) attributes it to "Ron Weinstein, an eminent academic pathologist." Another attribution is to Grady Booch, developer of the Unified Modeling Language.

262   Euripides, *Bacchæ*.

263   George Bernard Shaw, *Androcles and the Lion* (New York: Brentano's, 1910), preface.

264   Thomas Sowell, "Random Thoughts," *Townhall*, (November 29, 2005).

265   David Rosenberg, *Breakfast with Dave*, Gluskin Sheff, February 9, 2012.

266   Edwin Lefèvre, *Reminiscences of a Stock Operator*, Investment Classics (New York: John Wiley & Sons, 1993), 181. First published in 1923 by George H. Doran and Company (New York).

267   Bagehot, "Wink Wink," *The Economist*, July 24, 2008, summarizing research by social psychologists and behavioral economists.

268   Israeli-Palestinian summit, June 2003, quoted by Palestinian foreign minister Nabil Shaath in "George Bush: 'God told me to end the tyranny in Iraq,' *The Guardian*, October 7, 2005. The full quote: "I am driven with a mission from God. God would tell me, 'George, go and fight these terrorists in Afghanistan.' And I did. And then God would tell me 'George, go and end the tyranny in Iraq.' And I did ... And now, again, I feel God's words coming to me, 'Go get the Palestinians their state and get the Israelis their security, and get peace in the Middle East.' And, by God, I'm gonna do it." From Wikiquote (January 31, 2017), that has the following disclaimer: "These remarks were allegedly made by Bush outside the presence of reporters, and have not been confirmed by Bush's representatives nor denied by representatives of anyone present."

269   I assume hearing voices and/or having a split personality has some advantages. There is always someone around to debate the matters at hand: "I have opinions of my own—strong opinions—but I don't always agree with them." (George H. W. Bush, *Spin Magazine*, November 1992).

270   As quoted in N. B. Sen, *Wit and Wisdom of Socrates, Plato, Aristotle* (New Delhi: New Book Society of India, 1967), 140.

271   Mehdi Hasan, "The NS Interview: Nassim Nicholas Taleb," *NewStatesman*, June 18, 2010. Quotation is answer to "You've written a lot about chance and probability. Do you believe in God?" Full answer: "I'm in favor of religion as a tamer of arrogance. For a Greek Orthodox, the idea of God as creator outside the human is not God in God's terms. My god isn't the

god of George Bush." The description of Taleb in the text is his Twitter description, retrieved May 8, 2017.

272 Galileo Galilei, Letter to the Grand Duchess Christina of Tuscany, 1615.

273 David M. Darst, *The Little Book That Still Saves Your Assets* (Hoboken: John Wiley & Sons, 2013), 14.

274 H. L. Mencken, *Damn! A Book of Calumny* (New York: Philip Goodman, 1918).

275 John Maynard Keynes, *New Statesman and Nation*, July 15, 1933. On Keynes's arrogance: One economist, Murray N. Rothbard (1926–95), an Austrian economist with opposing views to Keynes, described Keynes as follows: "To sum up Keynes. Arrogant, sadistic, power besotted bully, deliberate and systemic liar, intellectually irresponsible, an opponent of principle, in favor of short term hedonism and nihilistic opponent of Bourgeois morality in all of its areas, a hater of thrift and savings, somebody who wanted to liquidate the creditor class, exterminate the creditor class, an imperialist, an anti-Semite, and a Fascist. Outside of that I guess he was a great guy." From a 1989 speech by Murray N. Rothbard, "Keynes the Man: Hero or Villain?", tongue firmly in cheek, presumably.

276 Quoted from Jonathan Duffy, "The Right to Be Downright Offensive," *BBC News Magazine*, December 21, 2004.

277 John Trenchard and Thomas Gordon, *Cato's Letters*, vol. 1 (1720). Spelling as in the original. The *Cato Letters* is a series of one hundred and forty-four essays that condemn corruption and lack of morality within the British political system and warning against tyranny. Full quote: "Without Freedom of Thought, there can be no such Thing as Wisdom; and no such Thing as publick Liberty, without Freedom of Speech: Which is the Right of every Man, as far as by it he does not hurt and control the Right of another; and this is the only Check which it ought to suffer, the only Bounds which it ought to know."

278 Bobby Henderson, *The Gospel of the Flying Spaghetti Monster* (London: Harper Collins, 2006), xi. Disclaimer about midgets.

279 Caskie Stinnett, *Out of the Red* (New York: Random House, 1960).

280 Isaac D'Israeli, *Curiosities of Literature* (London: J. Murray, 1791–1834). Emphasis in the original.

281 As quoted in *Reader's Digest* 140 (1992).

282 From Michael Lewis, *Liar's Poker: Rising through the Wreckage on Wall Street* (New York: Penguin Books, 1989). *Liar's Poker* is a gem, still readable and applicable. When I was very young, I once argued that if *Liar's Poker* were required reading in finance, all regulation would be obsolete. The full quotation of the anonymous trader contains more wisdom or, depending on your perception, more sarcasm: "When I'm trading, you see, I don't stop to pat myself on the back. Because when I pat myself on the back, the next sensation is usually a sharp kick lower down. And it isn't so pleasant." When asked the key to his success, he said, "In the land of the blind the one-eyed man is king." Best of all, he gave us a rule of thumb about information in the

markets that I later found useful: "Those who say don't know, and those who know don't say."

283   Tao Te Ching, representing the sole document generally attributed to Lao Tzu, Verse 56, translation by Stephen Mitchell. Full quote: "Those who know don't talk. Those who talk don't know. Close your mouth, block off your senses, blunt your sharpness, untie your knots, soften your glare, settle your dust. This is the primal identity. Be like the Tao. It can't be approached or withdrawn from, benefited or harmed, honored or brought into disgrace. It gives itself up continually. That is why it endures."

284   Charles Knight, *Knight's Quarterly Magazine*, volume III, August–November 1824.

285   Baltasar Gracián, *The Art of Worldly Wisdom* (n.p., 1647), clxvi.

286   In 1975, Brandon Gill published a memoir titled *Here at The New Yorker* (Random House, New York) that included in Chapter 6 the following passage: "In fact, not a shred of evidence exists in favor of the argument that life is serious, though it is often hard and even terrible. And saying that, I am prompted to add what follows out of it: that since everything ends badly for us, in the inescapable catastrophe of death, it seems obvious that the first rule of life is to have a good time; and that the second rule of life is to hurt as few people as possible in the course of doing so. There is no third rule." From Quote Investigator (January 31, 2017).

287   I assume this is a four-word summary of William James, *Pragmatism: A New Name for Some Old Ways of Thinking* (London: Longmans Green and Co, 1907). The original is "truth in our ideas means their power to work." The variant I use is part of a book title: Harvey Cormier, *The Truth Is What Works: William James, Pragmatism, and the Seed of Death* (Lanham: Rowman & Littlefield, 2000).

288   George Bernard Shaw, *The World*, July 18, 1894.

289   As quoted in Oscar Wilde, *The Illustrated Oscar Wilde*, ed. Roy Gasson (Poole, Dorset: New Orchard Editions, 1977), xxii.

290   P. J. O'Rourke, *Holidays in Hell* (New York: Atlantic Monthly Press, 1988).

291   From Jane Austen, *Emma* (London: John Murray, 1816), vol. 2, chapter 8: Emma to Mr. Knightley; a monologue that applies reasonably well to finance: "I do not know whether it ought to be so, but certainly silly things do cease to be silly if they are done by sensible people in an impudent way. Wickedness is always wickedness, but folly is not always folly.—It depends upon the character of those who handle it." Em-dash in the original.

292   George Bernard Shaw, *Man and Superman: A Comedy and a Philosophy* (Westminster: Archibald Constable & Co., 1903), Maxims for Revolutionists, 238.

293   Baltasar Gracian, *The Art of Worldly Wisdom* (n.p., 1647), ccxl.

294   Bertrand Russell, *Marriage and Morals* (New York: H. Liveright, 1929), 58. Full quote: "The fact that an opinion has been widely held is no evidence whatever that it is not utterly absurd; indeed in view of the silliness of the majority of mankind, a widespread belief is more likely to be foolish than sensible."

295 H. L. Mencken, *A Mencken Chrestomathy* (New York: Alfred A. Knopf, 1949).

296 As quoted in Doreen Chila-Jones, *Say What?* (Baltimore: Duopress, 2018).

297 Michel de Montaigne, Project Gutenberg's *The Essays of Montaigne*, book I, chapter XXXI. The full quotation deserves the endnote reader's attention. It reads: "The true field and subject of imposture are things unknown, forasmuch as, in the first place, their very strangeness lends them credit, and moreover, by not being subjected to our ordinary reasons, they deprive us of the means to question and dispute them: For which reason, says Plato, —[In Critias.]—it is much more easy to satisfy the hearers, when speaking of the nature of the gods than of the nature of men, because the ignorance of the auditory affords a fair and large career and all manner of liberty in the handling of abstruse things. Thence it comes to pass, that nothing is so firmly believed, as what we least know; nor any people so confident, as those who entertain us with fables, such as your alchemists, judicial astrologers, fortune-tellers, and physicians . . ."

298 Ludwig von Mises, *Epistemological Problems of Economics*, trans. George Reisman, edited and with a foreword by Bettina Bien Greaves and Introduction by Jörg Guido Hülsmann, 3rd ed. (Indianapolis: Liberty Fund, 2013), 179. Originally published in German as *Grundprobleme der Nationalökonomie* (Jena: Verlag von Gustav Fischer, 1933).

299 This quotation, or a variant thereof, has been attributed to both Thomas Dewar (1864–1930), a Scottish whisky distiller, as well as James Dewar (1842–1923), Scottish chemist and physicist (no relation). Barrypopik.com (December 27, 2020) traces the origin to the Louisville (KY) *Times* in 1927 with the original authorship being unknown.

300 Bertrand Russell, *Unpopular Essays* (London: George Allen and Unwin, 1950).

301 "Fere libenter homines id quod volunt credunt." Translated to: "In most cases men willingly believe what they wish." From De Bello Gallico, Commentarii de Bello Gallico (Commentaries on the Gallic War), book III, chapter 18. From Wikiquote (December 27, 2020). I use a popular variant of the quote.

302 No source could be found attributing this to Buddha. One source says it's a fake, another that it's a poor translation, twisting Buddha's meaning. It's still an applicable quotation; irrespective from where it originated.

303 Original: "Croyez ceux qui cherchent la vérité, doutez de ceux qui la trouvent; doutez de tout, mais ne doutez pas de vous-même." From André Gide, *Ainsi soit-il; ou, Les Jeux sont faits Texte imprimé* (Paris: Gallimard, 1952), 174. From Wikiquote (December 21, 2016). An advertisement by Insight Investment Management, a London-based financial consultant, read: "Believe those who are seeking the truth. Doubt those who find it." From *Financial Times*, June 25, 2012.

　　Disclaimer: this quote is self-serving in my case as I do research for a living and research of course involves searching for the truth.

304   Voltaire, Letter to Frederick William, Prince of Prussia (November 28, 1770).

305   What was first, Voltaire or the German proverb, I don't know. Voltaire might have been paraphrasing Madeleine de Scudéry (1607–1701), French author who ran a well-frequented salon in the 1650s: "Die Skepsis ist die Mutter der Gewissheit." (Skepticism is the mother of certainty.)

306   Originally published in 1959, but appearing in the collected works of of Erich Fromm, as "Der Kreative Mensch," In *Gesamtausgabe. Vol. 9: Sozialistischer Humanismus und humanistische Ethik*, ed. Rainer Funk (Stuttgart: Deutsche Verlags-Anstalt, 1980–81), 399–407.

307   Will Durant, *The Greatest Minds and Ideas of All Time*, compiled and edited by John Little (New York: Simon & Schuster, 2002), 26.

308   The resolution of independence was actually approved in a closed session of Congress on July 2.
      The most important freedom-related one-pager in history was Switzerland's Federal Charter from 1291. In terms of spirit, the two one-pagers from 1291 and 1776 are quite similar. Switzerland's Federal Charter is kept in a museum, a twenty-minute drive from where I live in central Switzerland. My ranking of important freedom-toting one-pagers, therefore, needs to be taken with a pinch of applied history salt. Britain's *Magna Carta* from 1215 was pretty important too.

309   George Iles, *Canadian Stories* (New York: George Iles, 1918), 167.

310   Mohandas K. "Mahatma" Gandhi, *Harijan* (Gandhi's weekly publication), February 17, 1940.

311   It's unclear whether Minsky ever said this. I assume it is a three-word summary from his 1992 paper "The Financial Instability Hypothesis." See Hyman P. Minsky, "The Financial Instability Hypothesis," the Jerome Levy Economics Institute Working Paper 74, May 1992.

312   Walter Raleigh, Letter to Sir Robert Cecil (May 10, 1593).

313   As quoted in Ralph Louis Woods, *The Modern Handbook of Humor* (New York: McGraw Hill, 1967), 493. There are many variants of this quote. It is not just attributed to Heine.

314   David Dreman, "Ben Graham Was Right—Again," *Forbes*, May 5, 1996.

315   John Webster, "The Alternative Balancing Act," *Greenwich Associates*, December 2003.

316   As quoted in Nina Colman, *The Friars Club Bible of Jokes, Pokes, Roasts, and Toasts* (New York: Hachette Books, 2001), 316.

317   Confucius, *The Analects*, as quoted in Gary Jones, *Chambers Dictionary of Quotations* (London: Chambers, 1997), 279. There are some variants in wording but not in content.

318   Michel de Montaigne, *Essais* (1600).

319   Thomas Fuller, *Gnomologia* (1732). Or as songwriter Bob Marley put it in what was not a finance-related context: "You ain't gonna miss your water until your well runs dry." From lyrics to "Could You Be Loved."

320 From a "Valedictory Address, Delivered to the Graduating Class of the Bellevue Hospital College" in 1871, reprinted in the *New York Medical Journal* 13: 426.

321 Quoted from Karen Weekes, *Women Know Everything!* (Philadelphia: Quirk Books, 2007), 142.

322 Gerald Ashley, *Uncertainty and Expectation: Strategies for the Trading of Risk* (Chichester: John Wiley & Sons, 2003), 98.

323 See for example: Tom Morris, *Philosophy for Dummies* (New York: Wiley Publishing, 1999), 49.

324 Sometimes attributed to Oscar Wilde without providing an original source.

325 From Ethan Reiff and Cyrus Voris, *Kung Fu Panda* (DreamWorks Animation, 2008). Original: "Oogway: There are no accidents. Shifu: [sighs] Yes, I know. You've already said that twice. Oogway: That was no accident either. Shifu: Thrice." From imdb.com (October 24, 2017).

326 From Gonzales (2003) referencing Perrow (1999).

327 I herein use a popular variant. The following quotation is often misattributed to Albert Einstein: "Any intelligent fool can make things bigger, more complex and more violent. It takes a touch of genius—and a lot of courage—to move in the opposite direction." This quotation was actually written by Ernst F. Schumacher in a 1973 essay titled "Small is Beautiful," which appeared in the *Radical Humanist*: volume 37, p. 22. Earliest published source found on Google Books attributing this to Einstein is: The *British Medical Journal* 319, 23 (October 1999): 1102. From Wikiquote (December 23, 2016).

328 *Institutional Investor Magazine*, September 2001.

329 Ken Griffin said in 2017 that he didn't appreciate the fragility of the US banking system in the lead-up to the 2008 financial crisis—a blip that amounted to the "biggest mistake" of his career. "I did not foresee a day where the government had to intervene to bail out basically everybody," Griffin said in a video interview with *Institutional Investor*'s Julie Segal. From Rachael Levy "Hedge Fund Titan Ken Griffin Describes the 'Incredibly Humiliating' Moment His Firm Nearly Went Under," *Business Insider*, July 5, 2017.

330 Quoted from Vince Farrell, "Why Risk/Reward Favors Investors," *CNBC Guest Blog*, September 30, 2008.

331 Some of the remarks in this chapter related to Wriston's law of capital draw on material from Alexander Ineichen, "Wriston's Law of Capital," IR&M, July 10, 2012.

332 Charles Churchill, *The Ghost* (1762), sometimes erroneously attributed to Winston Churchill.

333 Robertson Davies, *A Voice from the Attic: Essays on the Art of Reading* (London: Penguin Books, 1990).

334 This story was passed around in 2009. Original source unknown. Hat tip to Dennis Gartman.

335 George Bernard Shaw, *Back to Methuselah* (New York: Brentano's, 1921).

336   Graham Norton, *The Graham Norton Show*, June 6, 2018, commenting on Kim Kardashian visiting Trump in the Oval Office.

337   Urs Bühler interview with Charles Lewinsky, "Charles Lewinsky: 'Im Jüdischen Witz Liefert oft Gott die Pointe,'" *NZZ*, August 23, 2018. Translation is my own.

338   Khalil Gibran, *Sand and Foam* (New York: Alfred A. Knopf, 1926).

339   Thornton Wilder, *The Eighth Day* (New York: Harper & Brothers, 1967).

340   As quoted in Dan Kamin, *Charlie Chaplin's One-man Show* (Lanham, MD: Scarecrow Press, 1984), 37.

341   Edward Abbey, *A Voice Crying in the Wilderness* (New York: St. Martin's Griffin, 1989).

342   Marion Capron interview with Dorothy Parker, "Dorothy Parker, The Art of Fiction No. 13," *Paris Review* 13, Summer 1956.

343   Original source unknown. Wikiquote (January 5, 2017) points to some well-founded doubts that the origin of this quotation stems from Isaac Asimov.

344   Ludwig Wittgenstein, *Culture and Value*, trans. Peter Winch (Chicago: Chicago Press, 1980), originally Ludwig Wittgenstein, *Vermischte Bemerkungen* (Oxford: Basil Blackwell, 1977). A variant reads: "If people never did silly things, nothing intelligent would ever get done." From Wikiquote (January 5, 2017).

345   Jules Renard, "Cherchez le Ridicule en Tout, Vous le Trouverez." *Journal*, February 17, 1890.

346   Aldous Huxley, *Do What You Will* (London: Chatto & Windus, 1929).

347   Tobias Smollett, *The Adventures of Roderick Random* (London: J. Osborn, 1748). Sometimes quoted as "Some men are wise, and some are otherwise."

348   As quoted in Elon Foster, *New Cyclopædia of Prose Illustrations* (New York: Funk & Wagnalls, 1877).

349   Original: " tlhIngan Hol: tugh qoH nachDaj je chevlu'ta,'" Literal translation: "Soon a fool and his head will be separated." In case you were wondering. The Klingons are a fictional race in *Star Trek*, and *The Final Reflection* is a 1984 Star Trek tie-in novel by John M. Ford that emphasizes developments of Klingon language and culture. A proverb that originated closer to Earth states: "A fool and his money are soon parted."

350   As quoted in Winston Churchill, *The Irrepressible Churchill: Stories, Sayings and Impressions of Sir Winston Churchill*, ed. Kay Halle (London: Robson, 1987).

351   Thomas Aquinas, *Summa Theologica*, I, lxxvi, 1. From Will Durant, *The Story of Civilization, Volume 4: The Age of Faith* (Norwalk: Easton Press, 1992). First published in 1950 with Simon & Schuster (New York).

352   "History repeats itself" is an old proverb. However, the quote is very often attributed to Mark Twain but is not found in his works. The earliest publication yet located is a verse that might involve a deliberate invocation of poetic license in John Robert Colombo's poem, "A Said Poem," published in John Robert Colombo, *Neo Poems* (Winlaw: Sono Nis Press, 1970),

which reads: "'History never repeats itself but it rhymes,' said Mark Twain." From Wikiquote (January 28, 2021).

Mark Twain did use the prefatory phrase "History never repeats itself" in a novel he cowrote with his neighbor Charles Dudley Warner. The 1874 edition of *The Gilded Age: A Tale of To-Day* employed wonderfully vivid figurative language based on a kaleidoscope: "History never repeats itself, but the Kaleidoscopic combinations of the pictured present often seem to be constructed out of the broken fragments of antique legends." From Quote Investigator (January 2, 2017). Hat tip to Barry Popik.

353 George Santayana, *The Life of Reason, Volume 1* (Westminster: Archibald Constable & Co., 1905).

354 Will Durant, *The Story of Civilization, Volume 1: Our Oriental Heritage* (Norwalk: Easton Press, 1992). First published in 1935 with Simon & Schuster (New York).

355 John W. Gardner, quoted in Rhoda Thomas Tripp, *The International Thesaurus of Quotations* (New York: Thomas Y. Crowell Co., 1970), 280.

356 From a Toro cartoon, originally most likely published in *The New Yorker*. Emphasis in the original.

357 Roger Allers and Rob Minkoff, *The Lion King* (1994), Walt Disney Pictures. From imdb.com (April 5, 2017).

358 I herein use an abbreviated variant as quoted at the start of the last chapter of Margaret Reid, *The Secondary Banking Crisis 1973–1975: The Inside Story of Britain's Biggest Banking Upheaval* (New York: Macmillan Press, 1982). Original quotation: "Was die Erfahrung aber und die Geschichte lehren, ist dieses, daß Völker und Regierungen niemals etwas aus der Geschichte gelernt und nach Lehren, die aus derselben zu ziehen gewesen wären, gehandelt haben." From Johannes Hoffmeister, *Vorlesungen über die Philosophie der Weltgeschichte. Bd. 1: Die Vernunft in der Geschichte* (Hamburg: Felix Meiner Verlag, 1994), 19. There are some variant translations, one of which is the following: "What experience and history teach is this—that nations and governments have never learned anything from history, or acted upon any lessons they might have drawn from it." Georg Hegel, *Lectures on the Philosophy of History,* vol. 1 of 3, trans. H. B. Nisbet (Cambridge: Cambridge University Press, 1975). Originally published in 1832. Original quotations and sources are from Wikiquote (January 2, 2017). Aldous Huxley might have been quoting Hegel in 1959: "That men do not learn very much from the lessons of history is the most important of all the lessons that history has to teach." From Aldous Huxley, "A Case of Voluntary Ignorance," *Esquire*, October 1, 1956.

359 Hat tip to Pat Cross.

360 Aldous Huxley, *Music at Night and Other Essays* (Garden City, NY: Doubleday, 1931).

361 I herein use a shortened and simplified and somewhat punchier variant from Tyler O'Neil, "Bill de Blasio Wants to Turn New York City Into Venezuela," *PJ Media*, September 5, 2017. The original is from an interview by *New York Magazine*, September 4, 2017: "What's been hardest [to make

progress] is the way our legal system is structured to favor private property. I think people all over this city, of every background, would like to have the city government be able to determine which building goes where, how high it will be, who gets to live in it, what the rent will be. I think there's a socialistic impulse, which I hear every day, in every kind of community, that they would like things to be planned in accordance to their needs. And I would, too. Unfortunately, what stands in the way of that is hundreds of years of history that have elevated property rights and wealth to the point that that's the reality that calls the tune on a lot of development."

362   John Locke, *An Essay Concerning Human Understanding* (London: Tho. Basset, 1689), book IV. Full quotation: "'Where there is no property there is no injustice,' is a proposition as certain as any demonstration in Euclid: for the idea of property being a right to anything, and the idea to which the name 'injustice' is given being the invasion or violation of that right, it is evident that these ideas, being thus established, and these names annexed to them, I can as certainly know this proposition to be true, as that a triangle has three angles equal to two right ones."

363   See Niall Ferguson, "The 6 Killer Apps of Prosperity," TED talk, TEDGlobal (July 2011). The six killer apps are: "1. Competition, 2. The Scientific Revolution, 3. Property Rights, 4. Modern Medicine, 5. The Consumer Society, 6. The work Ethic."

364   Karl Marx and Friedrich Engels, *Manifesto of the Communist Party*, a thirty-page pamphlet first published in German (London: Kommunistischer Arbeiterbildungsverein, 1848), then translated into English by Helen Macfarlane and published in serial fashion in the periodical, *The Red Republican* (1850). In English, the work is commonly referred to as *The Communist Manifesto*. A popular English version is *The Communist Manifesto*, introduction by Francis B. Randall, trans. Samuel Moore, and edited by Joseph Katz (New York: Pocket Books, 1965). Strictly speaking, the quotation I use is not a sentence but an expression. Original: "In diesem Sinn können die Kommunisten ihre Theorie in dem einen Ausdruck: Aufhebung des Privat-Eigenthums zusammenfassen." "Eigenthum" is not a typo but an old version of "Eigentum," changed at the "Orthographischen Konferenz" of 1901. So the authors of the *Communist Manifesto* of 1848 can only be ridiculed for content, not orthography.

365   As quoted from *The Intelliquest Historical Biography Series*, "The World's Greatest People," vol. 1, disk 6 (Intelliquest, 1995).

366   James Madison, *Property, Chapter 16, Papers 14* (March 29, 1792), 266–68. Edits in the original.

367   No source was found. This is probably one of the cases Voltaire warned about in the preface; not all quotations found on the Internet are true. I left it attributed to Winston Churchill. It fits his style.

368   Milton Friedman, Free to Choose, PBS television series, 1980.

369   Margaret Thatcher, in a TV interview for *Thames TV This Week*, February 5, 1976.

370   Raw data is from Angus Maddison's work, and GDP per capita is measured
      in 1990 International Geary-Khamis dollars. Calculations are my own.
      By comparison, the United States grew by 62 percent in both periods
      mentioned in the text.

371   Matt Ridley, *The Rational Optimist: How Prosperity Evolves* (New York:
      HarperCollins, 2011).

372   Henry Kaufman, *On Money and Markets: A Wall Street Memoir* (New
      York: McGraw Hill, 2000), 263. Kaufman on Wriston: "Walter is a tall and
      rather lanky man, with an intense bearing and a dry wit. Economically
      and politically conservative, he had close ties to the Republican political
      leadership in his day." That's not the end of the story. Kaufman and
      Wriston were opposites in terms of credit creation. Kaufman was the
      warner, dubbed "Dr. Doom," while Wriston was pushing credit expansion.
      Conversation between the two: Wriston: "Is the world coming to an end yet,
      Henry?" Kaufman: "Not as long as Citicorp has access to the Fed's discount
      window." Walter Wriston on Henry Kaufman: "For Henry Kaufman, a
      senior officer of Salomon Brothers with a clear view of its trading floor, to
      deplore the creation of excess credit is like the piano player in the fancy
      house protesting that he didn't know what was going on upstairs." From
      Kaufman making reference to a 1986 *Wall Street Journal* article by Walter
      Wriston titled "Dr. Doom Takes a Dark View of Regulation."

373   Rich Karlgaard, "Predicting the Future: Part II," *Forbes*, February 13,
      2006. I first came across Walter Wriston in *The Gartman Letter*. George
      Soros said something similar to what I herein call Wriston's law of capital:
      "Financial capital is an essential ingredient of production, and it will seek to
      go where it is best rewarded." From George Soros, *The Alchemy of Finance:
      Reading the Mind of the Market* (New York: John Wiley & Sons, 2003),
      13. First published in 1987 by Simon & Schuster (New York). Many other
      economists and down-to-earth practitioners have said something similar.
      Some call it the iron law of capitalism. I have a preference for the Walter
      Wriston version because it is short and, more importantly, it includes
      everything related to capital; money, human capital, patents, ideas, business
      relationships, and everything. The origin of the idea, though, goes much
      further back than Wriston.

374   Diane Abbott, *This Week* [TV Show], BBC, February 21, 2008. This quote is
      actually not as stupid as it initially sounds. Russian leaders have denounced
      Stalin, but Chinese leaders, some of which are neo-Maoists, have not
      denounced Mao. Deng Xiaoping himself ringfenced Mao from the harshest
      criticism by declaring that his errors were outweighed by "his contribution
      to the revolution." Since Mao's death in 1976, the Chinese Communist
      Party's official line on the issue has been that he was "70 percent right and
      30 percent wrong." While many Westerners see Mao as a killing machine
      akin to Hitler and Stalin, many Chinese today do indeed apply the 70:30
      formula to Mao. The Great Leap Forward, Mao's disastrous campaign to
      accelerate China's industrialization by relying on manpower over machines,
      that led to a catastrophic famine that killed almost fifty million people,

belongs in the 30 percent bucket. Improving the status of women in China, improving literacy and education, getting rid of the Japanese, and trying to unite the country all belong in the 70 percent bucket.

375   The quotation used here is a political slogan derived from the *Communist Manifesto*, 1848, but is not in the original. The original last three sentences of the manifesto were: "Die Proletarier haben nichts in ihr zu verlieren als ihre Ketten. Sie haben eine Welt zu gewinnen. Proletarier aller Länder vereinigt Euch!" The last sentence was the battle cry, the end of the 1848 manifesto.

376   Jim Rogers, *Investment Biker: Around the World with Jim Rogers* (Chichester: John Wiley & Sons, 2000), 272. First published in 1994 by Beeland Interest (Miami).

377   Quoted in Hugh Carnegy, "France Vows to Maintain Tax Hit on Rich," *Financial Times*, December 30, 2012.

378   Quoted in Benedict Mander, "Trouble in Venezuela Brings Benefits to Its Neighbour," *Financial Times*, May 8, 2012. By 2012, it was the industrious and savvy who left Venezuela, benefiting the new host. However, by 2018, the influx of refugees from Venezuela became a problem for Colombia, not just a windfall.

379   Will Durant, *The Story of Civilization, Volume 6: The Reformation* (Norwalk: Easton Press, 1992). First published 1957 with Simon & Schuster (New York). Ellipses in the original. A committee wrote to the major cities of Germany, asking their advice as to whether the monopolies were harmful, and should they be regulated or destroyed. The quotation is from the response of Augsburg.

380   I herein use an often-cited variant. Original: "Learning is not compulsory; it's voluntary. Improvement is not compulsory; it's voluntary. But to survive, we must learn. The penalty for ignorance is that you get beat up. There is no substitute for knowledge." W. Edwards Deming, "Quality, Productivity, and Competitive Position," [seminar], Newport Beach, CA (February 24–28, 1986). From Frank Voehl, *Deming: The Way We Knew Him* (Boca Raton: St. Lucie Press, 1995).

381   Dennis Gartman, *The Gartman Letter*, June 24, 2016.

382   First use was in Alexander Ineichen, "Wriston's Law of Capital," IR&M, July 10, 2012.

383   Winston Churchill, Speech at the Scottish Unionist Conference, Perth, Scotland (May 28, 1948) in Winston Churchill, *Never Give In!: The Best of Winston Churchill's Speeches* (New York: Hyperion, 2003), 446.

384   Variously attributed also to Benjamin Franklin and Mark Twain. The earliest known occurrence, and probable origin, is from a 1981 text from Narcotics Anonymous: "Insanity is repeating the same mistakes and expecting different results." From Wikiquote (January 3, 2017). Sources commonly attribute the quotation to Einstein in his "Letters to Solovine: 1906–1955," although no one seems to be able to produce a page from that volume that holds the quotation. An earlier version of the quotation came from author Rita Mae Brown's novel *Sudden Death* (New York: Bantam,

1983). In the novel, Brown writes: "Unfortunately, Susan didn't remember what Jane Fulton once said. 'Insanity is doing the same thing over and over again, but expecting different results.'"

385 From Becker's Online Journal, January 3, 2017.

386 The following variant is misattributed to Winston Churchill: "If you're not a liberal when you're twenty-five, you have no heart. If you're not a conservative by the time you're thirty-five, you have no brain." Churchill himself once said, "I am an English Liberal. I hate the Tory Party, their men, their words, and their methods." These words are undermined by his two periods of political service in the Conservative Party, both before and after his time as a Liberal.

Clemenceau said on being told his son had joined the Communist Party: "My son is twenty-two years old. If he had not become a communist at twenty-two, I would have disowned him. If he is still a communist at thirty, I will do it then." As quoted in Bennet Cerf, *Try and Stop Me* (New York: Simon & Schuster, 1944). The variant I use, similar in content, is also attributed to Clemenceau, as quoted in Ralph Keyes, *Nice Guys Finish Seventh: False Phrases, Spurious Sayings, and Familiar Misquotations* (New York: HarperCollins, 1992).

W. Gurney Benham, *A Book of Quotations* (Philadelphia: J. B. Lippinscott, 1907) cites a statement by François Guizot as the earliest known expression of this general idea, stating that Clemenceau merely adapted the saying substituting socialiste for republicain: "N'être pas républicain à vingt ans est preuve d'un manque de cœur; l'être après trente ans est preuve d'un manque de tête." ("Not to be a republican at twenty is proof of want of heart; to be one at thirty is proof of want of head.")

The earliest example of this quotation is found in Jules Claretie's *Portraits Contemporains* (1875), where the following remark is ascribed to lawyer and academic Anselme Polycarpe Batbie: "Celui qui n'est pas républicain à vingt ans fait douter de la générosité de son âme; mais celui qui, après trente ans, persévère, fait douter de la rectitude de son esprit" ("He who is not a republican at twenty compels one to doubt the generosity of his heart; but he who, after thirty, persists, compels one to doubt the soundness of his mind"). From various sources, including Wikiquote (January 3, 2017).

387 Stuti Mishra, "Democrat Lawmaker's Gender Inclusive 'Amen and Awoman' Congressional Prayer Causes Stir," *The Independent*, January 4, 2021.

388 From Paul Wilmott and David Orrell, *The Money Formula: Dodgy Finance, Pseudo Science, and How Mathematicians Took Over the Markets* (Chichester: John Wiley & Sons, 2017), 218.

389 Robert Anton Wilson, *The Illuminati Papers* (San Francisco: And/Or Press, 1980).

390 I herein use a popular variant. Original: "People in Russia say that those who do not regret the collapse of the Soviet Union have no heart, and those that do regret it have no brain. We do not regret this; we simply state the fact and know that we need to look ahead, not backwards. We will not allow the past to drag us down and stop us from moving ahead. We understand

where we should move. But we must act based on a clear understanding of what happened." Interview with German television channel ARD and ZDF, May 2005. From Wikiquote (October 26, 2017).

391   Edward Young, *Love of Fame*, Satire II, line 281 (London: J. Tonson in the Strand, 1728).

392   Cicero, *Orator Ad M. Brutum*, chapter XXXIV, section 120 (46 BC). I use a shortened variant. Original: "Nescire autem quid ante quam natus sis acciderit, id est semper esse puerum. Quid enim est aetas hominis, nisi ea memoria rerum veterum cum superiorum aetate contexitur?" Translation: "Not to know what happened before you were born is to be a child forever. For what is the time of a man, except it be interwoven with that memory of ancient things of a superior age?" From Wikiquote (April 10, 2017).

393   Thomas Sowell, "Random Thoughts," townhall.com (March 25, 2004).

394   Karl Popper, "A Crucial Year: Marxism; Science and Pseudoscience," in *Unended Quest: An Intellectual Autobiography* (Glasgow: HarperCollins Distribution Services, 1976).

395   Fareed Zakaria, "Culture Is Destiny: A Conversation with Lee Kuan Yew," *Foreign Affairs* 73, no. 2 (Mar.–Apr. 1994), 119. From Graham Allison and Robert D. Blackwill, *Lee Kuan Yew: The Grand Master's Insights on China, the United States, and the World* (Cambridge, MA: MIT Press, 2013), 120.

396   Bill Freehan, *Behind the Mask: An Inside Baseball Diary* (Mountain View, CA: World Publications, 1970).

397   Kurt Cobain, *Journals* (New York: Penguin, 2003).

398   Edward Abbey, *A Voice Crying in the Wilderness* (New York: St. Martin's Griffin, 1989). A variant on the Internet reads: "It is the duty of the patriot to protect his country from its government." According to the Thomas Paine National Historical Association, this variant has been misattributed to Paine.

399   There is hardly any evidence that Keynes said or wrote this, despite the quotation fitting very well with both his personality as well as volatile experiences as a speculator. The earliest known written evidence for this saying appeared in a column by A. Gary Shilling in *Forbes* in February 1993. Keynes was not mentioned when the aphorism was employed by Shilling: "Above all, in 1993 remember this: Markets can remain irrational a lot longer than you and I can remain solvent." The journalist Jason Zweig was working at *Forbes* in 1993, and he believes that he heard the expression "numerous times" before Shilling's column appeared. He thinks the phrase was in use by the late 1980s. Loose variants of this quotation that include the word "irrational" are attributed to Keynes and can be traced as far back as 1964, i.e., eighteen years after his death in 1946. An original source has not yet been found. From Wikiquote, Quote Investigator, and barrypopik.com (January 3, 2017).

The walls of Gary Shilling's office are covered with framed quotations, of which some he originated. The one used here is dated from 1979. Gary Shilling has been using the phrase since then in *Forbes* columns, *Insight* reports and speeches. From A. Gary Shilling, *INSIGHT* (November 2015) and personal email correspondence (May 8, 2017).

400   Quoted from Amy Chua, *Day of Empire: How Hyperpowers Rise to Global Dominance—and Why They Fall* (New York: Anchor Books, 2007), 288.

401   Juvenal, *Satire VI.*

402   William R. White, quoted from John Mauldin and Johnathan Tepper, *Code Red: How to Protect Your Savings from the Coming Crisis* (Hoboken: John Wiley & Sons, 2014), 242.

403   Ludwig von Mises, "Lord Keynes and Say's Law," *The Freeman*, October 30, 1950.

404   Warren Buffett, Interview with Becky Quick, CNBC, July 7, 2011.

405   This quotation first appeared in John Galt, *Dreams Come Due: Government and Economics as If Freedom Mattered* (New York: Simon & Schuster, 1986), 312, written under the pseudonym of John Galt. It is there attributed to Jefferson, but is not found anywhere in his works. It bears a very vague resemblance to Jefferson's comment in a prospectus for his translation of Destutt de Tracy's *Treatise on Political Economy*: "To take from one, because it is thought that his own industry and that of his fathers has acquired too much, in order to spare to others, who, or whose fathers have not exercised equal industry and skill, is to violate arbitrarily the first principle of association,—the guarantee to every one of a free exercise of his industry, & the fruits acquired by it." From Wikiquote and *Thomas Jefferson Encyclopedia* (January 4, 2017).

406   Michael Hintze, "Global Review," *HedgeFund Intelligence*, Autumn 2013.

407   Vladimir Putin at that time proposed a penalty on Cypriot bank deposits, quoted from Ilya Arkhipov and Henry Meyer, "Putin Says Cyprus Bank-Deposit Levy Is Dangerous, Unfair," *Bloomberg*, March 18, 2013.

408   Thomas Sowell, "Random Thoughts on the Passing Scene," May 5, 2004, https://townhall.com/columnists/thomassowell/2001/12/21/random -thoughts-on-the-passing-scene-n873445.

409   Harry Browne, *Liberty A-Z* (Sacramento, CA: Advocates for Self-Government, 2004), 76.

410   Nassim Nicholas Taleb, "The Intellectual Yet Idiot," *medium.com* (September 16, 2016), extracted from *Skin in the Game*, forthcoming at the time. https://medium.com/incerto/the-intellectual-yet-idiot-13211e2d0577.

411   Herbert Spencer, *Essays on Education and Kindred Subjects* (London: Everyman's Library, 1861).

412   Dennis Gartman, *The Gartman Letter*, July 25, 2011.

413   Ludwig von Mises, *Human Action: A Treatise on Economics*, 4th ed. (San Francisco: Fox & Wilkes, 1996), 858. First published 1949 by Yale University Press.

414   Karen Weekes, *Women Know Everything!* (Philadelphia: Quirk Books, 2007), 140.

415 Matthew Lau, "Ontario's Minimum Wage Hike Has Been Disastrous, Especially for Disabled Workers," *Foundation for Economic Education*, July 2, 2018.

416 See Thomas Sowell, *Applied Economics: Thinking Beyond Stage One* (New York: Basic Books, 2004).

417 Thomas Sowell, *Ever Wonder Why? and Other Controversial Essays* (Stanford: Hoover Institution Press, 2006), 286.

418 Thomas Sowell, "A Defining Moment," *Real Clear Politics*, February 7, 2012.

419 Thomas Sowell, *The Thomas Sowell Reader* (New York: Basic Books, 2011), 144, originally in Thomas Sowell, "The Survival of the Left," *Forbes*, September 8, 1997.

420 *Braveheart* is a 1995 epic war film loosely based on the life of William Wallace, a fourteenth-century Scottish hero. The film won five Academy Awards in 1996, including the Academy Award for Best Picture. It stars Mel Gibson as William Wallace.

The upside-down Argentinian flag was most likely supposed to be the St. Andrew's Cross—the Scottish flag, the Saltire. Toward the end of the film, with Braveheart's face being full of blood and the blue hue being darker, the face painting actually resembles the Union Jack.

421 The proper German word for the Swiss is "Eidgenossen," which is often translated into English as "Confederates." Because French speakers couldn't pronounce "Eidgenossen," it became "Eyguenots," which later became "Huguenot," used later to refer to all French Calvinists. The official name of Switzerland is "Schweizerische Eidgenossenschaft." "Eid" in German means oath and is a reference to 1291 where the Swiss, simplifying a bit, decided to rule themselves.

422 I didn't make this up entirely. Arnold von Winkelried is historical fact. His involvement, action, and battle cries at the Battle of Sempach are legend only. Historical fact is that the Confederates (men from Lucerne and the surrounding cantons, then called "forest cantons" [because there was not much else there then] gave the knights of the Habsburg empire a real beating, killing eighteen hundred, including their leader, Duke Leopold III of Austria. The Habsburg rearmed and had another go at the Battle of Näfels on April 9, 1388. According to legend, and perhaps also according to history, the enemy outnumbered the Swiss by a factor of ten, and still lost. The Austrians, simplifying a bit, called it a day then, and the Swiss lived in freedom happily ever after.

The funny thing is that the three battles of Morgarten (1315), Sempach, and Näfels gave the Swiss a brutish and battlefield-savvy image, because all battles they won as the under-armed underdog against the then-state-of-the art military force. This tough, hard-hitting mountain-people image became quite important in later centuries, when wealth was created by supplying armies of Swiss mercenaries internationally; a wealth that is still visible in grandiose architecture in places close to where I live in central Switzerland. Swiss mercenaries were so popular for around three hundred to three hundred and fifty years that Swiss fought Swiss on the battlefield, as both adversaries recruited from there.

423 Margaret Thatcher, *Statecraft: Strategies for a Changing World* (New York: HarperCollins, 2002), 346.

424 Hat tip to anonymous. The Borg is a proxy for both, equality (as everyone is equally "assimilated") and unfreedom and tyranny (as "resistance is futile").

425 That said, it actually only takes four days to set up a company in France, according to data from the World Bank, down from forty-one days in 2003. However, one of the reasons entrepreneurs set up shop elsewhere is due to the stringent and inflexible labor laws; flexibility being an indispensable and essential condition for start-ups. That said, based on a report by EY's European Attractiveness Survey from June 2018, Paris actually overtook London for foreign investors to invest in. The British capital has claimed the top spot in the ranking of investors' favorite European cities since the survey began in 2003. One of the comical aspects about France is that once we adjust economic produce per capita by working hours (1472 per year in France versus 1783 in the US based on OECD estimates), France is doing rather well from a productivity perspective. Free people are free to choose between work and leisure. The French just opted for a bit more of the latter; as in early retirement, extensive holidays, lower working hours, joie de vivre, rather than burn-out at forty-five, etc. There's even a proverb to this effect, one that I believed originated in France: "The French work to live, but the Swiss live to work."

426 Michael Stothard, "Spring Arrives for Mélenchon Far-left Crusade," *Financial Times*, April 5, 2017. To be fair to Mr. Mélenchon, he was the first French politician to use holograms to speak at two places at the same time. (So now we know, nonsense can be leveraged too.) Mr. Mélenchon is a Hugo Chávez idealizer; which is quite fascinating, given the extraordinary misery caused by the Bolivian revolutionist: "Chávez c'est l'idéal inépuisable de l'espérance humaniste, de la revolution." ("Chávez is the inexhaustible ideal of humanist hope for revolution.") Mr. Mélenchon also has a free online video game and a large YouTube following. Socialists nearly everywhere find it difficult to cater to grownups. In the UK elections of June 2017, another Chávez admirer, Jeremy Corbyn, "won" because his party was able to mobilize the young. (He also won because, most brilliantly, the Labour Party campaign team replaced Corbyn's Mahmoud Ahmadinejad outfit [beige/gray-ish shirt with Harrington jacket] with a Donald Trump outfit [dark navy blue suit, white shirt, red tie]. (Corbyn on Chávez: "Thanks Hugo Chávez for showing that the poor matter and wealth can be shared. He made massive contributions to Venezuela and a very wide world." @jeremycorbyn, Twitter (March 5, 2013). Thanks, Hugo, indeed.

427 Peter Thiel, Speech, GAIM conference, Monaco (June 19, 2012).

428 "Life in the Old Continent Yet; An Unfashionably Optimistic History of Europe from across the Atlantic," *The Economist*, February 6, 2003.

429   As did Ayn Rand in a letter written on March 19, 1944: "Fascism, Nazism, Communism, and Socialism are only superficial variations of the same monstrous theme—collectivism."

430   Ludwig von Mises, *Human Action: A Treatise on Economics*, 4th ed. (San Francisco: Fox & Wilkes, 1996), 724. First published 1949 by Yale University (New Haven).

431   From a 1963 letter to his wife Gweneth, written while attending a gravity conference in communist-era Warsaw.

432   Raw data is from Angus Maddison's work. GDP per capita is measured in 1990 International Geary-Khamis dollars. Calculations are my own.

433   Norman Mailer, as quoted in Laurence J. Peter, *Peter's Quotations: Ideas for Our Time* (New York: William Morrow, 1977).

434   "How Chávez and Maduro have impoverished Venezuela," *The Economist*, April 6, 2017.

435   Karen Weekes, *Women Know Everything!* (Philadelphia: Quirk Books, 2007), 66.

436   Nelson Mandela, as quoted in *Time* magazine, February 25, 1985.

437   Warren Buffett, Berkshire Hathaway, 2016 letter to shareholders, February 25, 2017, 5–6.

438   Andrew Redleaf and Richard Vigilante, *Panic: The Betrayal of Capitalism by Wall Street and Washington* (Minneapolis: Richard Vigilante Books, 2010), 107.

439   Ayn Rand, *Capitalism: The Unknown Ideal* (New York: New American Library, 1966).

440   As quoted in *The Listener* (1978), a weekly magazine established by the BBC.

441   *Alternate History Discussion Board*, "Socialism: The Next Social Revolution," post by Jeffrey Evan Brooks, October 12, 2013.

442   Charles Murray, @charlesmurray, Twitter (November 17, 2019).

443   Based on data compiled by the Maddison Project, also known as the Maddison Historical Statistics Project, a project to collate historical economic statistics, such as GDP, GDP per capita, and labor productivity, named after Angus Maddison (1929–2010), a British economist specializing in quantitative macroeconomic history. Example: Egypt, similarly to Argentina often portrayed as one of the losers by economists over the past hundred years, went from $1 GDP per capita (in PPP terms) in the year 1 to $9.3 in the year 2016. The Netherlands, by comparison, went from $1 in the year 1 to $76 in 2016.

444   Lee Kuan Yew, "A Tryst with Destiny," speech given at the joint meeting of the Associated Chambers of Commerce and Industry of India, the Federation of Indian Chambers of Commerce and Industry, and the Federation of Indian Industries, New Delhi (January 5, 1996). Quoted from Graham Allison and Robert D. Blackwill, *Lee Kuan Yew: The Grand Master's Insights on China, the United States, and the World* (Cambridge, MA: MIT Press, 2013), 59.

445   Cato the Elder, *Plutarch's Life of Cato*.

446   Elbert Hubbard, *The Roycroft Dictionary and Book of Epigrams* (New York: Roycrofters, 1923).

447   Mohandas K. "Mahatma" Gandhi, *Young India*, March 12, 1931. *Young India* (published from 1919 to 1932) was an English periodical journal, published from Bombay as a biweekly, under Gandhi's supervision from May 7, 1919, and as a weekly from Ahmedabad, with Gandhi as editor from October 8, 1919.

448   As quoted in Ann Kannings, *Nelson Mandela: His Words* (Morrisville, NC: Lulu Press, 2014).

449   Charles Péguy, *Basic Verities, Prose and Poetry* (London: Kegan Paul, 1943).

450   As quoted in Maurice William Cranston, *Freedom: A New Analysis* (London: Longmans, 1953), 112.

451   Hippie, def.: "A hippie is someone who looks like Tarzan, walks like Jane, and smells like Cheetah." (Ronald Reagan)

452   As quoted in the *Week*, December 1, 2012, originally from the *Daily Mail*. *TV Guide* named J. R. number one in their 2013 list of The 60 Nastiest Villains of All Time. J. R. Ewing is, of course, a fictional character. But still, someone wrote the line.

453   Will Durant, *The Story of Civilization, Volume 6: The Reformation* (New York: Simon & Schuster, 1957). Durant references *The Muqaddimah*, also known as the *Muqaddimah of Ibn Khaldun* or *Ibn Khaldun's Prolegomena*, a book written by the Arab historian Ibn Khaldun in 1377 which records an early view of universal history. Durant wrote: "These are a few of the thousands of ideas that make the Muqaddama the most remarkable philosophical product of its century, Ibn-Khaldun has his own notions on almost everything but theology, where he thinks it unwise to be original."

454   Nassim Nicholas Taleb, *Antifragile: Things That Gain from Disorder* (New York: Random House, 2012), 246.

455   Murray Rothbard, *For a New Liberty: The Libertarian Manifesto* (London: Macmillan, 1973).

456   Those were not his exact words. The quotation is a simplification of an actual quote, first attributed to Lincoln in 2002. The simplification is a derivative from a speech by Lincoln titled "The Perpetuation of Our Political Institutions," known as the Lyceum Address of 1838 based on the location of its giving. Original: "At what point then is the approach of danger to be expected? I answer, if it ever reach us, it must spring up amongst us. It cannot come from abroad. If destruction be our lot, we must ourselves be its author and finisher. As a nation of freemen, we must live through all time, or die by suicide." From quora.com and Wikiquote (March 31, 2017). Full speech is on abrahamlincolnonline.org.

457   Thomas Sowell, *Controversial Essays* (Stanford: Hoover Institution Press Publication, 2002).

458   Neil deGrasse Tyson, @neiltyson, Twitter (March 19, 2017).

459   See Stephanie Condon, "Hank Johnson Worries Guam Could 'Capsize' After Marine Buildup," CBS News, April 1, 2010, allegedly not an April Fool's joke. During a House Armed Services Committee hearing on

March 25, 2010 concerning the US military installation on the island of Guam, Johnson said to Admiral Robert F. Willard, Commander of US Pacific Command, "My fear is that the whole island will become so overly populated that it will tip over and capsize," to which Admiral Willard replied, diplomatically brilliant: "We don't anticipate that." From Wikipedia (June 22, 2017).

460   Thomas Sowell, *Barbarians inside the Gates and Other Controversial Essays* (Stanford: Hoover Press, 1999), Random thoughts section.

461   As quoted in Barney Ronay, *The Manager: The Absurd Ascent of the Most Important Man in Football* (London: Sphere, 2009).

462   George W. Bush, Campaign speech, Florence, South Carolina (January 11, 2000).

463   George W. Bush, Speech, Beaverton, Oregon (September 25, 2000), discussing US oil imports.

464   Edgar Fiedler, "Commentary," *Across the Board* 14 (June 1977): 62–63.

465   Richard J. Evans, *In Defence of History* (London: Granta Books, 1997), 62.

466   Robert Zemeckis, director, *Forrest Gump* (Hollywood, CA: Paramount Pictures, 1994). Fun fact: The quotation is ranked fortieth in the American Film Institute's list of the top hundred movie quotations in American cinema. "I'll be back" is thirty-seventh. "We'll always have Paris" is forty-third. "Frankly, my dear, I don't give a damn," from *Gone with the Wind,* was first.

467   Forrest Gump receiving a letter from Apple with its then famous rainbow logo was a movie mistake as the scene was set in 1975, with the logo being designed in 1976 and Apple going public in 1981. But then, who cares? The film is still a classic.

468   From Mark Buchanan, *Ubiquity: Why Catastrophes Happen* (New York: Three Rivers Press, 2000), 140, with reference to OECD Economic Outlook, June 1993.

469   John Kenneth Galbraith, *Time* magazine, March 3, 1961, 20.

470   Margaret Thatcher, *Statecraft: Strategies for a Changing World* (New York: HarperCollins, 2002), 104.

471   The Quote Investigator (October 12, 2017) could not find the original source and argues that quotation experts and Twain scholars are skeptical as to the attribution to Twain. I left it there for the readers who, like myself, are currently raising teenagers.

472   Thomas Sowell, "A Childish Letter," *Jewish World Review*, August 17, 1998.

473   There are many variants of this quotation in relation to one's ignorance of ignorance. The origin of the idea, I believe, is from *The Analects*, Chapter II. The Analects are a collection of sayings and ideas attributed to the Chinese philosopher Confucius and his contemporaries, traditionally believed to have been compiled and written by Confucius's followers.

474   David Benioff and D. B. Weiss, directors, "Breaker of Chains," *Game of Thrones*, season 4, episode 3 (HBO, 2011–19).

475   *Poor Richard's Almanack* (1754).

476   Sydney J. Harris, *Pieces of Eight* (Boston: Houghton Mifflin Harcourt, 1982).

477   As quoted in Jack Schwager, *Market Sense and Nonsense: How the Markets Really Work (and How They Don't)* (Hoboken: John Wiley & Sons, 2013), 3–4.

478   Irvin Kershner, director. George Lucas, *Star Wars: Episode V—The Empire Strikes Back* (Burbank, CA: Twentieth Century Fox, 1980).

479   Daniel Kahneman, *Thinking, Fast and Slow* (New York: Farrar, Straus and Giroux, 2011), 24. The most important paper mentioned in the text is Kahneman and Tversky (1979) on loss aversion and decision-making under risk.

480   Karl Popper, "A Crucial Year: Marxism; Science and Pseudoscience," in *Unended Quest: An Intellectual Autobiography* (Glasgow: HarperCollins Distribution Services, 1976).

481   As quoted in Larry Chang, *Wisdom for the Soul of Black Folk* (Washington, DC: Gnosophia, 2007), 359.

482   Plato apparently. There is no other record of Socrates ever having said that; he didn't write things down.

483   William Shakespeare, *As You Like It* (1603).

484   The origin of this proverb is attributed manifold, including Michael Apostolius (1420–78), Greek teacher and writer, Desiderius Erasmus (1466–1536), Dutch philosopher, and translator of the Bible.

485   John Kay, "Cracks in the Crystal Ball," *Financial Times*, September 29, 1995.

486   Robert N. Veres, "The Vision Thing," *Investment Advisor*, June 1997.

487   Nassim Nicholas Taleb, *The Black Swan: The Impact of the Highly Improbable* (New York: Random House, 2007), 163.

488   As quoted in Will Durant, *The Story of Civilization, Volume 7: The Age of Reason Begins* (Norwalk: Easton Press, 1992). First published in 1961 with Simon & Schuster (New York). "Knave" herein means "a rogue, a rascal; deceitful fellow; a dishonest man."

489   Lance Roberts, "5 Universal Laws Of Human (Investment) Stupidity," *realinvestmentadvice.com* (May 11, 2017). "The Basic Laws of Human Stupidity" was an essay written in Italian by Cipolla in 1976 when he was a professor of economic history at the University of California, Berkeley.

490   Roberts, "5 Universal Laws Of Human (Investment) Stupidity."

491   William Gaddis, *Carpenter's Gothic* (New York: Viking, 1985).

492   Edward Abbey, *The Monkey Wrench Gang* (Philadelphia: Lippincott, 1975).

493   See Robson, *The Intelligence Trap*, chapter 9, 215.

494   Yuval Noah Harari, *21 Lessons for the 21st Century* (London: Jonathan Cape, 2018), 180.

495   *The Century Dictionary* (1903). Hat tip to Mardy Grothe and Marc Faber.

496   "Juncker Responds to Trump's Trade Tariffs: 'We Can Also Do Stupid,'" *Euronews*, March 3, 2018.

497   I herein use a variant. Original: "Some scientists claim that hydrogen, because it is so plentiful, is the basic building block of the universe. I dispute that. I say there is more stupidity than hydrogen, and that is the basic building block of the universe." Frank Zappa and Peter Occhiogrosso, *The Real Frank Zappa Book* (New York: Poseidon Press, 1989), 239. The

Quote Investigator (November 3, 2017) finds that Harlan Ellison (b. 1934), American author and media critic, used a version of the expression before Zappa. Einstein's reference to stupidity being infinite was a saying in the 1940s and was later ascribed to Albert Einstein. According to Wikiquote (November 3, 2017) the origin of the expression goes as far back as 1880 to Gustave Flaubert (1821–80), French writer and author of *Madame Bovary*.

    The earliest published attribution of a similar quotation to Einstein seems to have been in Gestalt therapist Frederick S. Perls' 1969 book *Gestalt Theory Verbatim*, where he wrote: "As Albert Einstein once said to me: 'Two things are infinite: the universe and human stupidity.' But what is much more widespread than the actual stupidity is the playing stupid, turning off your ear, not listening, not seeing."

498   Variant: "In politics, an absurdity is not a handicap"—In French: "En politique, une absurdité n'est pas un obstacle." As quoted in: *L'Opinion* 5, no. 1 (1912): 173.

499   As quoted in Matthew Parris, *Scorn: The Wittiest and Wickedest Insults in Human History* (London: Profile Books, 2016), 11.

500   As quoted on Wikiquote (May 15, 2017). There is a link to a YouTube video sequence with the original quote.

501   Nassim Nicholas Taleb, *The Black Swan: The Impact of the Highly Improbable* (New York: Random House, 2007), 150.

502   John Oliver talks to Stephen Hawking in the first installment of *Last Week Tonight's* "People Who Think Good" series, June 16, 2014.

503   Peter Drucker, *Management: Tasks, Responsibilities, Practices* (New York: Harper & Row, 1973).

504   Philip E. Tetlock and Dan Gardner, *Superforecasting: The Art and Science of Prediction* (New York: Crown Publishers, 2015), 6.

505   James Simons, Speech at Greenwich Roundtable 1999. Quoted from Hal Lux, "The Secret World of Jim Simons," *Institutional Investor* 25, no. 11 (November 2000): 38.

506   "The son of a shoe factory owner, Jim Simons grew up daydreaming about numbers. 'I wanted to do mathematics from the time I was three,' says Simons, who was raised in the Boston suburb of Newton. 'Literally. I would think about numbers and shapes.'" Quoted from Hal Lux, "The Secret World of Jim Simons," *Institutional Investor* 34, no. 11 (November 2000).

507   As quoted in Christopher Cerf and Victor Navasky, *The Experts Speak: The Definitive Compendium of Authoritative Misinformation,* expanded and updated edition (New York: Villard, 1998), 115, making reference to John Toland, *Adolf Hitler* (Garden City, NY: Doubleday, 1976).

508   Quoted in the *Chicago Daily News*, June 21, 1974. In the same year, Richard Burton mused: "Elizabeth and I have been through too much to watch our marriage go up in flames. There is too much love going for us ever to divorce." Quoted from Don Atyeo and Johnathon Green, *Don't Quote Me* (London: Hamlyn, 1981).

509   As quoted in "Atom Energy Hope is Spiked By Einstein/Efforts at Loosing Vast Force is Called Fruitless," *Pittsburgh Post-Gazette*, December 29, 1934.

510   2007 exchange between Microsoft CEO Steve Ballmer and David
      Lieberman of *USA Today* at their sixth CEO Forum.

511   Bryan Glick, "Timing Is Everything in Steve Ballmer's Departure—Why
      Microsoft Needs a New Vision," *Computer Weekly Editors Blog*, August 27,
      2013.

512   Jessamyn West, *To See the Dream* (New York: Harcourt, Brace & Co.,
      1957). Often erroneously attributed to Ralph Waldo Emerson (1803–82),
      American essayist.

513   Andrew S. Grove, *Only the Paranoid Survive* (New York: Doubleday
      Business, 1996).

514   Elon Musk, @elonmusk, Twitter (December 2, 2020).

515   Quoted from Ed Regies, "The Doomslayer," *Wired*, 5.02 (February 1997).

516   William Cunnings, "The World Is Going to End in 12 Years If We Don't
      Address Climate Change, Ocasio-Cortez says," *USA Today*, January 22,
      2019. Mrs. Ocasio-Cortez later said that she didn't mean it literally.

517   Deirdre N. McCloskey, "How Piketty Misses the Point," *Cato Policy Report*
      37, no. 4 (July/August 2015).

518   Denis Diderot, *Pensées philosophiques* (1746).

519   Benjamin Disraeli, Speech in the House of Commons (January 24, 1860).

520   William A. Sherden, *The Fortune Sellers: The Big Business of Buying and
      Selling Predictions* (New York: John Wiley & Sons, 1998), 190.

521   Nassim Nicholas Taleb, *The Black Swan: The Impact of the Highly
      Improbable* (New York: Random House, 2007), 154.

522   Harvard Economic Society, *Weekly Letter*, November 16, 1929. See
      Christopher Cerf and Victor Navasky, *The Experts Speak: The Definitive
      Compendium of Authoritative Misinformation*, expanded and updated ed.
      (New York: Villard, 1998) for more foolish predictions from the Harvard
      Economic Society.

523   I herein use a popular variant. One sourceable original reads: "I would
      rather be governed by the first two thousand people in the Boston telephone
      directory than by the two thousand people on the faculty of Harvard
      University." As quoted in Ralph Keyes, *The Quote Verifier* (New York: St.
      Martin's Griffin, 2006), 82.

524   Henry George, *A Perplexed Philosopher* (New York: Charles L. Webster and
      Co., 1892).

525   As quoted in Matthew Parris, *Scorn: The Wittiest and Wickedest Insults in
      Human History* (London: Profile Books, 2016), 8.

526   Philip E. Tetlock and Dan Gardner, *Superforecasting: The Art and Science
      of Prediction* (New York: Crown Publishers, 2015), 52. Emphasis in the
      original.

527   E. Joseph Cossman, *How I Made $1,000,000 in Mail Order* (New York:
      Prentice Hall, 1963).

528   Jan Tinbergen, "The Role of Errors in Scientific Development," *Review of
      Social Economy* 46 (1998): 225–30.

529   John Greenwald, "The Forecasters Flunk," *Time* (August 27, 1984).

530   Nassim Nicholas Taleb, *Fooled by Randomness: The Hidden Role of Chance in Markets and in Life*, 2nd ed. (New York: Thomson/Texere, 2004), 5.

531   John Kenneth Galbraith, *Money: Whence It Came, Where It Went* (Harmondsworth: Penguin Books, 1975), 315.

532   Thomas Jefferson, Letter to Charles Thomson, September 20, 1787.

533   Philip E. Tetlock and Dan Gardner, *Superforecasting: The Art and Science of Prediction* (New York: Crown Publishers, 2015), 15.

534   John Kay, "Economics—Rituals of Rigour," *Financial Times*, August 25, 2011.

535   Quoted from Michael Covel, *Trend Following* (Upper Saddle River, NJ: Prentice Hall, 2004).

536   See Philip E. Tetlock, *Expert Political Judgment: How Good Is It? How Can We Know?* (Princeton, NJ: Princeton University Press, 2005). Also: look up "The Good Judgment Project."

537   *Wall Street Journal*, January 22, 1993, C1.

538   Dan Lyons, *Disrupted: My Misadventure in the Start-Up Bubble* (New York: Hachette Books, 2016). From chapter eight: "The Bozo Explosion." Emphasis in the original. Steve Jobs coined the term "bozo explosion." It describes the phenomenon that "a company's mediocre early hires rise up through the ranks and end up running departments. The bozos now must hire other people, and of course they prefer to hire bozos."

539   Bertrand Russell, "The Triumph of Stupidity" (May 10, 1933), in *Mortals and Others: Bertrand Russell's American Essays, 1931–1935*, vol. 2, ed. Harry Ruja (London: Routledge, 1998), 28.

540   Shunryu Suzuki, *Zen Mind, Beginner's Mind* (New York: Weatherhill, 1970).

541   William J. Bernstein, *The Intelligent Asset Allocator* (New York: McGraw Hill, 2000).

542   Janet Yellen, Speech to Commonwealth Club of California, San Francisco (June 30, 2009).

543   Alan Greenspan, "Interview," *The Daily Show,* Jon Stewart, October 21, 2013.

544   As quoted in Dominic Lawson, "Flip-flop Phil Gets His Spreadsheets in a Twist," *The Times*, October 15, 2017.

545   Paul A. Samuelson and William D. Nordhaus, *Economics*, 13th ed. (New York: McGraw Hill, 1989), 837. I found some indication that the quote shown was used in Samuelson's textbook from 1961 to 1989. The fall of the Berlin Wall might have been an incentive to stop the praise for socialism.

546   Paul A. Baran, *A Collective Portrait* (New York: Monthly Review Press, 1964). In Kim Il-sung, Joan Robinson, a younger colleague of Keynes at the University of Cambridge, saw "a messiah rather than a dictator," lending support to the idea that intelligent people too can tend to romanticize things a bit. These quotes are good examples of *dysrationalia* mentioned in chapter one.

547   Paul Krugman, "Why Most Economists' Predictions Are Wrong," *The Red Herring*, June 10, 1998. Full quote: "The growth of the Internet will slow drastically, as the flaw in "Metcalfe's law"—which states that the number

of potential connections in a network is proportional to the square of the number of participants—becomes apparent: most people have nothing to say to each other! By 2005 or so, it will become clear that the Internet's impact on the economy has been no greater than the fax machine's." To be fair to Mr. Krugman, there is a debate as to the impact of computers and Internet with respect to an economy's productivity. Robert Solow (b. 1924), an American economist whose doctoral students were George Akerlof, Joseph Stiglitz, and Alan Blinder, among others, said as early as 1987: "You can see the computer age everywhere but in the productivity statistics." (Robert Solow, "We'd Better Watch Out," *New York Times*, July 12, 1987.) This is generally referred to as the "productivity paradox," the "Solow paradox," or the "Solow productivity paradox."

Fun fact: around the same time when Paul Krugman said the Internet is nothing, David Bowie (1947–2016), a singer, said the Internet would be huge, a game-changer.

548   Herbert Spencer, *Social Statics* (London: John Chapman, 1851).

549   Anthony de Mello, *The Way to Love* (New York: Doubleday, 1991).

550   Margaret Thatcher, television interview with Barbara Walters, ABC TV, March 18, 1987.

551   Full quote: "Your 'instincts' were correct. However, one day your intuition will fail, and you will finally understand that logic is primary above all else. 'Instinct' is simply another term for serendipity." Tuvok to Nelix, From Rick Berman, director. *Star Trek: Voyager,* "Rise" (Paramount Television, 1997). So, the joke was actually on Tuvok for not getting the idea that intuition might work well in decision-making. He probably hadn't read Malcom Gladwell's *Blink.*

552   James Lovelock, *Novacene: The Coming Age of Hyperintelligence* (London: Allen Lane, 2019), 18.

553   Rita Mae Brown, *Sudden Death* (New York: Bantam Books, 1983).

554   Johnathan Weil, "Geithner Downgrades His Own Credibility to Junk," *Bloomberg*, April 21, 2011, based on televised interview with Peter Barnes, Fox News, April 18, 2011. The downgrade to AA+ by S&P occurred on August 2, 2011.

555   While speaking to CNN, as quoted in James R. Barth, *The Rise and Fall of the U.S. Mortgage and Credit Markets* (Hoboken: John Wiley & Sons, 2009), 1.

556   Carl Gutierrez, "Fannie and Freddie Are Fine, Bernanke Says," *Forbes*, July 16, 2008. Fun fact: David Einhorn, an American hedge fund manager, on Ben Bernanke: "I got to ask him [Ben Bernanke] all these questions that had been on my mind for a very long period of time, right? And then on the other side, it was like sort of frightening because the answers weren't any better than I thought that they might be. I asked several things. He started out by explaining that he was 100 percent sure that there's not going to be hyperinflation. And not that I think that there's going to be hyperinflation, but it's like how do you get to 100 percent certainty of anything?" David Einhorn commenting on a dinner conversation on March 26, 2014, from Julia La Roche, "DAVID EINHORN: I Had Dinner With Bernanke And

What He Said Was 'Sort Of Frightening,'" *Business Insider*, May 6, 2014. Michael Faraday (1791–1867), English chemist and physicist, comes to mind: "A man who is certain he is right is almost sure to be wrong." From Bence Jones, *The Life and Letters of Faraday* (London: Longmans, Green, and Co., 1870).

557   Andrew Pierce, "The Queen Asks Why No One Saw the Credit Crunch Coming," *The Telegraph*, November 5, 2008.

558   George Akerlof and Joseph Stiglitz, "Let a Hundred Theories Bloom," *Project Syndicate*, October 26, 2009. Whether Mr. Akerlof shares his spouse's view on the Fed's forecasting ability being "second to none," I do not know.

559   Adair Turner, "Banks Are Safer but Debt Remains a Danger," *Financial Times*, September 11, 2018.

560   Mark Buchanan, "Economists Should Stop Being Quite So Certain," *Bloomberg*, April 11, 2018.

561   Warren Buffet, Berkshire Hathaway, 2016 letter to shareholders, February 25, 2017, 6.

562   Dwight Eisenhower, Radio and television address to the American people prior to departure for the Big Four Conference at Geneva (July 15, 1955).

563   Russell Napier, "Why We Can Learn More from Stupid People Than from Smart People: The Uses and Abuses of Financial History," Dinner presentation, 62nd Annual CFA Institute Financial Analysts Seminar, Chicago (July 24, 2017).

564   Leonardo da Vinci, *The Notebooks of Leonardo da Vinci*, trans. Jean Paul Richter (New York: Scribner and Welford, 1888), chapter XIX, "Philosophical Maxims. Morals. Polemics and Speculations: On Foolishness and Ignorance."

565   Nassim Nicholas Taleb, *Antifragile: Things That Gain from Disorder* (New York: Random House, 2012), 391.

566   I have been using this quotation for years. It is too convenient not to. However, this quotation is one of the many examples whereby a very convenient quotation is spread broadly over the Internet. For this book, I was not able to find the original source. I assume the quotation is a variant from the following: "He who knows does not speak. He who speaks does not know." From Lao Tzu, *The Way of Lao Tzu (Tao Te Ching)*, chapter 56, trans. Wing-Tsit Chan (Indianapolis: The Bobbs-Merrill Company, 1963). The Tao Te Ching is a Chinese classic text, sometimes referred to as Laozi. The text's true authorship and date of composition or compilation are still debated.

567   Kehlog Albran (Martin A. Cohen and Sheldon Shacket), *The Profit* (Los Angeles: Price/Stern/Sloan, 1973).

568   Thomas Malthus, *An Essay on The Principle of Population* (London: J. Johnson, 1798).

569   Paul Ehrlich, The Population Bomb (New York: Ballantine Books/Sierra Club, 1968). That said, given the tenacity of cockroaches of holding on to existence, they indeed will most likely survive us.

570   James Lovelock, as quoted in *The Economist*, July 27, 2019, in relation to
      Mr. Lovelock's new book, *Novacene,* which I strongly recommend. James
      Lovelock doesn't just think outside of the box. He thinks as if there is no
      box.

571   Cicero, *De Inventione* (84 BC). I used a shortened variant. The original
      quotation was translated as follows: "For it is not having insufficient
      knowledge, but persisting a long time in insufficient knowledge that is
      shameful; since the one is assumed to be a disease common to all, but the
      other is assumed to be a flaw to an individual." From Wikiquote (April 10,
      2017).

572   Nassim Nicholas Taleb, *Fooled by Randomness: The Hidden Role of Chance
      in Markets and in Life*, 2nd ed. (New York: Thomson/Texere, 2004), xxi.

573   Carl Sagan, *Cosmos* (New York: Random House, 1980), 4.

574   Albert Einstein, "What Life Means to Einstein: An Interview by George
      Sylvester Viereck," *The Saturday Evening Post*, October 26, 1929.

575   Ephraim Hardcastle, *Daily Mail*, July 22, 2003. The quotation is an answer
      to a question asked by pupils of Gillott's School in his constituency whether
      he would like the job of prime minister. Whether decapitation is an
      appropriate analogy to use with children, I'm not sure. Today's youth must
      know Elvis though. At another occasion he dropped Elvis: "As I never tire
      of saying, my chances of becoming prime minister are only slightly better
      than being decapitated by a frisbee, blinded by a champagne cork, locked
      in a fridge, or being reincarnated as an olive." From John Higginson, "Boris
      Johnson: I'm More Likely to be Reincarnated as an Olive than be PM,"
      Metro, June 5, 2012.

576   Will Rogers, as quoted in Laurence J. Peter, *Peter's Quotations: Ideas for Our
      Time* (New York: William Morrow, 1977), 524. There are many variants
      to this quote. Potentially the original states: "There is no credit to being a
      comedian, when you have the whole government working for you. All you
      have to do is report the facts. I don't even have to exaggerate." From P. J.
      O'Brian, *Will Rogers, Ambassador of Good Will, Prince of Wit and Wisdom*
      (Philadelphia: John C. Winston, 1935), 157.

577   Arthur C. Clarke, "Hazards of Prophecy: The Failure of Imagination,"
      essay first published in Arthur C. Clarke, Profiles of the Future (London:
      Pan Books, 1962). Clarke's second law: "The only way of discovering
      the limits of the possible is to venture a little way past them into the
      impossible." Clarke's third law: "Any sufficiently advanced technology is
      indistinguishable from magic." From Wikipedia (March 27, 2017).

578   Gerd Gigerenzer, *Risk Savvy: How to Make Good Decisions* (New York:
      Viking, 2014), 17.

579   Gigerenzer, *Risk Savvy*, 23.

580   William A. Sherden, *The Fortune Sellers: The Big Business of Buying and
      Selling Predictions* (New York: John Wiley & Sons, 1998), 123.

581   Anthony Gaubis, as quoted in Philip Jenks, 500 of the Most Witty, Acerbic
      and Erudite Things Ever Said about Money (Petersfield, England: Herriman
      House, 2002).

582   Peter Lynch, with John Rothschild, *One Up on Wall Street: How to Use What You Already Know to Make Money in the Market* (New York: Simon & Schuster, 1989), 85.

583   Robert A. Heinlein, *Time Enough for Love* (New York: G. P. Putnam's Sons, 1973).

584   Some aspects of expert failure (and illusory correlation) draw on material first published in Alexander Ineichen, "20th Century Volatility—A Review of the Stock and Derivatives Markets in the 20th Century," Warburg Dillon Read (December 1999), drawing quite heavily on David Dreman, *Contrarian Investment Strategies: The Next Generation* (New York: Simon & Schuster, 1998) at the time.

585   Howard Ruff, as quoted in Mark Skousen, *The Maxims of Wall Street*, 5th ed. (Washington, DC: Capital Press, 2017), 69. First published in 2011 with Skousen Publishing (Winter Park, FL).

586   David H. Freedman, *Wrong: Why Experts* Keep Failing Us—And How to Know When Not to Trust Them, *Scientists, Finance Wizards, Doctors, Relationship Gurus, Celebrity CEOs, High-powered Consultants, Health Officials and More* (New York: Little, Brown and Company, 2010).

587   From David Dreman, "The Not-So-Expert Expert," in *Classics: An Investor's Anthology*, ed. Charles D. Ellis with James R. Vertin (Homewood, IL: Business One Irwin, 1989) quoting Herbert Simon, "Theories of Decision Making in Economics and Behavioral Sciences," *American Economic Review* 49, no. 2 (June 1959): 253–83.

588   Herbert Simon, *Models of Man: Social and Rational* (New York: John Wiley & Sons, 1957).

589   Guru Grades, CXO Advisory, www.cxoadvisory.com/gurus/, retrieved on March 21, 2017.

590   See David Dreman, *Contrarian Investment Strategies: The Next Generation* (New York: Simon & Schuster, 1998), 86.

591   Ned Davis, *Being Right or Making Money*, 3rd ed. (Hoboken: John Wiley & Sons, 2014), 3. First published in 1991 by Ned Davis Research.

592   As quoted in William A. Sherden, *The Fortune Sellers: The Big Business of Buying and Selling Predictions* (New York: John Wiley & Sons, 1998), 259.

593   Rolfe Winkler and Justin Lahart, "How Do Pundits Never Get It Wrong? Call a 40% Chance," *Wall Street Journal*, February 26, 2018.

594   Ned Davis, *Being Right or Making Money*, 3rd ed. (Hoboken: John Wiley & Sons, 2014), 3. First published in 1991 by Ned Davis Research.

595   Nassim Nicholas Taleb, *The Black Swan: The Impact of the Highly Improbable* (New York: Random House, 2007), 277.

596   Alexander Hamilton, James Madison, John Jay, and Roy P. Fairfield. *The Federalist Papers: A Collection of Essays Written in Support of the Constitution of the United States: From the Original Text of Alexander Hamilton, James Madison, and John Jay* (Baltimore: Johns Hopkins University Press, 1981). Originally published as *The Federalist Papers* (1787–88).

597   David H. Freedman, *Wrong: Why Experts* Keep Failing Us—And How to Know When Not to Trust Them, *Scientists, Finance Wizards, Doctors, Relationship Gurus, Celebrity CEOs, High-powered Consultants, Health Officials and More* (New York: Little, Brown and Company, 2010), 84.

598   Howard Marks calls this "the greatest investment adage," in Howard Marks, *The Most Important Thing: Uncommon Sense for the Thoughtful Investor* (New York: Columbia University Press, 2011), 22.

599   William A. Sherden, *The Fortune Sellers: The Big Business of Buying and Selling Predictions* (New York: John Wiley & Sons, 1998), 265.

600   Though often attributed to John Kenneth Galbraith, as early as 1988 in *U.S. News & World Report*, the earliest publications of this statement, in the *Bulletin* (1984) and *Reader's Digest* (1985) attributes it to Ezra Solomon. From Wikiquote (March 21, 2017).

601   Edward Abbey, *A Voice Crying in the Wilderness* (New York: St. Martin's Griffin, 1989).

602   Often attributed to Stephen Hawking without a source, but originally from historian Daniel J. Boorstin. It appears in different forms in *The Discoverers* (New York: Random House, 1983), *Cleopatra's Nose* (New York: Random House, 1995), and the introduction to *The Decline and Fall of the Roman Empire* (New York: Modern Library, 1995). Boorstin was interviewed in the *Washington Post* in January 1984. He modestly referred to himself as an amateur historian because his primary background was the legal profession: "What an amateur is, is a lover of a subject. I'm a lover of facts. The fact is the savior, as long as you don't jam it into some preconceived pattern. The greatest obstacle to discovery is not ignorance—it is the illusion of knowledge." Boorstin employed different versions of the saying over the years, but he did not assert that the underlying idea was his own. Indeed, he once ascribed a similar notion to the well-known historian Edward Gibbon, and on another occasion, he called it an aphorism. From Wikiquote and Quote Investigator (March 17, 2017).

603   The distinction between objective and subjective model I got from J. Edward Russo and Paul J. H. Schoemaker, *Decision Traps: The Ten Barriers to Brilliant Decision-Making and How to Overcome Them* (New York: Simon & Schuster/Fireside, 1989).

604   Susan Cain, *Quiet: The Power of Introverts in a World That Can't Stop Talking* (New York: Random House, 2012), 52.

605   Howard Marks, "A Conversation with Howard Marks and Mike Milken," Milken Institute (May 1, 2013).

606   Bert Bacharach, "Now See Here!" *Coshocton Tribune*, August 4, 1968.

607   There are many variants of this quote, attributed to all sorts of people, including Mark Twain, Niels Bohr, Samuel Goldwyn, Yogi Berra, Nostradamus, among others. Quote Investigator (March 21, 2017) finds the earliest recording of this quotation in Denmark. The Danish politician Karl Kristian Steincke (1880–1963) referred to it in his autobiography, overheard in the parliamentary year of 1937–38, although no attribution was given.

608   First published in Alexander Ineichen, "Nowcasting and Financial Wizardry," IR&M (January 2015). An alternative definition of nowcasting is the following: "Now-casting is defined as the prediction of the present, the very near future, and the very recent past." From Marta Bańbura, Domenico Giannone, Michele Modugno, and Lucrezia Reichlin, "Now-Casting and Real-time Data Flow," *European Central Bank*, Working Paper Series, no. 1564 (July 2013). (The reason why it makes sense to forecast the most recent past is that official economic data is released with a long delay. Nowcasting, therefore, predicts the past before the past is known, sort of. There is empirical evidence that markets and the economic cycle are coincident, making the case for using nowcasting as an investment tool for asset allocation and/or risk management.)

609   James Picerno, *Nowcasting the Business Cycle: A Practical Guide For Spotting Business Cycle Peaks Ahead of the Crowd* (n.p.: Beta Publishing, 2014), 114. Emphasis in the original.

610   Richard Russell, as quoted in Barry Ritholtz, *The Big Picture*, October 22, 2012.

611   Yogi Berra, *The Yogi Book* (New York: Workman, 1998). In July 1973, when Berra's Mets trailed the Chicago Cubs by nine and a half games in the National League East; the Mets rallied to win the division title on the final day of the season.

612   The musical connection is with the familiar operatic role of Brunnhilde in Richard Wagner's *Götterdämmerung*, the last of the immensely long, four-opera Ring Cycle. Brunnhilde is usually depicted as a well-upholstered lady who appears for a ten-minute solo to conclude proceedings. "When the fat lady sings" is a reasonable answer to the question "When will it be over?", which must have been asked many times during Ring Cycle performances, lasting as they do upwards of fourteen hours. From phrases.org.uk (April 25, 2017).

613   Ed Gardner, *Duffy's Tavern*, American radio show in the 1940s.

614   Mark Spitznagel, "Picking Market Crashes Is Impossible, Spitznagel Says," Bloomberg TV, February 7, 2018.

615   Hyman P. Minsky, *John Maynard Keynes* (New York: Columbia University Press, 1975), 168.

616   Rudiger Dornbusch, "Growth Forever," *Wall Street Journal*, July 30, 1998.

617   Robert E. Lucas, Jr. "Understanding Business Cycles," paper prepared for the Kiel Conference on Growth without Inflation, June 22–23, 1976 (University of Chicago). *Carnegie-Rochester Conference Series on Public Policy* 5 (1977): 15.

618   Central bankers will beg to differ because they can, of course, change the wind, and repeatedly do so.

619   George Soros, "Fallibility, Reflexivity, and the Human Uncertainty Principle," *Journal of Economic Methodology* 20, no. 4 (2014): 309–29.

620   This quotation is most likely a variant, originated by Larry Summers in 2011. Original: "The crisis takes a much longer time coming than you think, and then it happens much faster than you would have thought." From a PBS

interview, January 2001. Rüdiger Dornbusch might have used a variant in connection with the European Monetary Union ("EMU"), for which he was a critic. In 1996 he said: "If there was ever a bad idea, EMU it is." From Rudi Dornbusch, "Euro Fantasies," *Foreign Affairs* 75, no. 5 (September/October 1996): 113.

Michael Covel, the author of *Trend Following* (London: Financial Times/ Prentice Hall, 2004), referred to the idea as "Dornbusch's law" in 2010 as it applies very well to trend following. It also applies very well to "nowcasting" that suggests one ought not to try and predict the difficult-to-forecast turning points, but measure them objectively. Paul Krugman referred to "Dornbusch's law" in relation to the Euro in 2012. From Paul Krugman, "Dornbusch's Law And The Euro," *New York Times*, July 20, 2012.

621 Title to Chapter 4 in Martin Zweig, *Winning on Wall Street* (New York: Warner Business Books., 1986), 42.

622 Martin Zweig, *Winning on Wall Street* (New York: Warner Business Books, 1986).

623 Ned Davis, *Being Right or Making Money*, 3rd ed. (Hoboken: John Wiley & Sons, 2014), 24–27 and 36–38. First published in 1991 by Ned Davis Research. Rules three through nine are: 3. Beware of the crowd at the extremes, 4. Rely on objective indicators, 5. Be disciplined, 6. Practice risk management, 7. Remain flexible, 8. Money management rules (for example, let profits run, cut losses short, among other rules), and 9. Those who do not study history are condemned to repeat its mistakes.

624 See Richard C. Grinold, "The Fundamental Law of Active Management," *The Journal of Portfolio Management* 15, no. 3 (Spring 1989): 30–37 and Richard C. Grinold and Ronald N. Kahn, *Active Portfolio Management: A Quantitative Approach for Producing Superior Returns and Controlling Risk*, 2nd ed. (New York: McGraw Hill, 2000). First published in 1995 as *Active Portfolio Management: Quantitative Theory and Applications* by Probus (Chicago).

625 I herein use a short and popularized variant of the original quote, which reads: "Investors operate with limited funds and limited intelligence: they do not need to know everything. As long as they understand something better than others, they have an edge." From George Soros, *The Alchemy of Finance: Reading the Mind of the Market* (New York: John Wiley & Sons, 2003), 55. First published in 1987 by Simon & Schuster (New York).

626 Jack Schwager, *The New Market Wizards: Conversations with America's Top Traders* (New York: HarperCollins, 1992).

627 Pyotr Ilyich Tchaikovsky, as quoted in Carl Fehrman, *Poetic Creation: Inspiration or Craft* (Minneapolis: University of Minnesota Press, 1980).

628 Dan Poynter, as quoted in Doreen Chila-Jones, *Say What?* (Baltimore: Duopress, 2018).

629 Robert A. Heinlein, *Time Enough for Love* (New York: G. P. Putnam's Sons, 1973).

630   "The early bird gets the worm" is a proverb. The quote I use in the text is often used in business administration when discussing the "second mover advantage," as for example Microsoft, Apple, Google, etc.

631   There are numerous variants to this quote. The Thomas Jefferson Encyclopedia finds no variant in the writings of Thomas Jefferson. Other attributions include: Stephen Leacock, Mark Twain, George Allen, Samuel Goldwyn, "old Amish saying." *The Yale Book of Quotations*, ed. Fred R. Shapiro (New Haven, CT: Yale University Press, 2006) attributes the earliest appearance to a F. L. Emerson, *Reader's Digest* (March 1947). It's also a line in *Fifty Shades of Grey*: "I don't subscribe to luck or chance, Miss Steele. The harder I work, the more luck I seem to have." The exact context of the latter is beyond the scope of this book.

632   Pamela Anderson, *Esquire*, January 2005.

633   Eddie Cantor, as quoted in James Nicholas, *A Book of Wisdom and Delight: How to Fall in Love With Life* (Bloomington, IN: iUniverse, 2008), 162.

634   Humphrey B. Neill, *The Art of Contrary Thinking: It Pays to Be Contrary!* 5th and enlarged ed. (Caldwell, ID: Caxton Press, 2001). First published in 1954 by Caxton Press.

635   Christopher Nolan, director, *The Dark Knight* (Hollywood, CA: Warner Brothers, 2008).

636   Richard Hamming, "You and Your Research," speech, from transcription of the Bell Communications Research Colloquium Seminar (March 7, 1986).

637   Rules #1–5 are: "1. Control your own destiny or someone else will. 2. Face reality as it is, not as it was or as you wish it were. 3. Be candid with everyone. 4. Don't manage, lead. 5. Change before you have to." From P. J. Smit, *Strategy Implementation: Readings* (Kenwyn : Juta Academic, 2000). Welch's rules #2 and #5 apply very well to finance.

638   Walter Kerr, *Journey to the Center of the Theater* (New York: Alfred A. Knopf, 1979).

639   Denzel Washington, *Ebony Man*, November 1987.

640   The original source is disputed. It has been attributed to Seneca since the 1990s. Some books ascribe the saying to either Darrell K. Royal (former American football player, born 1924) or Elmer G. Letterman (insurance salesman and writer, 1897–1982). However, it is unlikely either man originated the saying. A version that reads "He is lucky who realizes that luck is the point where preparation meets opportunity" can be found (unattributed) in 1912's *The Youth's Companion*: Volume 86. The quotation might be a distortion of the following passage by Seneca (who makes no mention of "luck" and is in fact quoting his friend Demetrius the Cynic): "The best wrestler," he would say, "is not he who has learned thoroughly all the tricks and twists of the art, which are seldom met with in actual wrestling, but he who has well and carefully trained himself in one or two of them, and watches keenly for an opportunity of practising them." (Seneca the Younger, *On Benefits*, vii. 1) From Wikiquote (June 27, 2017).

641   Pirithous of Greek mythology allegedly.

642 Marilyn vos Savant, as quoted in *Parade* magazine (1988). Private email correspondence with spokesperson of Mrs. Savant (September 21, 2017). I have been using a variant of this quote: "Skill is successfully walking a tightrope over Niagara Falls. Intelligence is not trying." The spokesperson assumed that someone altered the original quotation after the events of 9/11. As Voltaire said in the preface of this book, some quotes on the Internet are false.

643 Warren Buffett, Preface to Benjamin Graham's *The Intelligent Investor*, 4th ed., reprinted from the *Financial Analyst Journal* (November/December 1976).

644 Peter Lynch, with John Rothschild, *One Up On Wall Street: How to Use What You Already Know to Make Money in the Market* (New York: Fireside, 1989), 80–81.

645 Andrew Lo, "The Adaptive Market Hypothesis—Market Efficiency from an Evolutionary Perspective," *Journal of Portfolio Management* 30, no. 5 (2004): 15–29. The most important paper was: Daniel Kahneman and Amos Tversky, "Prospect Theory: An Analysis of Decision under Risk," *Econometrica* 47, no. 2 (1979): 263–91, as mentioned earlier in the book.

646 Charles T. Munger, *Poor Charlie's Almanack: The Wit and Wisdom of Charles T. Munger,* ed. Peter D. Kaufman, expanded 3rd ed. (Virginia Beach: The Donning Company Publishers, 2008), 423. From Talk Ten: USC Gould School of Law Commencement Address (May 13, 2007). Next three sentences: "The same requirement exists in lower walks of life. I constantly see people rise in life who are not the smartest, sometimes not even the most diligent. But they are learning machines." This last quote is consistent with curiosity being an important factor for success, as discussed earlier in the book in relation to Richard Feynman.

647 Bertie Charles Forbes, *Finance, Business and the Business of Life* (n.p., 1915). Original is from Benjamin Franklin: "Drive thy Business, or it will drive thee." *Poor Richard's Almanack* (November 1738).

648 Joost Swarte, *The New Yorker*, volume 82, 2006.

649 Bambi's mother when Bambi sighs in a long winter. From *Bambi* [Movie] (Burbank, CA: Walt Disney Animation Studios, 1942).

650 Martin Zweig, as quoted in "Stock Trader's Almanac," *Hirsch Holdings* (1992).

651 Anne Morrow Lindbergh, *The Wave of the Future, a Confession of Faith* (New York: Harcourt, Brace & Co., 1940).

652 Stephen Hawking, Oxford University graduation speech (1962).

653 Estimated casualties in WWII range from forty to eighty-five million and the war lasted 2193 days. I divided 50 million by 2193 in the text. The IISS Armed Conflict Survey 2017 puts the casualties from armed conflicts for 2014–16 at 180,000, 167,000 and 157,000 per year respectively, which averages around 460 deaths per day. (Around 152,000 people die each day.) The 460 deaths include wars and terrorism. As a comparison: around 18,000 people die <u>daily</u> by stroke, around 9,000 from alcohol, around 3,400 by road traffic accident, and around 1,100 die daily from murder, of which

Brazil and the United States have a "market share" of around 16 percent and 4 percent respectively. Around 680 illegal drug users die from drug overuse globally per day, of which the US has a "market share" of around 30 percent.

654   Own calculations using the S&P 500 and TOPIX price indices from *Bloomberg*. In this example, I made my life a bit easier by ignoring dividends and inflation. The former rises the compounding rate a bit, depending mainly on how the dividends are taxed and reinvested, while the latter reduces the compounding rate a bit. (An inflation rate of 2 percent cuts the capital's purchasing power in half within thirty-four years. At 5 percent, it takes fourteen years to halve capital in real terms. At 8 percent, a bit more than eight years.)

655   Mark Buchanan, *Ubiquity: Why Catastrophes Happen* (New York: Three Rivers Press, 2000), 239.

656   Adam Johnson, Bloomberg TV, October 9, 2013.

657   Warren Buffett, Berkshire Hathaway, 2008 annual letter to shareholders, February 27, 2009.

658   Ludwig von Mises, *Human Action: A Treatise on Economics*, 4th ed. (San Francisco: Fox & Wilkes, 1996), 106. First published in 1949 by Yale University.

659   "All models are wrong" is a common aphorism in statistics. It is generally attributed to the statistician George Box. The first record of Box saying "all models are wrong" is in a 1976 paper published in G. E. P. Box, "Science and Statistics," *Journal of the American Statistical Association* 71 (1976): 791–99. The paragraph containing the aphorism states: "Since all models are wrong the scientist cannot obtain a "correct" one by excessive elaboration. On the contrary following William of Occam he should seek an economical description of natural phenomena. Just as the ability to devise simple but evocative models is the signature of the great scientist so overelaboration and overparameterization is often the mark of mediocrity." From Wikipedia (June 1, 2017). The quotation I use is from G. E. P. Box and N. R. Draper, *Empirical Model Building and Response Surfaces* (New York: John Wiley & Sons, 1987), 424.

660   This quotation is frequently used in the financial literature, has many variants, but its origin is disputed. Large losses when the bubble burst, as far as I can judge from the various sources I use, is factual. Wikiquote (May 12, 2017) mentions the following: "Disputed: 'I can calculate the motions of erratic bodies, but not the madness of a multitude.' Such a statement is indicated as Newton's response to a question regarding the financial fiasco known as the South Sea Bubble, in 'Mammon and the Money Market,' in *Church of England Quarterly Review* (1850), p. 142."

I have seen this quotation used to make a case against quantitative finance, in a sense, that one can be numerically brilliant, but still get market forces horribly wrong, as being numerically brilliant might at times not be an applicable skill. Being numerically brilliant can be like the flopping of a fish on dry land at times.

661   Roger Lowenstein, *When Genius Failed: The Rise and Fall of Long-Term Capital Management* (New York: Random House, 2000), 61.

662   Lillian Chew, "Shock Treatment," *Risk* 7, no. 9 (1994): 63–70.

663   James Thurber, "The Fairly Intelligent Fly," *New Yorker*, February 4, 1939.

664   Arthur Zeikel, "On Thinking," *Financial Analyst Journal* 44, no. 3 (May–June 1988): 11–17.

665   Steve Blumenthal, "Louis Gave—An Important Paradigm Shift Which Will Define the 21st Century," *Valueweek*, April 8, 2018.

666   Gerd Gigerenzer, *Risk Savvy: How to Make Good Decisions* (New York: Viking, 2014), 31.

667   Didier Sornette, *Why Stock Markets Crash: Critical Events in Complex Financial Systems* (Princeton, NJ: Princeton University Press, 2003), 3–4.

668   Warren Buffett, Berkshire Hathaway, 2016 letter to shareholders, February 25, 2017, 6.

669   Warren Buffett, Berkshire Hathaway, 2016 letter to shareholders, February 25, 2017, 6.

670   Clint Eastwood, *Magnum Force* [Movie] (Hollywood, CA: Warner Brothers, 1973).

671   Oscar Wilde, *An Ideal Husband* (London: Leonard Smithers and Company, 1899).

672   Ken Griffin, "Over Uno, Citadel's Griffin Reveals His Mistakes of 2008," video interview with Institutional Investor's Julie Segal, in which the pair partake in a game of Uno, July 5, 2017.

673   Jack Schwager, *Market Wizards* (New York: CollinsBusiness, 1993), 288. First published in 1989 by the New York Institute of Finance.

674   Douglas Adams, *The Hitchhiker's Guide to the Galaxy* (London: Pan Macmillan, 1979), from the introduction.

675   David Robson, *The Intelligence Trap: Revolutionise Your Thinking and Make Wiser Decisions* (London: Hodder & Stoughton, 2019), 257.

676   Sophocles, *Aletes*, fragment 99.

677   Marie von Ebner-Eschenbach, *Aphorisms*, trans. D. Scrase and W. Mieder (Riverside, CA: Ariadne Press, 1994). German original, *Aphorismus*, published 1880. Original: "Ein Aphorismus ist der letzte Ring einer langen Gedankenkette."

678   F. A. Hayek, *The Road to Serfdom* (New York: Routledge Classics, 2006), 246. First published in 1944 by George Routledge Sons (New York). The quote is from the conclusion of the book.

679   Stephen Hawking, *Brief Answers to the Big Questions* (London: John Murray Publishers, 2018), 189–90.

680   J. P. Donleavy, *The Ginger Man* (Paris: The Olympia Press, 1955).

681   Voltaire, *Le Dîner du Comte de Boulainvilliers* (n.p., 1767).

INDEX